OSPREY AIRCRAFT OF THE ACES • 68

Bf 109 Defence of the Reich Aces

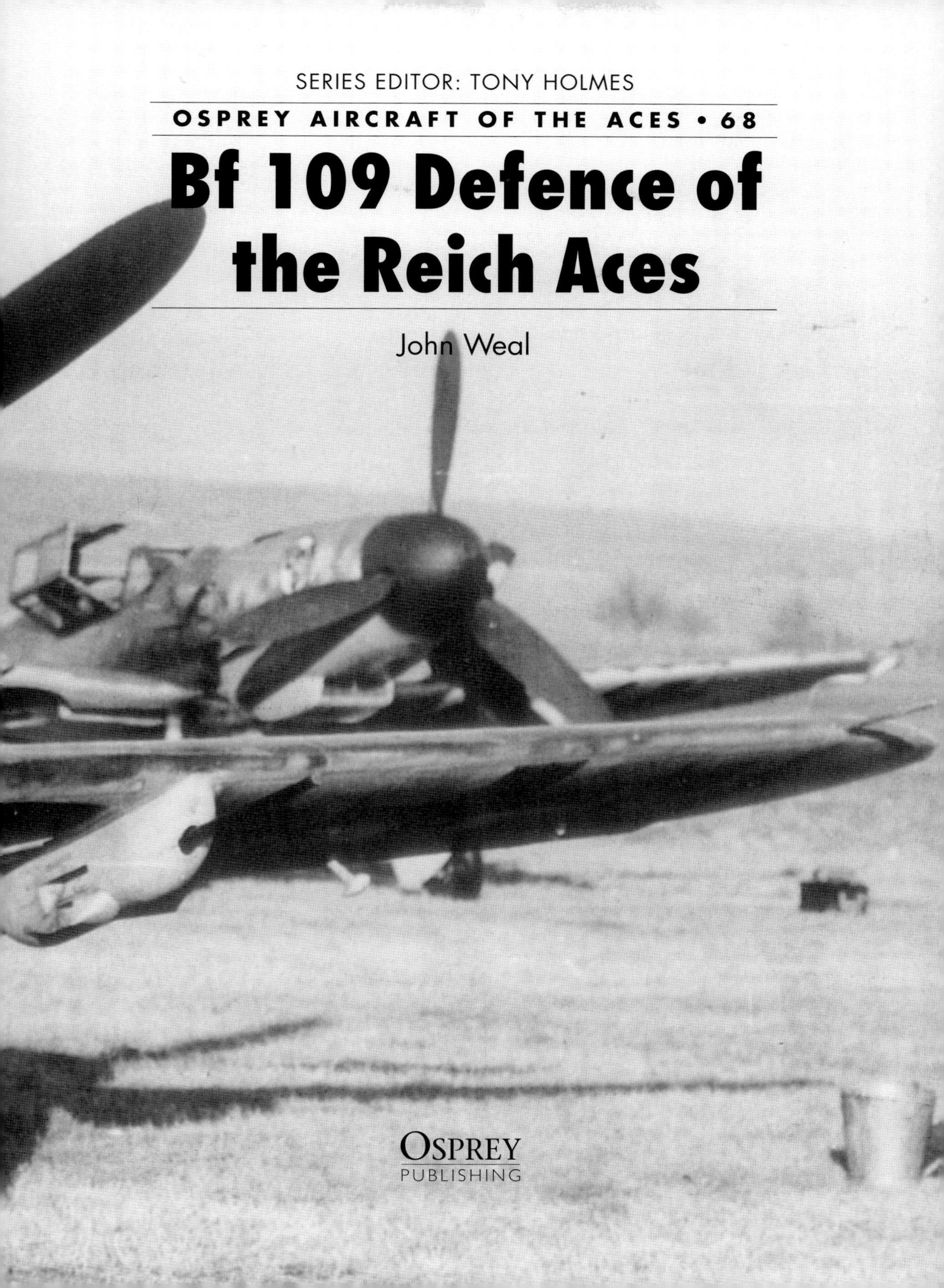

SERIES EDITOR: TONY HOLMES

OSPREY AIRCRAFT OF THE ACES • 68

Bf 109 Defence of the Reich Aces

John Weal

OSPREY
PUBLISHING

Front cover

On 17 August 1943, over 200 B-17 Flying Fortresses of the Eighth Air Force's 1st Bomb Wing were despatched to attack a vital target – the Reich's major ball-bearing factories at Schweinfurt. The bomber crews were expecting trouble. Their take-off had been delayed by bad weather, and they were a critical three hours or more behind the B-17s of the 4th Bomb Wing, which were heading for Regensburg. They knew the defending Luftwaffe fighters would be fully alerted and ready for them. And they were right.

At Eupen, a small Belgian town less than ten miles from the German border, the bombers 'short-legged' P-47 Thunderbolt escorts were forced to turn back. The Fortresses pressed on alone into Germany. It was the moment the Luftwaffe fighter pilots had been waiting for.

Among the first to attack were the 12 rocket-armed Bf 109G-6s of 5./JG 11 down from Jever. Oberleutnant Heinz Knoke's 'Black 1' was hit by heavy Browning 0.50-calibre machine gun fire as the *Staffel* jockeyed into position astern of the bombers. With his port wing damaged and left-hand rocket tube (nicknamed a 'stovepipe' by German fighter pilots) shot away, Knoke launched his remaining missile, but without result. Then the rest of the *Staffel* bored in.

According to Knoke's subsequent account of the action, both Feldwebel Erich Führmann, illustrated here in his 'Black 9', and Feldwebel Wilhelm Fest scored hits on B-17s which blew up in mid-air. However, post-war research suggests that the two 92nd Bomb Group (BG) Flying Fortresses hit in this engagement suffered only slight damage and later fell victim to conventional fighter attack.

Despite his damaged wing, Heinz Knoke took off again later to attack the bombers returning from Schweinfurt. He is credited with bringing down the 305th BG's flak-damaged B-17F 42-30159 *Settin' Bull*, which crashed in Belgium, before finally writing-off his own 'Black 1' in a forced landing near Rheinbach (*Cover Artwork by Mark Postlethwaite*)

First published in Great Britain in 2006 by Osprey Publishing
Midland House, West Way, Botley, Oxford, OX2 0PH
443 Park Avenue South, New York, NY 10016, USA

ISBN 1 84176 879 0

Edited by Tony Holmes
Page design by Tony Truscott
Cover Artwork by Mark Postlethwaite
Aircraft Profiles by John Weal
Index by Alan Thatcher
Origination by PPS Grasmere, Leeds, UK
Printed and bound in China through Bookbuilders

06 07 08 09 10 10 09 08 07 06 05 04 03 02 01

For a catalogue of all books published by Osprey please contact:
NORTH AMERICA
Osprey Direct, C/o Random House Distribution Center,
400 Hahn Road, Westminster, MD 21157
E-mail:info@ospreydirect.com

ALL OTHER REGIONS
Osprey Direct UK, P.O. Box 140 Wellingborough, Northants, NN8 2FA, UK
E-mail: info@ospreydirect.co.uk
www.ospreypublishing.com

ACKNOWLEDGEMENTS
The author would like to thank the following individuals for their generous help in providing information and photographs:

Roger Freeman, Chris Goss, Manfred Griehl, Rolf Hase, Uwe Hausen, Helmut Kern, Hal Lester, Walter Matthiesen, Axel Paul, Tomás Poruba, Dr Alfred Price, Jerry Scutts, Robert Simpson, Nigel Smith and Andrew Thomas

CONTENTS

THE STAGE IS SET

The start of the Luftwaffe's 820-day Defence of the Reich campaign coincided with one of the major turning points of the war. The opening shots were exchanged on 27 January 1943 when 53 American B-17 Flying Fortresses bombed the North Sea naval base of Wilhelmshaven. This was the first time that the Eighth Air Force had attacked a target within Germany itself. Six days later, and over 1500 miles to the east, the last emaciated survivors of *Generalfeldmarschall* von Paulus' *6. Armee* – once a third of a million strong – surrendered to Soviet troops at Stalingrad. Never before had Hitler's forces suffered such a crushing defeat. And after this date never again would they win a major victory.

The aerial battle in defence of the Reich would thus be played out against a backdrop of the continual reverses and withdrawals taking place on all the other fighting fronts.

By the spring of 1945 German troops in the east, who had once stood at the very gates of Moscow and Stalingrad, would have been pushed back into the heart of their own capital, Berlin. In the Mediterranean, Axis forces in North Africa had long ago surrendered, setting in train the invasions of Sicily and Italy and the subsequent slow, stubborn retreat northwards into the shadow of the Austrian Alps. And in north-west Europe those defenders of Normandy who had managed to escape the killing fields around Falaise had been forced back to the Rhine and beyond, to the Elbe.

But for the Luftwaffe *Jagdgruppen* defending the daylight skies of the Greater German Reich there was nowhere to retreat to. They stood their ground and traded the US heavy bombers blow for blow. And the outcome, far from being a foregone conclusion, would hang in the balance for many months. It was to be almost a full year before the growing weight of American superiority – not least in the sleek cruciform shape of the P-51 Mustang escort

The gateway to the Reich. Both the RAF and USAAF chose Wilhelmshaven as their first target on mainland Germany. This is the later raid of 11 June 1943, and smoke pots are already beginning to form a screen below the approaching Flying Fortresses

fighter – began to tell irrevocably against them. But even then another year and more of desperately fought actions was to pass before they too were finally and conclusively beaten.

On 25 April 1945 a combined total of 1414 USAAF and RAF heavy bombers flew their last bombing raids of the European war. Not one of the 15 'heavies' lost in these operations fell to the guns of a defending Luftwaffe fighter. By this time the *Jagdwaffe* was a totally spent force. And five days later – as proof positive that all was indeed lost – Adolf Hitler committed suicide in his Berlin bunker.

The wreckage of one of the four No 107 Sqn Blenheim IVs lost in the RAF's first bombing raids of the war is recovered from the bottom of Wilhelmshaven harbour. N6184 was brought down by flak from the German heavy cruiser *Admiral Hipper*

It had all been so very different in the beginning. Within hours of Great Britain's declaring war on Germany on 3 September 1939, Hampdens and Wellingtons of RAF Bomber Command were scouring the German Bight for enemy naval vessels. Although no sightings were made on this first day of hostilities, some 29 bombers were despatched against Wilhelmshaven and Brunsbüttel 24 hours later. Seven failed to return, three having been brought down by the Nordholz-based Bf 109Es of II./JG 77.

For the RAF – firm believers in the pre-war dictum that 'the bomber will always get through' (and presumably back again?) – the loss of nearly a quarter of its attacking force gave serious pause for thought. More than three weeks were to pass before the next attempt was made. On 29 September 11 Hampdens set out to search for German naval units reported to be at sea in the area of Heligoland. This time almost half the attackers were wiped out when Bf 109Ds of I./ZG 26 (a *Zerstörergruppe* awaiting delivery of its first Bf 110s) intercepted a formation of five Hampdens south of Heligoland and shot down every one of them.

There followed another lull while the RAF chiefs considered their options. They cited a whole number of reasons for the recent heavy losses – the accuracy of the German Navy's anti-aircraft fire, the often atrocious weather conditions, the attackers' lack of numbers – they even went so far as to suggest that some pilots were 'straggling' rather than keeping in close formation. The one possibility that they seemed reluctant to consider, let alone acknowledge, was that their bombers were being blown out of the sky by enemy fighters.

Nevertheless, all nine of the armed bomber sweeps carried out over the course of the next eight weeks had orders not to approach too close to the German mainland, but to remain on the outer periphery of the Bight. These operations, flown over open water along a wide arc between the Frisian islands of Borkum in the west to Sylt in the north, were completely uneventful. Not a single German warship was spotted, no bombs were dropped and not one aircraft was lost to enemy action.

It appeared that the RAF had decided to restrict its North Sea activities to the same level of routine patrolling as that being carried out along the

Oberstleutnant Carl Schumacher was tasked with organising the aerial defences of the German Bight

Franco-German border which had already given rise to the phrase 'Phoney War'. But this was far from the case. The War Cabinet in London was eager to see the sinking of one of the enemy's capital ships – for morale purposes alone, if nothing else – and plans were already in hand for Bomber Command to return to the German coast in force.

Meanwhile, the Luftwaffe had not been idle. Upon the outbreak of war fighter strength in the whole of north-west Germany had comprised fewer than a dozen *Staffeln*, the majority equipped with obsolescent Bf 109Ds. These units came under the direct control of *Luftgaukommando XI* headquartered in Hannover. But the aggressive stance adopted by the RAF right from the outset soon led to changes.

Early in November 1939 Oberstleutnant Carl Schumacher, *Gruppenkommandeur* of II./JG 77, was tasked with setting up a completely new *Jagdgeschwaderstab* (Fighter Group HQ). Based at Jever, Schumacher's *Stab* JG 1 was unusual in that, at first, it did not possess any component *Gruppen* of its own. Instead, Schumacher was given control of all fighter units stationed along the North Sea coastal belt.

By mid-December this composite force had reached formidable proportions. It comprised two *Jagdgruppen* of Bf 109Es, a third flying a mix of Ds and Es, a semi-autonomous *Staffel* of Bf 109Ds, plus a *Zerstörergruppe* equipped with long-range Bf 110Cs. And it was this heterogeneous collection, composed mainly of the most modern fighters in the Luftwaffe's armoury – and backed up by a fledgling early-warning radar system – that was ready and waiting when Bomber Command next approached the German coastline.

5./JG 77's Leutnant Winfried Schmidt is carried shoulder-high from his 'Red 1' after claiming one of the fourteen Wellingtons credited to II./JG 77 in the 'Battle of the German Bight' of 18 December 1939

The attacking force on 14 December was as mixed a bunch as the defenders. The 42 RAF bombers despatched – 23 Hampdens, 12 Wellingtons and 7 Whitleys – constituted the biggest Bomber Command effort of the war so far. But their extra numbers availed them little. Neither the Hampdens nor the Whitleys sighted the enemy. The Wellingtons did find a coastal convoy in the Schillig Roads, north of Wilhelmshaven, only to lose five of their number – all to the Bf 109Es of II./JG 77. A sixth was so badly damaged that it crashed when attempting to land back at base.

Four days later an all-Wellington force was sent out to search for shipping in the same sea area off Wilhelmshaven. Of the 22 bombers

In fact, 'only' 12 Wellingtons were lost on 18 December. No 9 Sqn's N2971/WS-B was lucky not to have been among them. Flg Off W J MacRae was awarded an immediate DFC for getting his bomber back to North Coates with two wounded aboard and despite extensive damage to both wings and the rear fuselage

that reached the target area, 12 were shot down by Schumacher's pilots (for a more detailed account of the 18 December 'Battle of the German Bight' see *Osprey Aircraft of the Aces 11* and *25*).

The RAF could no longer ignore the evidence. The Wellington was the best bomber it possessed. Yet of the 36 machines of this type that had been despatched on the two sweeps of 14 and 18 December, exactly half had been destroyed by enemy fighter action – and this without their even venturing inland over German territory! The concept of the mutually supporting, self-defending daylight bomber formation had, quite literally, been shot to pieces.

The result was a fundamental change in RAF policy. Henceforth, with but a few notable exceptions, Bomber Command would restrict its strategic offensive against Germany to the hours of darkness. It seemed as if the Luftwaffe had won the daylight Defence of the Reich battle almost before it had begun. It is certainly no exaggeration to say that, for the next three years, Germany's North Sea coastal belt remained very much a backwater as the air war expanded ever further afield.

During the spring and summer of 1940 the focus of air operations shifted westwards, first with the invasion of the Low Countries and France and then the Battle of Britain. By year's end Luftwaffe units were also being sent south to the Mediterranean and Balkan regions. During this period, and well into 1941, Carl Schumacher's *Stab* JG 1 continued to guard the Reich's northern seaboard using a miscellany of temporarily-attached *Jagdgruppen* and *Staffeln*, many of which were either on their way to – or resting from – deployment on other fronts.

Since the occupation of the Netherlands Schumacher's area of responsibility had been extended to include the Dutch coastal regions. Throughout 1941 and 1942, it was this western half of JG 1's defensive domain that was to see almost all of the action as the RAF's medium bombers stepped up their campaign against offshore shipping and selected land targets in the Low Countries.

It was also at this time that the first moves were made to establish Oberstleutnant Schumacher's motley command on a more permanent basis. Two previously semi-autonomous *Jagdstaffeln* stationed in the area

Nosed over in the soft turf of De Kooy airfield near Den Helder, in the Netherlands, early in 1941, 3./JG 1's 'Yellow 3' adopts the classic pose commonly known in the Luftwaffe as a *Fliegerdenkmal,* or 'airman's monument'

had already been redesignated as 1. and 2./JG 1. A third *Staffel* (3./JG 1) was activated from scratch in the early spring of 1941. The three *Staffeln* remained on their widely separated bases for several months, however, and it was not until September 1941 that they began operating together as a *Gruppe* under their recently-appointed *Kommandeur*, Major Dr Erich Mix. This new I./JG 1 should not be confused with the original I./JG 1 of the early months of the war, which had been redesignated III./JG 27 in July 1940 (see *Osprey Aviation Elite Units 12*).

Hitler's invasion of the Soviet Union in June 1941 had resulted in the bulk of the Luftwaffe being transferred to the eastern front. The only fighter units remaining in northwest Europe were JGs 2 and 26, who were responsible for the defence of the French and Belgian coastal regions, and JG 1, whose area of operations now stretched from the Netherlands, along Germany's North Sea coastline and up into Denmark and southern Norway.

It was the pilots of JGs 2 and 26 who bore the brunt of the RAF's 1941 'lean into Europe'. The majority of the enemy's missions during this period were the so-called 'Circuses' – small formations of medium bombers, heavily escorted by fighters, whose primary object was to draw the Luftwaffe's fighters up into combat – and these simply did not possess the range to penetrate Reich airspace.

'Operation 77' was different, however. Mounted on 12 August 1941, and purportedly part of a drive to relieve the pressure on the west's newly-acquired Soviet ally (in retrospect, something of a forlorn hope!), 'Operation 77' was an all-Blenheim daylight raid despatched against two power stations located on the outskirts of Cologne. It was not an unqualified success. Of the 54 attackers, ten failed to return, and neither target suffered long-lasting damage. Although the Blenheims' course took them across southern Holland, most of those brought down by Luftwaffe fighters fell victim to JG 26.

Several Bf 109Es of 2./JG 1 had been scrambled from Katwijk, on the Dutch coast, shortly before midday, but they had failed to intercept the incoming bombers. A second scramble some 60 minutes later had more success. This time the Bf 109 pilots sighted 'a group of six Blenheims running for the coast'. 2./JG 1's Unteroffizier Siegfried Zick got on the tail of one of the fleeing bombers and shot it down over Zouteland. It was a first, not only for future Defence of the Reich *Experte* Zick, but also for 2. *Staffel*.

Nearly a month was to pass before 2. *Staffel* claimed a second victory. But the Blenheim credited to Feldwebel Albert 'Ali' Griener on 5 September was something of a rarity. Coming down near the island of Borkum, it was the only one of I./JG 1's two dozen confirmed kills of 1941 to be caught *inside* German airspace. The following week I./JG 1's Dutch-based *Staffeln* was ordered to Jever. For the first time they would be operating together as a *Gruppe*. But the move to Jever had taken them further away from the scene of action, and the next three months remained almost entirely uneventful. The only break in the monotony, and the only victory gained in the last quarter of 1941, was an 'intruder' Hampden of No 106 Sqn shot down by 1./JG 1's Oberfeldwebel Werner Gerhardt on 21 December – again over Holland.

Exactly a fortnight before Hampden AE151 crashed at Schoonebek, however, an event on the other side of the world had ensured that in the space of little more than a year, I./JG 1's North Sea patrol area would be transformed from an operational backwater into the frontline of the Reich's aerial defences.

The Japanese attack on the US Navy's Pacific Fleet in Pearl Harbor on the morning of 7 December 1941 opened up the war on a truly global scale. The United States and Great Britain officially declared war on Japan 24 hours later. And at 1500 hrs on 11 December Hitler announced to the members of the Reichstag that Germany was standing by her Tripartite Axis Asian ally by declaring war on America.

Despite the wave of public outrage that swept across the United States in the wake of the Japanese attack, President Roosevelt was persuaded that the first priority should be the defeat of Nazi Germany and the liberation of Europe. And one of the earliest moves towards this end was to be the establishment of an American strategic bomber force in the United Kingdom. On 20 February 1942 Brig Gen Ira C Eaker and six other USAAF officers arrived in England to set up the first American bomber command.

Eaker resisted pressure from British Prime Minister Winston Churchill to have his embryonic VIII Bomber Command join the RAF in its 'mass' night bombing raids. The Americans had implicit faith in the ability of their heavily-armed four-engined bombers, the B-17 Flying Fortress and B-24 Liberator, not merely to survive by day in the hostile skies of Europe, but to attack specific targets with pin-point precision.

The US Air War Plans Division drew up a list of 177 selected military and industrial targets, grouped within seven categories, whose destruction, it was confidently predicted, would deny Germany the means to wage war. The first category was 'German Aircraft Plants'. The Americans' primary objective would be to destroy the Luftwaffe, both in the air and on the ground, as a prerequisite to the planned invasion of Europe. It was a task similar to that attempted by Göring's Luftwaffe in the Battle of Britain in the summer of 1940. The Luftwaffe had failed to knock out the RAF – but only by the narrowest of margins. Would the USAAF be more successful over mainland Europe?

It was not a programme that could be embarked upon overnight. To start with, the strength of Eaker's command would have to be built up, and then operational experience gained. The first heavy bomber mission flown by VIII Bomber Command took place on 17 August 1942 when a dozen B-17Es (one carrying Brig Gen Ira Eaker himself) bombed the Rouen-Sotteville marshalling yards in France from an altitude of 23,000 ft (7000 m). All 12 Fortresses returned to their Northamptonshire base, two having sustained superficial flak damage over the target area. For the remainder of the year VIII Bomber Command's 'heavies' continued to hone their operational skills on the 'nursery slopes' of occupied northwest Europe. It would cost them over 30 of their number, mostly to Luftwaffe fighters and flak. But it prepared crews for the ordeal that lay ahead.

On the other side of the North Sea things remained fairly quiet during 1942. There had, however, been some significant organisational changes early in the year. On 5 January Oberstleutnant Carl Schumacher relinquished command of JG 1 to take up the appointment of *Jafü Norwegen* (Fighter-Leader Norway). It therefore fell to his successor, Major Erich von Selle, to oversee JG 1's transition from little more than a caretaker *Stab* into a full four-*Gruppe Geschwader*.

Hauptmann Hans von Hahn's Bf 109F-equipped I./JG 3 had been withdrawn from the eastern front in September 1941 for rest and refit in the Reich. Two months later it was transferred to two airfields on the Dutch coast – Katwijk and Vlissingen (Flushing). On 15 January 1942 the *Gruppe* was redesignated to become II./JG 1.

The origins of von Selle's last two *Gruppen* were less straightforward. By this stage of the hostilities almost every Luftwaffe *Jagdgeschwader* had formed its own rear-area *Ergänzungsgruppe*. Perhaps best described as 'in-unit OTUs', the task of these *Gruppen* was to prepare newly-trained fighter pilots for frontline service with their parent *Geschwader*. In turn, each such *Gruppe* had set up its own *Einsatzstaffel* (operational squadron), composed of instructors and selected trainees, which could be called upon to fly combat missions as and when the need arose. And it was from the *Ergänzungsgruppen* and *Einsatzstaffeln* of JGs 2, 26, 27, 51, 52 and 53 that III. and IV./JG 1 were created.

JG 1 was somewhat unusual in being one of onlytwo *Jagdgeschwader* currently made up of *four* component *Gruppen* (the other

A much more serious incident than the one illustrated on page ten resulted in the death of Unteroffizier Erwin Grütz of IV./JG 1 on 4 July 1942 when his Bf 109F-4, 'White 6', crashed into a building during an emergency scramble from Bergen-op-Zoom, in Holland. The fighters were responding to an incoming raid on the airfield by RAF Bostons

being JG 51 on the eastern front). The reason for JG 1's additional strength was no doubt the length of North Sea coastline it was assigned to protect. The *Geschwader's* area of operations now stretched in an unbroken arc from the Netherlands up into southern Norway.

In mid-1942 Major von Selle's three new *Gruppen* began converting from their Bf 109s on to Fw 190As. Only the original I./JG 1 remained on Messerschmitts, gradually exchanging its earlier E and F models for pressurised, high-altitude G-1s.

Hauptmann Fritz Losigkeit, *Kommandeur* of IV./JG 1, was photographed here soon after his *Gruppe* had completed its conversion from the Bf 109 to the Fw 190 in September 1942

Operationally, 1942 was very much a continuation of 1941. The bulk of the 90+ victories credited to JG 1 during the course of the year were scored over the Low Countries, where the RAF mediums were intensifying their attacks on targets in the coastal provinces and along the inshore shipping lanes. I./JG 1 claimed six victims over this westernmost sector – one, for example, being the Hudson shot down off the Dutch island of Texel on 17 February by Oberfeldwebel Gerhardt, the *Gruppe's* leading scorer. This took his total to nine.

But it was the 11 RAF machines brought down by I./JG 1 during the latter half of the year *inside* German airspace that was the true indication of how the daylight air war was edging inexorably closer to the Reich's northern borders. The majority of these claims were for solo reconnaissance intruders, including three high-flying Mosquitos. Based at Jever, at the very centre of the *Geschwader's* defensive arc, and equipped with brand new pressurised *Gustavs*, the *Gruppe* was ideally positioned and equipped to deal with such incursions.

Although they themselves had not yet been confronted by a formation of US heavy bombers, the pilots of I./JG 1, commanded since September 1942 by Hauptmann Günther Beise, had studied the intelligence summaries and read the combat reports of their fellow pilots of JGs 2 and 26 who had already seen action against the American 'heavies' over France and the Low Countries. These had gone a long way towards dispelling the mystique that had previously surrounded the US 'wonder' bombers. The B-17s and B-24s were far from invulnerable to determined fighter attack, as their casualties over northwest Europe proved.

The US bomber crews were well aware that they would soon be sent to attack a target inside Germany. Beise's pilots knew with equal certainty that they would be coming. For both sides it was just a matter of time.

And that time arrived on 27 January 1943.

A well-known, but nonetheless intriguing, shot of a Bf 109E of I./JG 1. 'Black 13' sports the *Gruppe* badge below the cockpit and carries a 250-kg bomb on a ventral rack. The purpose of the former is clear, but the reason for the latter less so. As far as is known, the unit was never engaged on *Jabo* ops. Could obsolescent *Emils* such as this, one or two of which remained on strength until the winter of 1942-43, have been employed in early aerial-bombing trials?

STRUGGLES AND EARLY SUCCESSES

The target chosen for the USAAF's first daylight raid on Germany was the same as that selected by the RAF over three years earlier – the naval base of Wilhelmshaven on the North Sea coast.

VIII Bomber Command's Mission No 31 on 27 January 1943 called for a maximum effort from all six of its bomb groups. A mixed force of 64 B-17s and 27 B-24s was despatched, but a combination of bad weather and poor navigation resulted in the Liberators failing to find the target. While searching, they ran foul of Fw 190s of II. and IV./JG 1 off the Dutch coast and two B-24s were shot down.

Meanwhile, 53 of the Flying Fortresses had made it through to Wilhelmshaven. Nine miles away at nearby Jever, Hauptmann Beise's I./JG 1 had been the first *Gruppe* to receive the order to scramble. Clawing for height in their pressurised *Gustavs*, they made contact with the bombers in broken cloud at an altitude of some 25,000 ft. But in the action that followed, their inexperience showed. At subsequent debriefings many bomber crewmen made particular reference to the heavy, but largely ineffective, flak which had tracked them in over the Frisian islands and stayed with them during their run across the mainland. The Luftwaffe's fighters, however, 'hadn't pressed home their attacks like those guys stationed in France usually did'.

Despite this less than glowing endorsement from the enemy, five of Beise's pilots claimed to have brought down a Flying Fortress. In reality, although well over half of the B-17s that bombed Wilhelmshaven suffered minor combat damage, only one failed to return. The dubious distinction of being the first American casualties of the Defence of the Reich campaign fell to Capt Vance Beckham and his crew of the 305th BG B-17F 41-24637.

Exactly who shot Beckham down is more open to question. One of the five claims was later downgraded to an unconfirmed. As to the other four, at least one reference source suggests that the victor was 2. *Staffel's* Feldwebel Siegfried Zick. If this is indeed the case, it was Zick's second kill (his first had been the Blenheim downed during the RAF's daylight raid on the Cologne power stations back in August 1941). He would add a further 17 'heavies' to his score during subsequent service with III./JG 11, the

Oberleutnant Hugo Frey of 2./JG 1 was one of the four claimants for the first B-17 downed over Wilhelmshaven on 27 January 1943. He is pictured here (bareheaded, second from right) as *Kapitän* of 7./JG 11 a year later. He would be shot down and killed in his Fw 190 during the first major USAAF raid on Berlin on 6 March 1944

last seven of them after converting to the Fw 190. His overall total stood at 32 when he was seriously wounded on the western front in the summer of 1944.

On the other side of the coin, the action of 27 January 1943 also resulted in the first Luftwaffe losses in the daylight Defence of the Reich. Five of I./JG 1's *Gustavs* went down, with three of the fighters taking their pilots into the depths of the North Sea with them.

Despite the jubilation back at VIII Bomber Command HQ that only three of the original 91 bombers despatched had failed to return, and notwithstanding the fact that 24 hours later the German armed forces communiqué triumphantly announced the destruction of *nine* bombers, neither side could have been entirely happy with the results of the Wilhelmshaven mission. Little more than half the attacking force had managed to locate the assigned target, and the damage they inflicted was slight. For the defenders, their performance had fallen far short of the 50 per cent casualty rate inflicted upon the RAF Wellingtons that had raided Wilhelmshaven three years earlier. The loss of three bombers was not going to persuade the USAAF to abandon its daylight offensive against the Reich and join the RAF under cover of darkness. The B-17s and B-24s would be back.

As a final postscript to 27 January, mention should also be made of the overclaiming by both sides. While the Luftwaffe pilots submitted claims for nine bombers destroyed, the gunners manning the US 'heavies' filed for no fewer than 22 enemy fighters shot down, plus 14 probables and a further 13 damaged. JG 1's combat losses in fact totalled just six. Registering on the mind in the heat of battle, and subsequently made in all good faith, such inflated claims are perhaps understandable – particularly in the case of the air gunners, where there could be six or more crew members aboard every bomber in each formation blazing away at the same hapless fighter as it barrelled past them.

Exaggerated claiming was to be a permanent feature of the Defence of the Reich campaign. And the figures would become even more distorted as the total of aircraft involved on each side grew to ten times or more the numbers participating in the early raids.

On 2 February 1943 Brig General Eaker sent his crews out on another maximum effort. But the atrocious weather conditions over the North Sea proved a greater deterrent than the Luftwaffe's fighters and all six groups were forced to turn back. Two days later they made a second attempt to get through to the same objective – the Hamm marshalling yards near Dortmund, in the Ruhr. The weather had scarcely improved in the interim, however, and the two Liberator groups were forced to abort due to severe icing.

Abandoning any hopes of reaching Hamm, over half the B-17 force diverted to the North Sea port of Emden as a last resort. They were

First published in a wartime Dutch newspaper, this photograph shows one of the five B-17Fs lost in the Emden raid of 4 February 1943. Damaged by flak and then attacked by Bf 109s and Bf 110s, the 91st BG's 41-24589 *Texas Bronco* crash-landed on the sands of the Dutch Frisian island of Terschelling

intercepted not only by elements of the same three *Gruppen* of JG 1 that had engaged them over Wilhelmshaven, but also by a number of Bf 110s of NJG 1. Thrown in as a stop-gap measure to bolster defensive numbers, it was the first time that twin-engined nightfighters had been sent up against the USAAF by day.

Although all three *Staffeln* of I./JG 1 were scrambled, only 3./JG 1 found a formation of B-17s in the thick cloud. Unteroffizier Otto Werner was credited with the destruction of one of the Fortresses southeast of Emden. The Fw 190 *Gruppen* claimed a further six, against two combat fatalities of their own. Dominated by the weather, it had been another inconclusive and unsatisfactory encounter for both sides.

The weather continued to restrict operational activity for the next three weeks. During that time VIII Bomber Command made another abortive attempt to attack the Hamm yards, but did manage to mount two missions against coastal targets in France. Then, on 26 February, it was back to Germany.

The briefed target for Mission No 37 was Bremen, but the weather again put paid to the VIII's carefully-laid plans. Thick cloud obscured the objective and all six bomber groups turned instead to a target of opportunity – the U-boat yards at Wilhelmshaven. This time the Fw 190 *Gruppen* were ordered off first, but they were able to down only one of the incoming bombers over open water. I./JG 1's *Gustavs* caught the 'heavies' as they were crossing the coast, and in less than 20 minutes claimed eight – four Liberators and four Flying Fortresses – without loss to themselves.

The first Liberator fell to a determined onslaught by 2. *Staffel's* Leutnant Heinz Knoke. His initial frontal attack had resulted in just a few hits on the B-24's right wing, and so;

'I went in for a second pass, again head on, but this time from a little below. I kept on firing until I had to break away to avoid colliding with the bomber. As I did so, I saw flames spreading along the bottom of its fuselage. It sheered away from the formation in a wide turn to the right. I followed it down, attacking twice more, this time from above and behind the tail. Ignoring the return fire from the Liberator's gunners, I watched my cannon shells rake along the top of its fuselage and right wing.

'The fire spread out along right wing. The inboard propeller windmilled to a stop. And then, suddenly, the whole wing broke off. The Liberator went spinning down almost vertically, a long black trail of smoke marking its descent. At an altitude of 900 metres there was a tremendous explosion. The bomber had disintegrated. The blazing wreckage landed just outside the perimeter of Bad Zwischenahn airfield.'

Although the Liberator was Heinz Knoke's third confirmed victory, it was his first heavy bomber. It was also the first B-24 to be lost over the Reich. By a cruel twist of fate, there had been 11 men aboard the bomber. For many weeks past a group of US newspaper correspondents had been requesting permission to fly on a bombing mission. The Eighth Air Force had finally given the go-ahead on 26 February. Five of the correspondents elected to ride with the Flying Fortresses. The sixth, Robert B Post of the *New York Times*, chose to accompany Capt Howard F Adams and his crew aboard their 44th BG B-24D 41-23777 *Maisey*. There were two survivors from *Maisey's* final mission to Wilhelmshaven. Neither of them was Post.

Coming initially from JG 52, Heinz Knoke served throughout almost all of the Defence of the Reich campaign, latterly as a hauptmann and *Gruppenkommandeur* of III./JG 1

Only two Liberators were lost on the 26 February raid, not the four claimed by I./JG 1. The second was *Maisey's* sister-ship, *Sad Sack* (41-23804), sent down over Oldenburg by 3. *Staffel's* Unteroffizier Leo Demetz two minutes later. It is also highly unlikely that all four of the B-17s credited to the *Gruppe* on this date were, in fact, destroyed. VIII Bomber Command's admitted losses were five B-17s and two B-24s – less than half of the 15 claimed by the Luftwaffe fighters (13 shared between JG 1s four *Gruppen* and two by NJG 1's nightfighters, who had again been called upon to lend their support).

Thus ended the first month of the Defence of the Reich campaign . The dominant feature throughout had been the appalling weather. This affected the US bomber crews more than the Luftwaffe's fighter pilots. Many of the former had still been training in the cloudless blue skies of the southern United States only months earlier. Some of the latter had been stationed on the North Sea coast for two years or more and were wise to the vagaries of the German Bight in all its moods, summer and winter.

It had certainly been the atrocious conditions which had restricted VIII Bomber Command's activities to just three raids, all against targets on the North Sea coastline. The 15 combat losses sustained during these missions had done nothing to dent American confidence in unescorted daylight bombing. Not that they were in a position to do anything about it if it had. The short-legged Spitfire VBs with which the embryonic VIII Fighter Command was currently equipped would have been able to do little more than wave the bombers goodbye and wish them *bon voyage* as they reached the limit of their range halfway across the North Sea.

For their part, although I./JG 1 had accounted for some half-dozen of the enemy's losses, Hauptmann Beise's pilots had already come to realise that their new Bf 109G-1s were proving far from ideal bomber-killing machines. The early *Gustav's* armament of a single engine-mounted 20 mm MG-151/20 cannon and two 7.9 mm MG 17 fuselage machine guns lacked the punch to despatch a heavy bomber cleanly – as demonstrated by the four passes required by future Knight's Cross winner Heinz Knoke to bring down his first B-24. Several attempts were made to improve the G-1's firepower.

One or two of the *Gruppe's* fighters were fitted with a pair of underwing gondolas containing MG 151/20 cannon. Others were later equipped with rocket launchers. A few even had bomb racks attached to their bellies so that trials could be carried out into the feasibility of dropping bombs onto the American heavy bomber formations from above! For the time being, however, it was business as usual for both sides. And the month of March would also see just three incursions into Reich airspace.

On 4 March VIII Bomber Command finally made it to the Hamm marshalling yards – or, rather, one bomb group did. It was to have been

A pair of unidentified I. *Gruppe* machines equipped with drop tanks and underwing cannon gondola patrol the skies of western Germany in the spring of 1943

an all-Flying Fortress strike, with the Liberators flying a diversionary mission on this date. But the four B-17 groups became separated in the omnipresent heavy cloud over the North Sea. Three decided to bomb Rotterdam as an alternative. The 91st BG plugged on alone on instruments until breaking out into clear weather over Germany.

I./JG 1's participation in the day's action was confined to 3. *Staffel*, which engaged the 'heavies' west of the target area and reported one *Gustav* damaged by return fire. But the sole claim for a B-17 destroyed, by Unteroffizier Günther Range, is not corroborated by US records.

A fortnight was to pass before enemy bombers were next reported to be approaching across the North Sea. Their target was the Vegesack U-boat yards on the River Weser, south of Bremen. All three *Staffeln* of I./JG 1 were scrambled, and they intercepted a formation of incoming B-24s south of Heligoland. In the 25-minute running battle that ensued between the island and the coast, three pilots of 2. *Staffel* claimed a Liberator apiece, although only one B-24 was subsequently reported missing. Two G-1s also went down. Despite being wounded, both pilots managed to take to their parachutes. One, Oberleutnant Hortari Schmude, the *Staffelkapitän* of 1./JG 1, was picked up safely. The injuries suffered by the other, 2. *Staffel's* Leutnant Dieter Gerhardt, were so severe that he died in his dinghy before help could reach him.

Forty minutes later, and some 75 miles off the Dutch coast, another Bf 109 pilot, Unteroffizier Max Winkler of 2./JG 27, was credited with shooting down one of a group of B-17s heading back to England.

The *Afrika* badge on the cowling of this early *Gustav* 'gunboat' clearly shows it to be an aircraft of I./JG 27, then based at Leeuwarden, in March 1943

Since being withdrawn from North Africa in November 1942, I./JG 27 had been stationed in northern France (see *Osprey Aviation Elite Units 12*). On 15 March 1943 Oberleutnant Josef Jansen's 2. *Staffel* had then been transferred to Amsterdam-Schiphol on temporary attachment to JG 1. It was the first of many units that would be fed into the Defence of the Reich organisation as the daylight battle of the skies of Germany intensified. And Winkler's B-17 was just the first of nearly 200 US heavy bombers that I./JG 27 would claim in the course of that campaign.

VIII Bomber Command's Mission No 46 of 22 March was another maximum effort against a familiar target – Wilhelmshaven. The approaching bombers were first engaged by Fw 190s of JG 1 north of the Dutch Frisian Island of Texel. Then I. *Gruppe's Gustavs* received the order to scramble, only to be recalled when uncertainty arose as to the enemy's intended objective. While the Messerschmitts were being readied for a second take-off, Leutnant Heinz Knoke seized his opportunity.

Although he has since attributed the original idea of aerial bombing the US formations from above to his great friend Dieter Gerhardt – with whom he had been conducting test flights in the interim – the latter's recent death meant that it had fallen to Knoke himself to put the theory into practice. Hurriedly calling for his groundcrew to arm his machine with a 250-kg bomb, Knoke sat fuming and fidgeting in his cockpit as the armourers struggled to attach the bomb to the *Gustav's* belly rack. He watched his *Staffel* scramble and head for the coast. Then, finally:

'"Ready!" Easing the throttle forward, I trundle heavily to the far side of the field. With the weight of the bomb beneath my fuselage, I have got to take off into the wind. But as I turn to do so my machine suddenly tips to the left – a tyre has burst! I send up a red flare. My groundcrew over at dispersal immediately grasp what has happened. Twenty or thirty men pile into a small truck and race across the field towards me. They put their backs under the left wing and heave it up. With the engine still running, the tyre is changed in a matter of seconds.

'"All clear!" The men quickly jump out of the way. I push the throttle forward and start to pick up speed. The kite begins to sag to port again, but after a 200-metre run I manage to haul it off the ground, missing the roof of Number 2 hangar by a hair's breadth.

'I climb out over the sea at full throttle into a cloudless blue sky. High above me – at 23,000 ft – I can see the ruler-straight contrails of the *Amis* (Americans), as well as those of our own fighters curving in to attack. The battle is already in progress, the unaccustomed heavy load is making my crate damned sluggish. It takes me almost 25 minutes to stagger up to 29,500 ft. The *Amis* have already dropped their bombs on Wilhelmshaven as the fire and smoke far below clearly indicate. Now they are retreating out over Heligoland.

An armourer poses for the camera just prior to hoisting a 250-kg bomb onto the ventral rack of Leutnant Heinz Knoke's 'Black 1'. The overall lack of urgency suggests that this is in preparation for a practice mission, not the emergency scramble described in the text

'I creep forward above the formation until I am level with the lead B-17. I have been under fire from below for some minutes now as I try to take a rough aim, dipping first the left wing and then the right to keep the formation in sight. Two, three bullet holes blossom in my left wing.

'I fuse the bomb, take aim one last time and press the bomb-release button on the control stick. My bomb plummets downwards. Climbing steeply, I bank so that I can watch its fall. It explodes right in the middle of a group of three Boeings. A wing is torn off one of them, and the other two dive away in alarm. Some 19 miles west of Heligoland, my third heavy bomber plunges into the sea (Knoke was one of three claimants during the recent Vegesack raid). There has been no sign of fire. The torn-off wing follows it down, fluttering like an autumn leaf.'

Although JG 1 was credited with four B-17s on this date, only one actually went down. All the evidence points to the day's sole Fortress casualty – the 91st BG's B-17F 42-29659 *Liberty Bell* as having fallen victim to Knoke as described above. Some sources have suggested that Knoke's fighter was armed with rockets rather than a bomb, but this is at complete variance with the Luftwaffe pilot's own later accounts of the action, all of which maintain that the B-17 was downed by a single bomb.

Whatever impact the bomb may have had on the remaining 17 Fortresses in the 91st BG formation, its detonation reverberated up the Luftwaffe chain of command right to the very top.

Immediately after landing back at Jever, Leutnant Knoke was instructed to report to the *Geschwaderkommodore*. Oberstleutnant Dr Erich Mix had also been in the air at the time, and had witnessed the demise of the B-17;

'My word, Knoke, you ought to try that with the whole *Staffel*!'

'That's the plan, sir'.

'Do you think it will work?'

Knoke was cautious;

'If today wasn't just a fluke, we ought to be able to bring down a few more *dicke Autos* ('fat cars', i.e. heavy bombers) the same way.'

Next, the *Jafü Deutsche Bucht (*Fighter-Leader German Bight), Oberst Karl Hentschel, telephoned;

'I'm delighted, my dear Knoke, magnificent show, congratulations!'

Then, during the night, Knoke's bedside telephone rang. It was the duty switchboard operator;

"Herr Leutnant, I have a top-priority call for you from the OKL (Luftwaffe High Command)!'

'"What! For me?" 'I state my name. A Major of the *Reichsmarschall's* staff is on the other end of the line. "It was you who brought down the enemy machine today by bombing, was it not?"

'"Jawohl, Herr Major." I am asked to give full details – the type of bomb used, what kind of fuse, how had I carried out the attack, what were the results. Then, "Who ordered the bombing operation to be flown?" Ordered? "Nobody, Herr Major, I simply went up and dropped the bomb."

'There is a long silence. I realise for the first time that I had acted completely without authority. Nobody had ordered a bomb-carrying mission to be flown. I could smell trouble brewing. The Major came back on the line. "I am putting you through to the Herr *Reichsmarschall*!" His words hit me like a bolt from the blue. Lying in bed, wearing only a pyjama jacket, I freeze to attention horizontally and bark out my name, rank and unit. "I am delighted by the initiative you displayed and wish to express to you my personal appreciation." "Most obedient thanks, Herr *Reichsmarschall*!" And that was that.'

Although Knoke was later chewed out for his unauthorised action by *General der Flieger* Josef Kammhuber, GOC XII. *Fliegerkorps*, Göring's personal interest in the matter ensured that the idea was taken further. The test centre at Rechlin was ordered to carry out trials to establish the proper tactics for air-to-air bombing, and several such missions were reportedly flown by *Jagdgruppen* based in the Mediterranean. Here, they proved a complete failure. Firstly, US bombers in the southern theatre did not fly such tight formations. Secondly, and much more importantly, they often enjoyed the luxury of fighter protection. Over the Reich, air-to-air bombing operations against VIII Bomber Command's unescorted 'heavies' would sputter on for a little longer before the concept was finally abandoned altogether.

Less spectacular, but of much greater benefit to the Defence of the Reich organisation in the long run, was the steady infusion of strength as further *Jagdgruppen* were added to its order of battle.

Major Reinhard 'Seppl' Seiler's III./JG 54 (see *Osprey Aviation Elite Units 6*) was a veteran Russian front Bf 109 unit which had been part of an experiment aimed at exchanging one complete eastern front *Jagdgeschwader* with a western-based one. The impracticalities of the scheme soon revealed themselves, however, and it was called off after just one reinforced *Gruppe* from each *Jagdgeschwader* had swapped places. But whereas I./JG 26 was promptly recalled from Russia, III./JG 54, whose members had arrived by rail at Vendeville, in France, on 12 February 1943, would remain in the west. After receiving a full complement of new Bf 109G-4s, III./JG 54 was transferred to Oldenburg, south of Wilhelmshaven, on 27 March 1943.

Four days later JG 1's four component *Gruppen* were split into two, with a new III. *Gruppe* to be added to each pair, thus effectively creating two *Jagdgeschwader* out of one. The redesignations of the three Fw 190 *Gruppen* are irrelevant here. Suffice it to say that, as of 1 April 1943, Hauptmann Beise's Jever-based I./JG 1 was renumbered to become II./JG 11.

The 'new' JG 11 now became responsible for the German sector of the North Sea coastline, while the reconstituted JG 1 guarded the more westerly Dutch seaboard approaches to the Reich. The two new III. *Gruppen* – both created from scratch and both initially equipped with Bf 109G-6s – would later join their parent *Geschwader* in their respective areas of operations, Major Karl-Heinz Leesmann's III./JG 1 taking up residence at Deelen, in Holland, and Hauptmann Ernst-Günther Heinze's III./JG 11 forming at Neumünster, north of Hamburg.

Then, for the first time in the Defence of the Reich campaign, Bf 109-equipped *Gruppen* would outnumber those flying the Fw 190 (by four to three). In addition, there were also two other *Staffeln* on Bf 109s – 2./JG 27, which had now moved from Amsterdam-Schiphol to Leeuwarden, and the *Jagdstaffel* Helgoland. As its name implies, the latter was based on the island of Heligoland (or, to be more exact, on the

Pictured here earlier as a hauptmann with II./JG 77, Major Anton Mader was appointed *Kommodore* of JG 11 upon the *Geschwader's* activation on 1 April 1943

smaller eastern island of Helgoland-Düne which, in comparison to the red sandstone bulk and towering cliffs of its neighbour, was little more than a sandbank).

Activated on 7 April 1943 and commanded by Oberleutnant Hermann Hintzen, *Jagdstaffel* Helgoland was unique in being equipped with the Bf 109T. This was a navalised, extended-span conversion of the basic Bf 109E originally intended for service aboard the never-to-be-completed aircraft carrier *Graf Zeppelin*.

This reorganisation of the Reich's aerial defences quickly paid dividends. The Americans' only incursion into German airspace in April was to result in their heaviest losses to date.

The target for the four Flying Fortress groups flying Mission No 52 on 17 April 1943 was the Focke-Wulf aircraft manufacturing plants on the outskirts of Bremen. All but eight of the 115 B-17s despatched bombed their assigned targets, causing severe damage to the works and the destruction of many completed Fw 190 fighters. But the Fortress crews also reported the strongest opposition yet encountered.

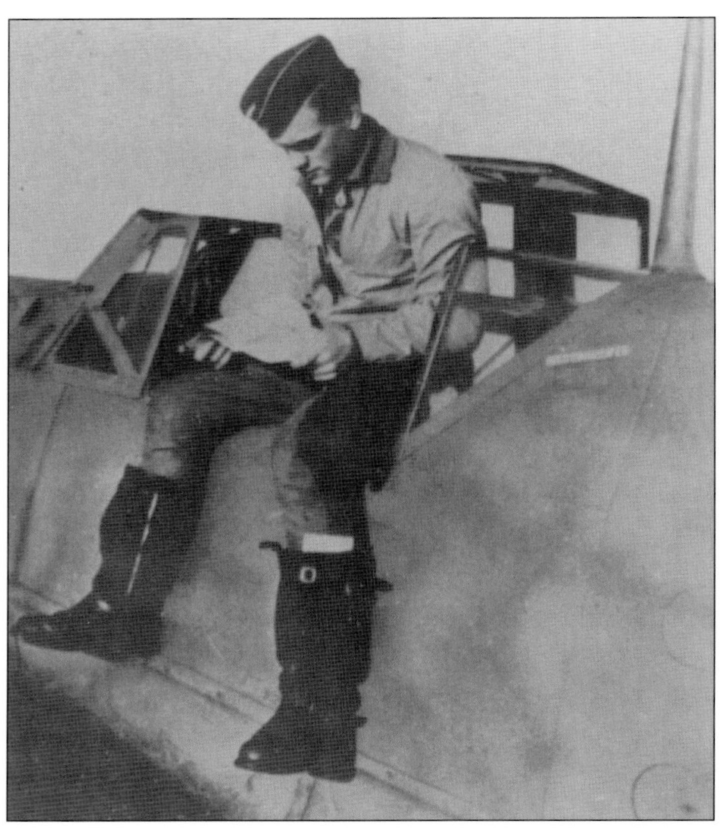

Perched on the cockpit sill of his Bf 109T (note twin access panels at lower right for the GM-1 high-altitude boost system), Leutnant Erich Hondt served briefly as the *Kapitän* of *Jasta* Helgoland during the summer of 1943 before taking command of 2./JG 11. With more than ten four-engined bombers among his final total – most, if not all, scored on the Fw 190 – Erich Hondt ended the war flying Me 262s with JV 44

That opposition included two Fw 190 *Gruppen*, plus the Bf 109s of II./JG 11 (together with the attached *Jasta* Helgoland), III./JG 54 and 2./JG 27, as well as twin-engined nightfighters from NJGs 1 and 3. For more than two hours – from the time they neared the coast until well back out to sea again – the B-17s were subjected to waves of attacks from the defending Luftwaffe fighters. No fewer than 16 heavy bombers went down, six of these from the 91st BG's 401st BS alone.

The first *Gruppe* to make contact were the veterans of the Bight, albeit now operating as II./G 11 and led by a new *Gruppenkommandeur*. Wearing the Knight's Cross with Oak Leaves, Major Adolf Dickfeld had spent the early years of the war serving with JG 52 (see *Osprey Aviation Elite Units 15*). Latterly, he had commanded II./JG 2 (see *Osprey Aviation Elite Units 1*) in Tunisia. Putting this combined experience to good use, Major Dickfeld was credited with the first B-17 to be downed on 17 April. It took his overall total to 134.

In the formation behind Dickfeld, 5. *Staffel's* Heinz Knoke had still not given up entirely on the idea of air-to-air bombing. But the missile he had so laboriously hauled aloft failed to find a target. It then took Knoke three firing passes to bring down the day's second Flying Fortress. Evidence suggests that this was the 91st BG's B-17F 41-24459 *Hellzapoppin*, one of the six 401st BS machines that failed to return from Bremen.

Altogether, II./JG 11's pilots were credited with the destruction of six B-17s, with Unteroffizier Ewald Herhold of *Jasta* Helgoland adding a seventh. In return, four Bf 109G-1s were damaged in emergency landings, mainly due to lack of fuel after the lengthy engagement. One Bf 109T was lost in combat, crashing into the sea north of the island of Norderney after Unteroffizier Oskar Menz had successfully bailed out.

Of the other Bf 109 units involved, III./JG 54 claimed four B-17s in exchange for four *Gustavs* damaged and one lost. The fighter that went down was that flown by Knight's Cross holder Hauptmann Hans-Ekkehard Bob, the *Staffelkapitän* of 9./JG 54. Leading his *Staffel* in for a second frontal attack as the bombers withdrew from the target area, Bob misjudged his distance by a fraction and ended up ramming his chosen victim. Escaping from the mangled fuselage of his fighter, he found himself floating earthwards surrounded by ten other parachutes – the entire crew of the stricken B-17 had also wasted little time in bailing out!

Suffering from delayed shock, Bob meekly allowed himself to be rounded up with the others. It was not until they were all standing in line and he began automatically to unzip his flying overalls that one of his captors shouted, 'There's an *Ami* here wearing the Knight's Cross!' Suddenly coming to his senses, Hauptmann Hans-Ekkehard Bob quickly identified himself as a Luftwaffe officer.

Oddly, American records make no mention of an aerial collision among the day's losses, but additional details provided by Bob, plus the location (southwest of Bremen), suggest that his victim was the 306th BG's 42-29643. Whatever its true identity the Flying Fortress – victory number 57 for Hans-Ekkehard Bob – was the only four-engined kill of his long and illustrious career.

The pilots of 2./JG 27 also claimed two B-17s (one unconfirmed) north of the Dutch island of Ameland for no loss to themselves.

In addition to the Bf 109 successes detailed above, the Fw 190 *Gruppen* and the nightfighters were credited with a further 13 victories between them. The Luftwaffe's claims thus totalled 25 – nine more than the actual US losses. Once again, however, the gunners aboard the bombers far outdid their opponents, submitting claims for no fewer than 63 fighters destroyed, plus 15 probables and 17 damaged – 95 in all! This was an indication perhaps of just how rattled the bomber crews had been by the unaccustomed ferocity of the Luftwaffe's attacks. The true German casualties were five fighters lost (including two Bf 110s of NJG 1 which had collided in poor visibility far from the scene of the action), one written-off in an emergency landing and nine damaged.

The losses suffered by VIII Bomber Command over Bremen were double those for any previous mission. They represented a casualty rate of 15 per cent. Attrition on such a scale could not be borne over the longer term. For the first time questions began to be asked about the bombers' ability to survive unprotected in enemy airspace.

For the time being, however, there was little that could be done to remedy the situation. VIII Fighter Command had flown its last Spitfire missions in early April when the P-47 made its operational debut. Although the range of the heavyweight Thunderbolt exceeded that of the British fighter, it still could not proceed beyond the German-occupied Low Countries (where two P-47s had already fallen victim to an Fw 190

Hauptmann Adolf Dickfeld claimed his first Defence of the Reich B-17 on 17 April 1943 – the very day he assumed command of II./JG 11. He would add a second before taking up a staff appointment with the RLM in Berlin the following month

Hans-Ekkehard Bob (right) congratulates Wilhelm Schilling on completing 9./JG 54's 500th operational mission. Both would be wearing the Knight's Cross – awarded in Russia, where this photograph was taken – by the time they arrived in the west with III./JG 54 to take up Defence of the Reich duties in early 1943

A flight of Thunderbolts disport for the press at an airfield in the UK in the early spring of 1943. Their entry into service would be too late to save B-17F 41-24459 in the foreground. The 91st BG's *Hellzapoppin* would go down south of Bremen on 17 April 1943

of II./JG 1). The bubble of the 'heavies'' invulnerability may have been pricked, but it had not yet been burst. Many still looked upon the advent of the new fighter as little more than a useful adjunct to VIII Bomber Command's operations. Before long everybody – not least the bomber crews themselves – regarded its presence as essential, and desperate efforts were being made to increase the P-47's range by the use of drop tanks.

Confident that they had hit the Americans hard over Bremen, the Luftwaffe fighter units awaited the bombers' next incursion. But it would be nearly a month before the enemy reappeared over the Reich. In the interim a third heavy bomber wing had been added to VIII Bomber Command's order of battle. This increase in numbers allowed it to mount multiple raids, attacking several widely separated targets at the same time in an attempt to fragment the Germans' fighter defences.

14 May's Mission No 56 was one such multiple effort. While groups of heavy bombers, some with fighter protection, were despatched against objectives in the Low Countries, the main force of unescorted B-17s and B-24s – over 100 strong – were sent against the submarine yards at Kiel, the major naval base on the Baltic Sea.

Once again, the Bf 109s of II./JG 11 (plus the attached *Jasta* Helgoland) provided the first line of defence. Among them was Leutnant Heinz Knoke, who had been appointed *Staffelkapitän* of 5./JG 11 a fortnight earlier. Still anxious to prove the validity of air-to-air bombing, Knoke led his entire *Staffel* high above the Flying Fortresses as they crossed the Schleswig-Holstein peninsula towards the target. But every time he attempted to manoeuvre his *Staffel* into position directly overhead a formation of bombers, it would weave out of the way 'as if they realised what we were trying to do'.

By now the leading B-17s were nearing their objective – the Germania shipyards on the eastern side of the port's inner basin. Having been unable to carry out a formation drop, Knoke ordered his pilots to bomb singly once the enemy had cleared the target area. When his own bomb failed to detonate, Knoke resorted once more to his cannon. A first frontal attack against a group of B-17s flying a little distance apart from the main formation proved unsuccessful, but a second head-on pass a few minutes later hit home.

According to Knoke, 'the Fortress reared up like a stricken animal, before falling away in steep spirals to the right'. Fellow bomber crews who witnessed the demise of the 92nd BG's B-17F 42-30003 reported last seeing it 'circling and going down under control with one engine out and a stabiliser missing'. The bomber came down near Husum, on the western coast of Schleswig-Holstein. Whether the crew survived the crash-landing, or had bailed our during the descent, is unknown, but all ten duly became prisoners-of-war. It was Leutnant Heinz Knoke's fifth heavy bomber kill in the space of less than three months. It made him the first Bf 109 ace of the Defence of the Reich campaign.

Two more B-17s went down into the North Sea between Amrum and Heligoland shortly afterwards. One was credited to Hauptmann Egon Falkensamer, *Staffelkapitän* of 6./JG 11. Other fighter units had also joined the fray by this stage, and two Fw 190 pilots of I./JG 11, plus a nightfighter crew of NJG 3, also entered claims for Flying Fortresses.

Trailing the B-17s in over the target area, the 17 B-24Ds of the 44th BG – the only Liberator group involved in the Kiel mission – flew into a veritable hornets' nest of flak and fighters. Five bombers were shot down and every one of the other twelve damaged. The Bf 109s of II./JG 11 and III./JG 54 claimed seven Liberators between them, but lost five of their own number. One machine of 6./JG 11, damaged by return fire from a B-24, crashed west of Kiel after its pilot successfully bailed out. III./JG 54 reported two pilots killed, and they were almost certainly flying the two *Gustavs* of 9. *Staffel* which were seen to collide over the town itself.

Undeterred by the losses incurred on the Kiel mission (half those of the previous trip to Bremen), VIII Bomber Command despatched its nine Flying Fortress groups on another operation 24 hours later. It was to be a twin-pronged attack on the North Sea ports of Wilhelmshaven and Emden. But the Wilhelmshaven force ran into ten-tenths cloud before reaching the target area and was forced to seek alternative targets. Most opted for the offshore airfields an the islands of Helgoland-Düne and Wangerooge.

With smoke from the Germania yards marking the B-17s' previous passage, two vics of Liberators cross Kiel on 14 May 1943

The Luftwaffe responded by sending up the same units as it had done the day before. The two Bf 109 *Gruppen*, II./JG 11 and III./JG 54, claimed four and five victories respectively. One of II./JG 11's kills provided the last of the 135 victories amassed by Major Adolf Dickfeld, whose operational career was now about to come to an end with his appointment to the Staff of the RLM. A second B-17 fell to Dickfeld's successor as *Gruppenkommandeur*, Hauptmann Günther Specht (who had also claimed a B-24 over Kiel the previous day).

Specht was no stranger to the northern coastline, having scored his first kills as a *Zerstörer* pilot with I./ZG 26 over this very area in September 1939. Two months later he had himself been shot down and lost his left eye. Despite this disability he was now back on operations, and would become one of the leading *Experten* in Defence of the Reich.

II./JG 11's other two kills were credited to Heinz Knoke and one of his 5. *Staffel* pilots, Unteroffizier Helmut Lennartz. According to his own account of the action, Lennartz had brought his Flying Fortress down by air-to-air bombing. If true (the Americans made no mention of the incident), it was one of the relatively few successful attacks of its kind.

Was it one of the six B-24s seen in the photograph on page 25 that provided the second Defence of the Reich heavy bomber kill for Hauptmann Günther Specht, the new *Gruppenkommandeur* of II./JG 11?

For the past six weeks II./JG 11 had gradually been replacing its original Bf 109G-1s with G-6s equipped with underwing cannon gondolas. And it was with these harder hitting 'gunboats' that the *Gruppe* was now scoring the majority of its successes.

In contrast to II./JG 11, which suffered no casualties, III./JG 54's five victories had been dearly bought. It lost four *Gustavs* and had two pilots killed. Both of the latter were Knight's Cross holders, recently decorated for their previous service on the eastern front. Since arriving in the west Leutnant Friedrich Rupp had been credited with two heavy bombers, but Hauptmann Günther Fink had failed to add to his Russian score. Both had gone down into the North Sea off Heligoland – a telling indication

Oberleutnant Heinz Knoke poses for the camera in front of a new Bf 109G-6 'gunboat'. The individual number of this machine is not known, but it is clear from the tiny fragment just visible above the leading-edge of the wing that it is not his usual 'Black 1'. Note the narrow red band around the rear fuselage

that the air battles over the Reich were no respecter of reputations. Nor would these two be the last. It was a lesson that many more newcomers drafted in to homeland defence duties from other fighting fronts, tyros and highly decorated veterans alike, were to learn to their cost in the final two years of the war.

During the next week VIII Bomber Command's B-17s were sent out on two more double raids on northern ports – Kiel and Flensburg on 19 May, Wilhelmshaven and Emden two days later. With their confidence growing, the Bf 109 units of the Reich's Defence, still comprising just two *Gruppen* and two *Staffeln*, were credited with the destruction of 25 of the B-17s engaged in these operations (18 were actually lost) at minimum cost to themselves. It was a similar story in the first half of June when the next two such raids were mounted, also within a 72-hour period – Wilhelmshaven and Cuxhaven were attacked on 11 June, followed by Bremen and Kiel on 13th. But June was notable for other reasons.

Firstly, four more Bf 109 *Gruppen* were added to the defenders' order of battle. 11 June finally saw the long-awaited combat debut of Major Leesmann's III./JG 1 when it was sent up against the B-17 force approaching Wilhelmshaven. Only one bomber was claimed – that by Leutnant Eugen Wintergerst, *Staffelkapitän* of 9./JG 1. It was victory 21 for Wintergerst, his 20th having been a Soviet MiG-3 fighter downed on the eastern front in September 1941. And a lot had happened to Wintergerst in the intervening 21 months.

On 24 September 1941 he had collided with fellow 4./JG 77 pilot Leutnant Herwig Zuzic behind enemy lines. Both were quickly captured by the Russians. But while prisoners together they decided to take a huge gamble. They would pretend to convert to the communist cause and allow themselves to be 'turned'. It worked. Once their Soviet captors were convinced that the pair had seen the political light, they were parachuted back into Rumania to operate as spies and saboteurs.

Instead, they immediately reported to the nearest German authorities. The questioning they were then subjected to was almost as harsh as the sessions they had undergone on the other side of the lines. Eventually, however, their interrogators were satisfied and they were allowed to return to operational duty. But they were not permitted to serve on the eastern front for fear of being captured again. They had therefore been posted to IV./JG 1 in the west. And from here it was but a short move to the newly forming III. *Gruppe*, where both were appointed *Staffelkapitäne*, Herwig Zuzic of 8. and Eugen Wintergerst of 9./JG 1.

Wintergerst's single victory of 11 June was overshadowed by the ten claims made by the veteran II./JG 11, including one each for Hauptmann Specht and Oberleutnant Knoke. And a B-17 reported by the

Hauptmann Günther Fink, pictured here (left) with Oberfeldwebel Rudolf Klemm in Russia, was one of many experienced pilots who would fail to make the transition from eastern front to west. He went down over the North Sea before being able to achieve a single victory in Defence of the Reich

Americans as having been lost in a mid-air collision with an Fw 190 had almost certainly also fallen victim to a Bf 109. After carrying out a frontal attack on his chosen target, 9./JG 54's Unteroffizier Werner Büscher attempted to roll away above it, but his wing smashed into the nose of the 379th BG Flying Fortress. Both bomber and fighter went down, each minus a wing. Although wounded, Büscher managed to bail out.

Another Bf 109 unit new to the German Bight that scored its opening Defence of the Reich victories on this date was Hauptmann Kurt Ruppert's III./JG 26. Flying in from Belgium in late May, and bringing with it a wealth of experience gained from combatting the 'heavies' over the Low Countries, III./JG 26 had taken up residence at Nordholz, south of Cuxhaven. Its first successes were a brace of B-17s credited to two of Ruppert's NCO pilots, Feldwebel Niese and Unteroffizier Stutt.

With over 250 B-17s despatched, VIII Bomber Command's Mission No 62 of 11 June had been its heaviest raid to date. Adding credence to the 'safety in numbers' camp, only eight Flying Fortresses had been shot down by flak and fighters.

In stark contrast, of the 60 B-17s that attacked Kiel two days later, a staggering 22 failed to return. Scrambling from Jever at 0854 hrs, it was the pilots of II./JG 11 who, yet again, were among the first to engage the incoming bombers – although it was Unteroffizier Ewald Herhold of the attached *Jasta* Helgoland who sent the *Gruppe's* first Flying Fortress down west of Neumünster. The second was reported by some sources as 'probably being hit by an aerial bomb'. If this is the case, it was most likely that credited to Leutnant Kilian, the only member of Heinz Knoke's 5. *Staffel* to make a claim on this date.

Over the target area the pilots of II./JG 11 added six more B-17s to the unit's collective scoreboard. Their only casualty was Unteroffizier Rohe, who had been wounded and bailed out near Neumünster. Ewald Herhold's Bf 109T had also been hit by return fire during the two passes that had been required to bring down his 95th BG Flying Fortress. Injured in the knee, he too was forced to take to his parachute. A second *Jasta* Helgoland pilot made an emergency landing in his damaged *Toni* on the island of Föhr.

III./JG 54 equalled II./JG 11's score of eight on this occasion, while III./JG 26's five victories against the 95th BG had all been achieved in the space of little more than ten minutes. The unit's sole casualty was Hauptmann Ruppert – the first Bf 109 *Gruppenkommandeur* to be lost in

Gustavs of 9./JG 11 prepare to take off from Oldenburg in the summer of 1943. 'Yellow 4' in the foreground is possibly the machine in which Unteroffizier Alfred Thieme was shot down north of Osnabrück on 28 July

the Defence of the Reich. His place was taken temporarily by acting-*Kommandeur* Hauptmann Rolf Hermichen.

The loss of over a third of the Kiel attacking force came as a huge shock to the Americans, especially after the perceived success of the Wilhelmshaven mission 48 hours earlier. The events at Kiel underlined the pressing need for adequate long-range fighter protection. But the machine that would, it was fervently hoped, be able to provide such protection was still a good six months away. Meanwhile, desperate efforts were being made to produce an auxiliary fuel tank that would at least enable VIII Fighter Command's existing Thunderbolts to poke their noses beyond the German border. And all the while the Luftwaffe was strengthening its Reich defences.

After the original I./JG 3 had been withdrawn from the Russian front in September 1941 for re-equipment and subsequent redesignation as II./JG 1, an entirely new I./JG 3 had been created in preparation of the eastern front's summer offensive of 1942. By year end this had taken the *Gruppe* as far as Stalingrad, after which it too was returned to the Reich for rest and re-equipment. Having spent several weeks at Döberitz, near Berlin, working up on Bf 109G-4s, I./JG 3, commanded by Hauptmann Klaus Quaet-Faslem, had been transferred to München-Gladbach (today's Mönchengladbach) in April 1943. Here, it took delivery of its first G-6 'gunboats' and was incorporated into the Defence of the Reich organisation. The *Gruppe's* introduction to the air war over the homeland came on the day the enemy launched his first major attack on the Ruhr.

The main part of VIII Bomber Command's Mission No 65 of 22 June was a raid by ten B-17 groups on the synthetic-rubber plant at Hüls. The bombers' route to the Ruhr sidelined the Bf 109s of II./JG 11 far to the north. The bulk of the defensive burden fell on the Dutch-based Fw 190s of JG 1, who were credited with 15 B-17s downed. In addition, III./JG 54 claimed one and the 'newcomers' of I./JG 3 three more.

Amongst the Hüls raiders were examples of the USAAF's latest defensive weapon for its bomber formations – the YB-40. Somewhat ironically, while Heinz Knoke and his *Staffel* had been trying to turn their Bf 109 fighters into bombers, the USAAF had been experimenting with the use of the B-17 bomber as an escort fighter in the form of the YB-40!

In an attempt to improve the defensive capabilities of the otherwise unescorted Flying Fortress formations, 20 B-17s were equipped with additional gun turrets, armament and armour. Literally 'Flying Fortresses', these YB-40s had first been used over France in 1943. Eleven of them made the trip to Hüls, where they suffered their only combat loss – to flak. Like 5./JG 11's bomb-carrying Bf 109s, however, the heavily-laden YB-40s were not a success. Incapable of keeping up with the normal B-17 bombers in climb and combat cruise, they were withdrawn from service in August. Some were reconverted back into their original form, while others went on to serve as gunnery trainers.

On 25 June the B-17s returned to their more familiar North Sea stamping grounds. But heavy cloud over the mainland obscured the primary targets and the bombers were restricted to attacking two coastal convoys off the Frisian Islands. The defenders nonetheless put up eight *Gruppen* in opposition. Among them for the first time were the Bf 109G-6s of III./JG 11, this *Gruppe* being credited with two bombers –

one fell to Oberleutnant Hugo Frey, *Staffelkapitän* of 7./JG 11, and the other to Feldwebel Siegfried Zick (both of whom had been claimants for the first B-17 downed over Wilhelmshaven on 27 January).

Of the other Bf 109 *Gruppen* engaged, III./JG 54 achieved a single victory and III./JG 26 three, while II./JG 11 and III./JG 1 claimed six and seven respectively. The *Gruppenkommandeure* of the latter two, Hauptmann Günther Specht and Major Karl-Heinz Leesmann, were both successful with one bomber apiece. This took Specht's tally of heavy bombers since joining to five. But their units suffered disproportionately. II./JG 11 had just one pilot wounded (the indefatigable Heinz Knoke, hit in the hand while in the process of downing his ninth heavy bomber). III./JG 1 reported two pilots killed – including Leesmann's *Gruppen-Adjutant*, Oberleutnant Friedrich Hardt, who had claimed his first victory only moments before he was himself hit – and three wounded.

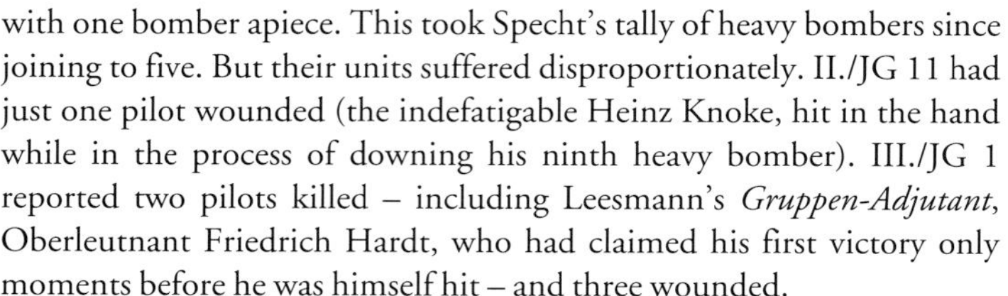

In contrast to the purposeful air of the photograph on page 28, 8./JG 1's 'Black 8' enjoys a welcome siesta in the Leeuwarden sun. In addition to the *Staffel* badge (see colour profile 4) immediately aft of the *Beule*, this machine sports an example of a less commonly seen *Rotte* emblem (a *Rotte* was a formation of two aircraft). The leader of the pair, Feldwebel Josef Kehrle, carried the silhouette of a skinny huntsman in a shield below the cockpit of his 'Black 7'. The wingman, Unteroffizier Rudolf Einberger, displayed a more portly version of the same huntsman, which is just visible here beneath the shadow of the sunshade. Einberger would be killed in this aircraft when shot down in error by German flak over Bremen on 8 October 1943. A wounded Josef Kehrle wrote off his 'Black 7' in an emergency landing after tangling with P-47s over Holland on 1 April 1944

For the next month there was very little operational activity over the Bight – just one major raid, and that was thwarted by solid cloud cover across the whole of northwest Germany – as RAF and USAAF Bomber Commands prepared themselves for Operation *Gomorrah*/'Blitz Week'. This was to be a six-day, round-the-clock combined bombing offensive against targets inside the Reich. While the RAF concentrated its nocturnal efforts against Hamburg, culminating in the devastating firestorm raid on the night of 27/28 July, the US Flying Fortresses were despatched against a range of military and industrial targets by day.

The weather on 25 July was still far from ideal. It forced two of the VIII Bomber Command formations to seek alternatives to their primary objectives at Hamburg and Kiel, and the third to abandon its mission against Warnemünde altogether.

Although the defending fighters were up in force, most units did not make contact until the B-17s were turning back out towards the sea. In a series of separate engagements, together lasting well over an hour, the Bf 109 *Gruppen* claimed a total of 14 bombers destroyed. II./JG 11 (plus the attached *Jasta* Helgoland) were responsible for six of them, but had four of its own pilots wounded. II./JG 26's three claims were made without loss. But III./JG 1's trio of B-17s cost the unit its *Gruppenkommandeur* when Major Karl-Heinz Leesmann's Bf 109G-6 was hit and crashed into the sea shortly after his 37th, and final, victim had gone down.

Twenty-four hours later the bombers' main targets were the Continental and Nordhafen rubber works in Hannover and the U-boat yards at Hamburg. The Bf 109 units almost replicated their previous day's performance with claims for a total of 15 Flying Fortresses destroyed. Among the familiar names adding to their growing tally of heavy bombers were Günther Specht and Hugo Frey of II./JG 11.

Less well known, perhaps, were two III./JG 1 pilots, both of whom were credited with their first B-17 kills on this date, thereby taking the overall score of each to exactly 40. Both were veterans of JG 3 and the eastern front. One, Feldwebel Alfred Miksch, had only recently been transferred to 8./JG 1 at Leeuwarden. The other, already wearing the Knight's Cross, was Oberleutnant Robert Olejnik, who had been a *Staffelkapitän* in the original I./JG 3 when it was withdrawn from Russia in September 1941 and redesignated to become II./JG 1. Since promoted to hauptmann, this was Olejnik's first day as *Gruppenkommandeur* of III./JG 1 in place of the fallen Karl-Heinz Leesmann.

On 28 July VIII Bomber Command despatched 15 Flying Fortress groups against two aircraft manufacturing plants – the Fieseler works at Kassel and the AGO factory at Oschersleben. The bombers' approach route took them over the North Sea where, as so often in the past, II./JG 11's Bf 109s up from Jever were the first to engage. In a running battle lasting less than 20 minutes, a dozen B-17s went down. *Gruppenkommandeur* Günther Specht was among those to score, as was the *Staffelkapitän* of 4./JG 11, Oberleutnant Gerhard Sommer. This took Sommer's total to double figures, including six heavy bombers.

Portrayed here as an Oberleutnant with JG 52 at the time of winning his Knight's Cross, Major Karl-Heinz Leesmann, *Gruppenkommandeur* of III./JG 1, was lost over the North Sea on 25 July 1943

But it was Heinz Knoke's 5. *Staffel* who claimed the lion's share, with no fewer than seven Flying Fortresses destroyed. All 11 of the *Staffel's Gustavs* were reportedly carrying bombs, and it was Unteroffizier Wilhelm 'Jonny' Fest who was credited with a remarkable treble. His missile apparently struck the 385th BG's B-17F 42-30257, which immediately careered out of control into the path of two other bombers, B-17Fs 42-3316 *Betty Boom* and 42-30285 – the unfortunately named *Roundtrip Ticket*. All three went down into the North Sea.

Many American sources, it should be pointed out, are at variance with the above description of events. Some maintain that the first B-17 suffered a direct flak hit. This is certainly possible if, as at least one report suggests, the bombers were not far west of the heavily-defended island of Sylt at the time of the incident. Others describe 42-30257 as being the victim of rocket attack, which is also feasible. Fw 190s of a test unit (*Ekdo.* 25) equipped with underwing rocket launchers had been attached to I./JG 1 for the past month and had already claimed the destruction of several Flying Fortresses.

The 21-cm air-to-air rocket – based on a German army weapon – would prove a valuable addition to the Luftwaffe's anti-bomber armoury. But, as far as is known, the first Bf 109 units did not receive this weapon until August.

Whatever the truth of the matter, the losses over the North Sea were only the start of the bombers' problems as they continued on over the German mainland. A total of ten *Jagdgruppen*, six flying Bf 109s, were deployed against them. Even before the last machines of II./JG 11 had broken contact, the *Gustavs* of III./JG 26 bored in, claiming three more B-17s. III./JG 11 got another two near Hannover, while I./JG 3 and III./JG 54 were credited with one apiece.

Having landed to refuel and rearm, a number of Bf 109s of II./JG 11 (and *Jasta* Helgoland) set off after the bombers again, catching up with them as they retired from the target area and adding another three to their collective day's score more than an hour after their first engagement.

But the sting of Mission No 78 lay in its tail. The bombers' return route took them out over Holland. As they approached the Dutch border the B-17s were still under attack from Fw 190s. Suddenly, near the town of Emmerich, the Focke-Wulfs were pounced upon by a group of P-47s! The US fighters had been fitted with jettisonable fuel tanks adapted from stocks of unpressurised ferry tanks. Although rudimentary, these added a crucial 30 miles or more to the P-47D's radius of action and, for the first time, allowed the Thunderbolts to penetrate German airspace.

While not entirely unexpected, the appearance of enemy fighters over the homeland came as a rude shock to the Luftwaffe. It may not have been as a direct result of this latest development – coincidences *do* happen – but 24 hours later the other two *Staffeln* of Hauptmann Ludwig Franzisket's I./JG 27 were pulled back from France and the entire *Gruppe* took up station at Münster-Handorf, less than 60 miles due east of the point where the P-47s had crossed the border. The Defence of the Reich's Bf 109 *Gruppen* now numbered seven.

VIII Bomber Command's targets on 29 July were the submarine yards at Kiel and the Heinkel aircraft works at Warnemünde, both on the shores of the Baltic. The response of the Luftwaffe was muted. III./JG 26 claimed four B-17s of the Kiel force close to the target area, including a brace for Hauptmann Hermann Staiger, *Kapitän* of 12. *Staffel*, but II. and III./JG 11 did not engage the retreating bombers until they were passing Heligoland on their way back out across the North Sea. Unusually, II./JG 11 failed to register a single success, but III. *Gruppe* was credited with three victories for one pilot wounded.

The following day saw the final raids of 'Blitz Week'. VIII Bomber Command's Mission No 80 took it back to the main Fieseler works at Kassel. I./JG 3 intercepted the bombers as the crossed into German airspace above the Eifel hills, and despite repeated attacks over the next 30 minutes its pilots succeeded in bringing down just two B-17s.

For some reason III./JG 1 and III./JG 11 were not scrambled until nearly two hours after I./JG 3 had been sent up. By that time the Flying Fortress formations had already bombed their targets and turned for home. They were not far short of Emmerich and the Dutch border when the Bf 109s finally engaged them. At almost the same moment large numbers of Thunderbolts appeared from the west.

Despite this intervention – three entire groups of P-47s, over 100 fighters in all, had been fitted with drop tanks and despatched to support the bombers' withdrawal – the two Bf 109 *Gruppen* managed to claim two B-17s apiece. But then they found themselves embroiled in what was arguably the first major fighter confrontation of the Defence of the Reich campaign (although much of the action actually spilled over into Dutch airspace).

III./JG 1 escaped with three *Gustavs* damaged, two of which had to be written off, but no pilot injuries. III./JG 11 was less fortunate, having four machines damaged, with one pilot wounded and one killed. The only success was the P-47 credited to 9./JG 1's Leutnant Eugen Wintergerst. The identity of his victim, the first US fighter to be claimed by a Reich's Defence Bf 109, is unfortunately not known – both the 56th and 78th FGs lost a single P-47C in combat on this date. But the incident marked the opening of a new phase in the escalating battle for Germany's skies.

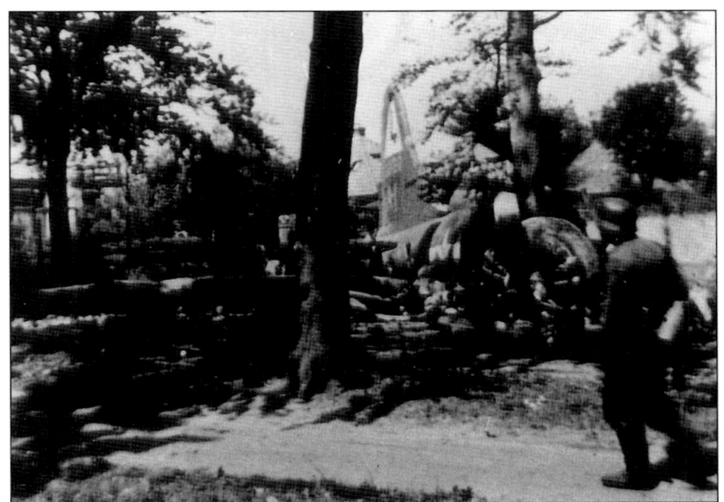

USAAF fighters were unable to prevent the loss of this flak-damaged Flying Fortress, picked off by fighters while returning from another raid on Kassel on 30 July. The vertical tail surfaces of the 381st BG's B-17F 42-3100 can just be made out between the trees alongside the Apeldoorn to Zutphen road in Holland

For the best part of the next fortnight, however, those skies remained quiet. During this period another of JG 3's *Gruppen* was withdrawn from the eastern front and added to the homeland's aerial defences.

III./JG 3 had served in Russia almost without a break since the invasion of June 1941. It numbered among its members several Knight's Cross holders and two 'centurions' (pilots with over 100 victories). The *Gruppe* had recently lost its long-serving *Kommandeur* when Major Wolfgang Ewald had been forced to bail out of his flak-damaged fighter behind Soviet lines. On 3 August III./JG 3 flew in to Münster-Handorf to be welcomed by Ewald's replacement: Hauptmann Walther Dahl. Its stay was intended to provide a brief period for rest and re-equipment, allowing the *Gruppe* to complete the process of conversion from the Bf 109G-4 to G-6 already begun in Russia. But within days its pilots would find themselves facing the massed firepower of US heavy bombers.

Two other Bf 109 *Gruppen* were also established at this time. Initially designated *Jagdgruppe Nord* and *Süd (Ost)*, *Jagdgruppen* 25 and 50 were special units specifically set up to combat another menace currently plaguing Germany's defenders – high-flying reconnaissance Mosquitos (see *Osprey Combat Aircraft 13*). They were led by two of the Luftwaffe's most experienced fighter pilots. JGr 25, activated at Berlin-Staaken and operating out of Gardelegen, was led by Major Herbert Ihlefeld.

Shown here wearing the Oak Leaves and Swords (awarded in 1942 for 101 victories with I./JG 77), Major Herbert Ihlefeld commanded the special high-altitude JGr 25 during its brief period of existence from August to December 1943

Based at Wiesbaden-Erbenheim, JGr 50 was headed by Major Hermann Graf. Soon the latter was also being tasked with developing new methods of combatting VIII Bomber Command's growing bomber strength. Its *Gustavs* were among the first to be equipped with underwing rocket launchers. And to assist him in his efforts, Hermann Graf – the 202-victory eastern front *Experte* who had already added a Mosquito and a B-17 to his score since arriving back in the west – had the clout to ensure that some of the most successful of his old *Staffel* comrades from 9./JG 52 in Russia joined him at Erbenheim.

On 12 August VIII Bomber Command reappeared over the Reich, 16 groups of B-17s being divided between two separate targets – a cluster of towns in the Ruhr and the city of Bonn, on the Rhine. Once again the weather intervened. The poor ground visibility forced many of the bombers to seek targets of opportunity in their respective areas. Only two B-17s were lost against Bonn, but no fewer than 23 of those attacking the Ruhr failed to return.

Based far to the north, II. and III./JG 11 were not involved in this day's action. But five of the Reich's other Bf 109 *Jagdgruppen* were scrambled against the bombers. Their fortunes, too, were mixed. III./JG 1, for example, was unable to claim a single success. The first *Gruppe* to engage was I./JG 3, which hit the bombers to the south of Wuppertal. The result

These pressurised Bf 109G-5s, each bearing its individual number on the rudder, are believed to be machines of JGr 25, photographed at Gardelegen

was one B-17 shot out of the formation by Oberfeldwebel Gerhard Schütte of 2./JG 3, which was then finished off by 3. *Staffel's* Leutnant Franz Schwaiger some 25 minutes later.

It might be worthwhile here to summarise briefly the three types of 'victory' that could be claimed against a US heavy bomber, each of which was worth a set number of points towards the conferring of awards and decorations. Firstly, there was the confirmed kill – a bomber seen to explode or disintegrate in mid-air, crash, ditch or make a forced landing (four points). Next came the so-called *Herausschuss* – literally the 'shooting out'. This meant damaging a bomber to such a degree that it dropped out of formation and became a straggler, with little or no hope of making it back to friendly territory (two points). Third, and last, was the *endgültige Vernichtung* – 'final destruction' – which was little more than the *coup de grâce* administered to any such lone straggler chanced upon (one point). The first two categories also counted as kills on a pilot's personal scoreboard. The last one did not.

Returning to 12 August, from Münster-Handorf I./JG 27 and the more recently arrived III./JG 3 took off together. Although the newcomers were able to get only a dozen *Gustavs* aloft for this, their first Defence of the Reich operation, they managed to claim three B-17s. The first fell to Leutnant Hans Schleef. It was victory 95 for Knight's Cross holder Schleef (whose previous kill had been a Soviet Yak-1 fighter downed over the Ukraine just 11 days earlier). Meanwhile, Hauptmann Ludwig Franzisket's I./JG 27, which was also operating for the first time in its entirety over the homeland, continued to harry the Ruhr attack force as it withdrew from the target area in a wide curve back towards the Belgian border. By the end of the 30-minute engagement its pilots had added six more B-17s to the *Gruppe's* collective total.

Five days later the Flying Fortresses went to Schweinfurt.

To be more precise, they went to Schweinfurt and Regensburg, for although Mission No 84 of 17 August 1943 was the most ambitious mounted by VIII Bomber Command to date, it followed the usual formula of striking at two targets simultaneously in order to split the

JGr 25's sister unit, JGr 50, was based at Wiesbaden-Erbenheim and commanded by an even higher-scoring Oak Leaves and Swords wearer than Major Ihlefeld – the 202-victory Major Hermann Graf

Luftwaffe's defences. While the nine Flying Fortress groups of the 1st Bomber Wing attacked the ball-bearing plants at Schweinfurt, the seven groups of B-17s making up 4th Bomb Wing would be despatched against the Messerschmitt factories at Regensburg. An added embellishment was that the latter would not then retrace their steps back to the UK, but continue on southwards across the Mediterranean to land in North Africa.

The business end of the underwing launcher for the 210 mm air-to-air rocket. The nose of the missile can just be seen inside the tube

The planners attended to every detail, including the provision of marginally improved drop tanks for the P-47s which would enable them to venture just that little bit further into German airspace, at least as far as Aachen. But they had no control over the fickle English weather. While most of western Europe enjoyed clear skies, a dense layer of very low cloud descended over VIII Bomber Command's East Anglian bases. It was considered too much of a risk for nearly 400 'heavies' to take off and try to assemble in such conditions.

The start of the mission was therefore delayed, but the Regensburg force could be kept waiting for only so long if it was to arrive in far-off Algeria before the onset of darkness. Reluctantly, the order was given for the 4th Bomb Wing to take off, but for the 1st Bomb Wing to await the forecast improvement in the weather. It was a recipe for disaster. And a disaster is exactly what followed.

The interval of several hours between the formations' crossing Germany afforded the defending Luftwaffe fighters with two opportunities to maul the Regensburg groups – 24 'heavies' would fail to reach North Africa, although several of these were forced down by lack of fuel or mechanical failure. Following the first attacks, the *Gruppen* landed and refuelled in readiness for a second attack as the heavy bombers fought their way back to the UK. But, of course, the Regensburg B-17s did not reappear (at least, not on this date – they returned to England a week later via France, bombing a Luftwaffe airfield *en route*). It meant, however, that the Defence of the Reich's *Jagdgruppen* were fully armed and fully alerted when the delayed Schweinfurt force finally arrived on the scene.

The bombers' approach had been carefully monitored as they crossed the North Sea towards the Scheldt Estuary. JG 11 had not been involved in the earlier actions

The firing cable was attached to the rear inner support strut of the launcher, and from there fed round through the backplate of the tube. This weapon was nicknamed the 'stovepipe' by the *Jagdwaffe* crews that used them in combat

against the Regensburg force, but had been moved down from their bases in northern Germany to airfields in Holland and Belgium in anticipation of the bombers' return back out over the Low Countries. Instead, they now found themselves being scrambled against a second incoming formation following some three-and-a-half hours late on the heels of the first.

The rockets were timed to detonate after a set distance had been travelled. These missiles have exploded harmlessly well behind the Flying Fortress formation they were aimed at

Lifting off from Gilze-Rijn shortly after 1430 hrs., Hauptmann Günther Specht's II./JG 11 sighted the enemy bombers near Antwerp. For almost 30 minutes they shadowed the Flying Fortresses across northeast Belgium, patiently waiting for the escorting fighters to reach the limit of their range. At Eupen, just south of Aachen, the Thunderbolts duly turned back, rocking their wings in salute as they peeled away, leaving the B-17s to continue on alone.

It was the moment the Luftwaffe pilots had been waiting for. II./JG 11 bored straight in, claiming three bombers within seconds of each other. These were almost certainly Flying Fortresses of the 381st BG, which was flying in the low group position of the leading wing on this day and suffered four of the first five losses to go down after Eupen. One of them had fallen to *Gruppenkommandeur* Günther Specht, who was also credited with a second some 20 minutes later.

It would seem that Oberleutnant Heinz Knoke had finally abandoned his flirtation with air-to-air bombing. His 5. *Staffel* was now equipped with underwing rocket launchers, but they achieved little success with the new weapon. Knoke's single missile failed to find a target (the other launch tube had already been shot away by return fire from the bombers). And although he has since described two of his pilots scoring direct hits – 'their bombers exploded in mid-air' – the two B-17s in question were only damaged. They were, however, forced to leave formation and both were picked off as stragglers later in the action.

The 27 minutes that elapsed between the departure of the P-47s at Eupen and the bombers crossing the River Rhine south of Mainz was the most ferocious part of the battle. In this short space of time 21 B-17s were shot down. This represented nearly 60 per cent of all the losses suffered by the Schweinfurt force. Over the rolling hills of the Eifel and Hunsrück regions, B-17s were going down at an average rate of almost one a minute!

They came under assault by fighters from up to a dozen *Jagdgruppen*. At the height of the battle it was estimated that they were being directly engaged by elements of at least nine of these units at the same time. The Luftwaffe pilots were practically queuing up to launch their frontal attacks. In seemingly endless succession, waves of fighters – mostly in line abreast, and 12 to 15 strong – hurled themselves at the struggling B-17s.

Not surprisingly, it was the leading wing of bombers that bore the brunt of the casualties, with 22 of its 57 aircraft failing to return from Schweinfurt, whereas the fourth and trailing wing lost just four out of 53.

Two of the Schweinfurt Flying Fortresses downed on 17 August provided victories 16 and 17 for Hauptmann Günther Specht

Among the other Bf 109 *Gruppen* that attacked the B-17s west of the Rhine, III./JG 11 was able to achieve only one victory. III./JG 26 was much more successful.

Commanded now by Hauptmann Klaus Mietusch, this *Gruppe* had been transferred from Nordholz down to Amsterdam-Schiphol on 13 August. Having been up against the Regensburg force – and claiming six bombers, including a pair for Knight's Cross holder Oberfeldwebel Heinz Kemethmüller – III./JG 26 was scrambled a second time at the approach of the Schweinfurt formation. It was *Gruppenkommandeur* Mietusch himself who downed the first, some 24 miles beyond Aachen, and exactly four hours after Kemethmüller's double from the earlier raid. Hauptmann Mietusch then added a second, possibly another unfortunate of 381st BG, which came down just short of the Rhine. Two of his pilots also scored, taking the *Gruppe's* Schweinfurt tally to four.

Although Luftwaffe opposition eased noticeably once the bombers were beyond the Rhine, they were still being subjected to intermittent attack. It was at this stage that III./JG 1 claimed two B-17s to add to the Regensburg straggler that 8. *Staffel's* Feldwebel Helmut Fröhlich had despatched earlier in the day. Up from München-Gladbach, I./JG 3 had also been in action against the Regensburg formation. With two B-17s already to its credit, a successful attack on the Schweinfurt force now raised the *Gruppe's* total to four – and its day wasn't over yet.

Perhaps the most contentious claims of all were the 16(!) victories ascribed by at least one source to Major Hermann Graf's JGr 50. It has been suggested that at least some of these kills rightfully belong to instructors (themselves experienced frontline pilots) of the various nearby training establishments who often flew operations under the tactical control of JGr 50. A number of such smaller Bf 109 units, school *Einsatzstaffeln* and factory defence flights, are known to have participated in the Schweinfurt-Regensburg actions. Of JGr 50 itself, although Hermann Graf did not add to his score on this date, one of his ex-9./JG 52 veterans, Oberleutnant Alfred Grislawski – now *Kapitän* of his 1. *Staffel* – was credited with a B-17 from each of the raiding forces.

By the time the Flying Fortresses reached Schweinfurt, most of the single-engined fighters that had been in action against them had landed to refuel and rearm, unsure whether the B-17s would reverse course and return to the UK or disappear southwards as the Regensburg formation had done. When it became clear that the enemy was heading west back towards the Rhine, small groups of fighters went up to intercept them.

Despite his damaged wing Oberleutnant Heinz Knoke took off from Bonn-Hangelar at the head of an *ad hoc* formation and managed to score II./JG 11's fourth, and final, victory of the day. At München-Gladbach the *Gustavs* of I./JG 3 scrambled for a third time in less than six hours. And, as on the previous two missions, they returned with a brace of B-17s under their collective belt, thus bringing the *Gruppe's* score for the day to six. Hauptmann Quaet-Faslem's pilots had been fortunate, however – not in bringing down the two Flying Fortresses, both of which fell near Maastricht, in Holland – but in escaping without casualties themselves. For at long last, after battling for more than two hours unescorted through enemy airspace, the Schweinfurt bombers had finally made rendezvous with their withdrawal support P-47s southeast of Aachen.

The ordeal of the B-17 crews was almost over. The last act of the Schweinfurt drama was to be a battle between the fighters – P-47s versus the Luftwaffe – over a wide tract of the Belgian-Dutch border to the north of Liège.

III./JG 3's part in the day's proceedings so far had been anything but successful. Initially scrambled from Münster-Handorf shortly after 1200 hrs, Hauptmann Walther Dahl's *Gruppe* had failed to find the Regensburg force. They landed at Woensdrecht in Holland an hour later. From here they took off again some 90 minutes later still to intercept the incoming Schweinfurt formation – only to be misdirected by ground control straight into a large gaggle of RAF Spitfires over northern Belgium. While Dahl's pilots were otherwise busily engaged – losing a pair of Bf 109G-6s, but suffering no pilot casualties – the Flying Fortresses sailed past high overhead some 12 miles away.

The two B-17Fs downed by JGr 50's Oberleutnant Alfred Grislawski on 17 August 1943 took his victory tally to 111. This photograph was taken the following month, by which time kill number 112 had been added – a B-17F claimed southeast of Stuttgart on 6 September. Note the machine's individual number on the aft fuselage behind the *Balkenkreuz*

By the time of its third take-off late in the afternoon, III./JG 3 was able to put only two *Schwärme* (eight aircraft) into the air. Led by Hauptmann Wilhelm Lemke, *Kapitän* of 9. *Staffel*, they tried to attack a force of some '80 bombers' but were thwarted by the arrival of a group of Thunderbolts. In the ensuing free-for-all III./JG 3 achieved its first victories of the day – a trio of P-47s for no loss to themselves. Two of the Thunderbolts went to Wilhelm Lemke. They brought the eastern front veteran's score to 127.

Some 30 minutes later, a long and determined chase by Unteroffizier Hinz was finally rewarded by his being credited with one of the 'heavies'. His victim was probably the 305th BG's B-17F 41-24564 'Patches', which crashed near Diest, in Belgium. It was the last Schweinfurt B-17 to come down on European soil (two more were subsequently forced to ditch in the North Sea before reaching England's shores).

The Luftwaffe's fighters had been remarkably successful in combatting the Schweinfurt-Regensburg raids. They had also sustained remarkably few losses. Although a number of Bf 109 pilots had been wounded, only four had been killed – two each from III./JG 26 and JGr 50.

For VIII Bomber Command it was a different story altogether. Mission No 84 had been intended to mark the first anniversary of the operational debut of the command's B-17s over Rouen/Sotteville exactly one year earlier. Instead, it had turned into an unmitigated disaster. The combined loss of 60 bombers in the two raids, plus very nearly three times that number damaged (out of a total 376 despatched), came as a staggering blow. Hard as it was to accept, the stark fact was that the B-17s could *not* survive on their own in hostile airspace. The voices of even the most fervent adherents of the 'unescorted self-defending bomber formation' policy were stilled. There were to be no more deep penetrations into the Reich until adequate fighter protection could be provided.

COLOUR PLATES

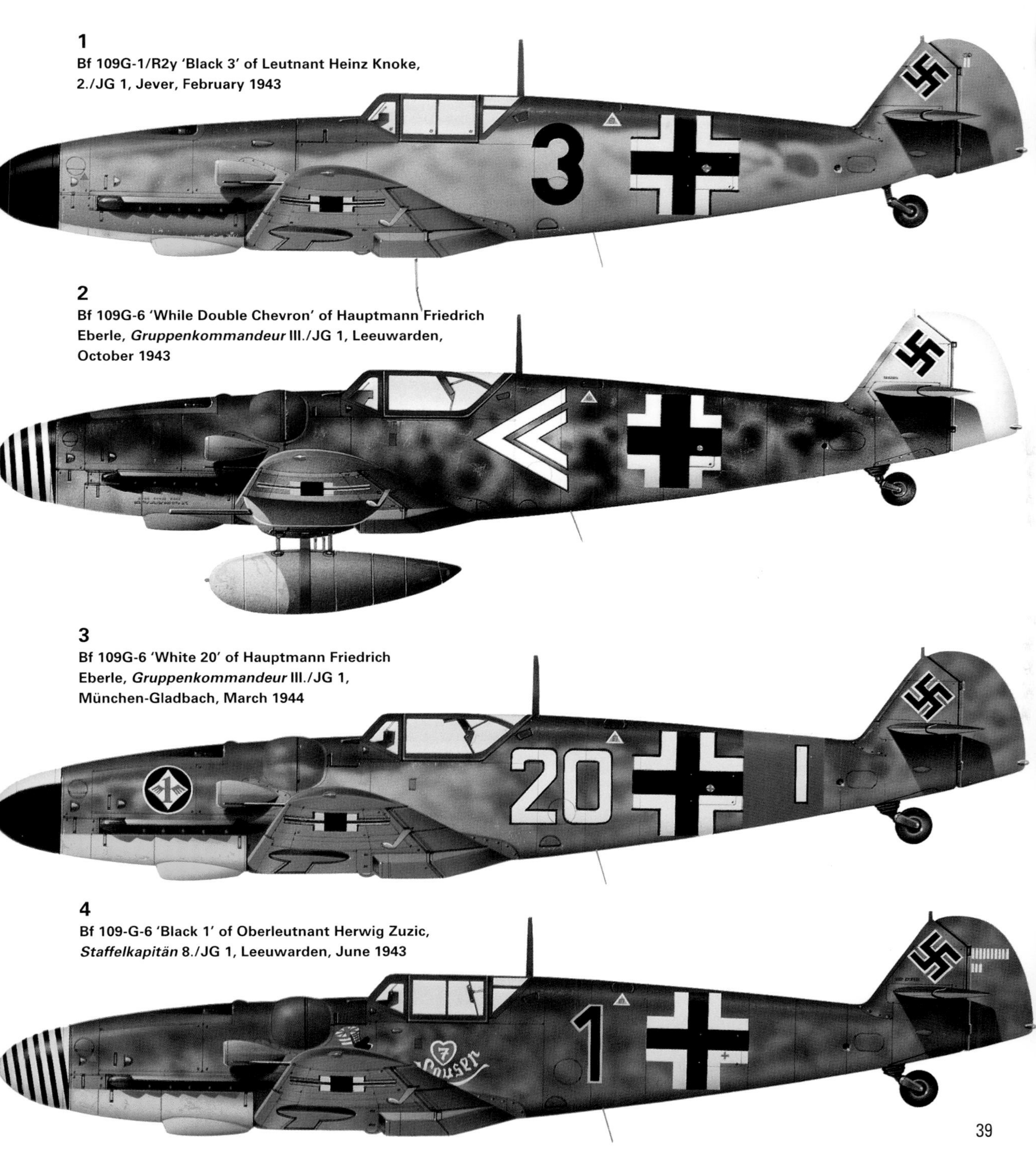

1
Bf 109G-1/R2y 'Black 3' of Leutnant Heinz Knoke, 2./JG 1, Jever, February 1943

2
Bf 109G-6 'While Double Chevron' of Hauptmann Friedrich Eberle, *Gruppenkommandeur* III./JG 1, Leeuwarden, October 1943

3
Bf 109G-6 'White 20' of Hauptmann Friedrich Eberle, *Gruppenkommandeur* III./JG 1, München-Gladbach, March 1944

4
Bf 109-G-6 'Black 1' of Oberleutnant Herwig Zuzic, *Staffelkapitän* 8./JG 1, Leeuwarden, June 1943

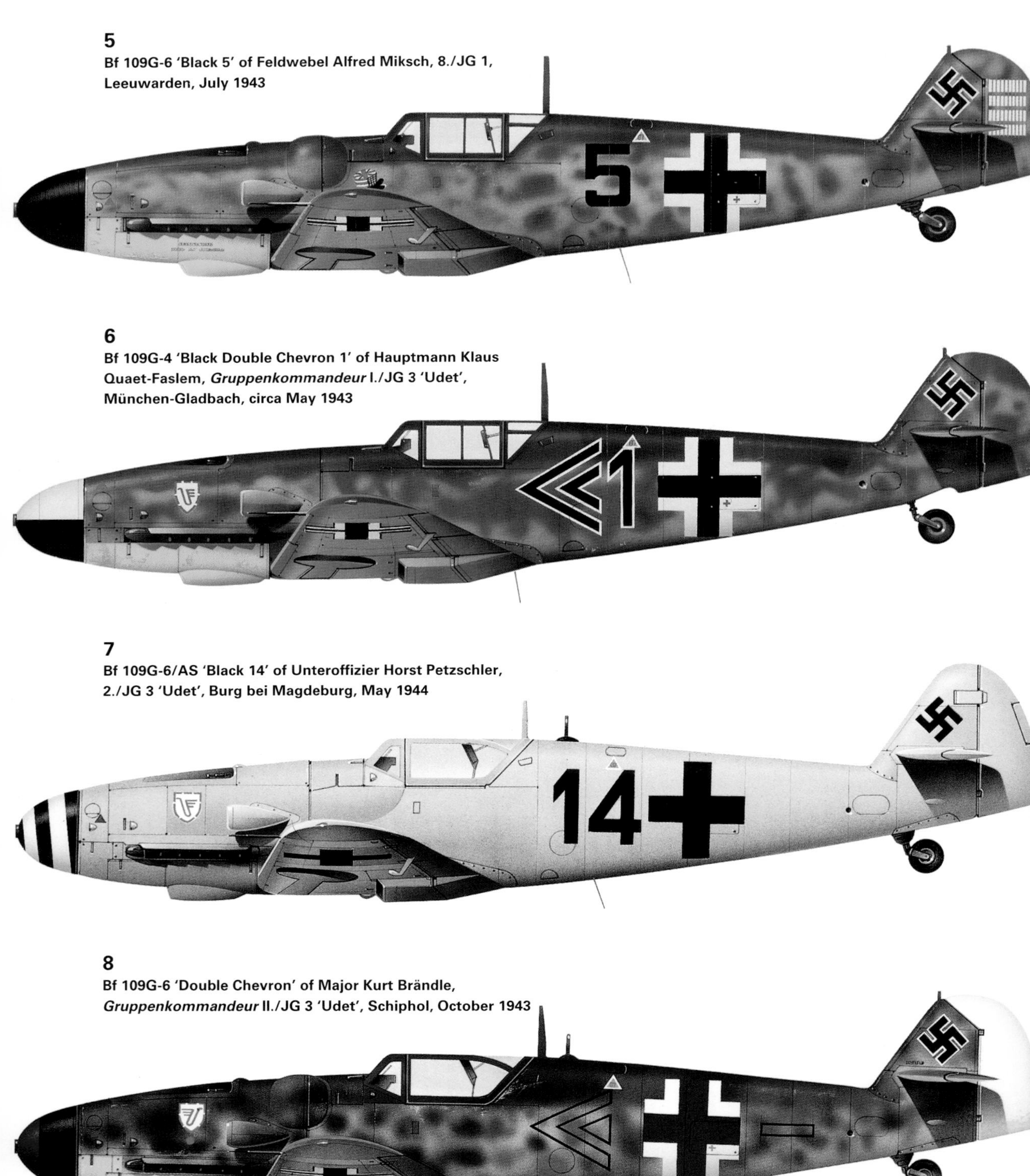

5

Bf 109G-6 'Black 5' of Feldwebel Alfred Miksch, 8./JG 1, Leeuwarden, July 1943

6

Bf 109G-4 'Black Double Chevron 1' of Hauptmann Klaus Quaet-Faslem, *Gruppenkommandeur* I./JG 3 'Udet', München-Gladbach, circa May 1943

7

Bf 109G-6/AS 'Black 14' of Unteroffizier Horst Petzschler, 2./JG 3 'Udet', Burg bei Magdeburg, May 1944

8

Bf 109G-6 'Double Chevron' of Major Kurt Brändle, *Gruppenkommandeur* II./JG 3 'Udet', Schiphol, October 1943

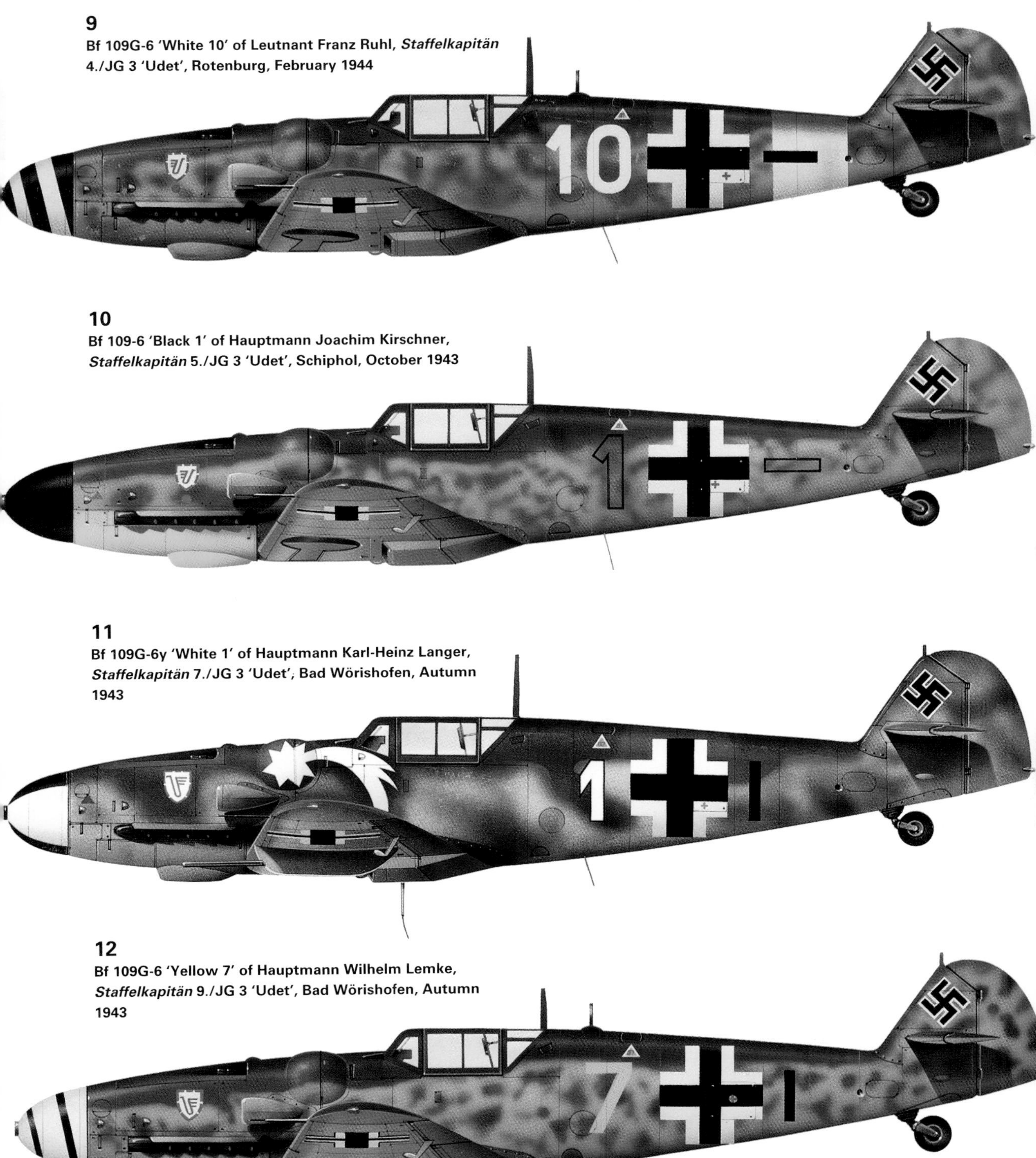

9

Bf 109G-6 'White 10' of Leutnant Franz Ruhl, *Staffelkapitän* 4./JG 3 'Udet', Rotenburg, February 1944

10

Bf 109-6 'Black 1' of Hauptmann Joachim Kirschner, *Staffelkapitän* 5./JG 3 'Udet', Schiphol, October 1943

11

Bf 109G-6y 'White 1' of Hauptmann Karl-Heinz Langer, *Staffelkapitän* 7./JG 3 'Udet', Bad Wörishofen, Autumn 1943

12

Bf 109G-6 'Yellow 7' of Hauptmann Wilhelm Lemke, *Staffelkapitän* 9./JG 3 'Udet', Bad Wörishofen, Autumn 1943

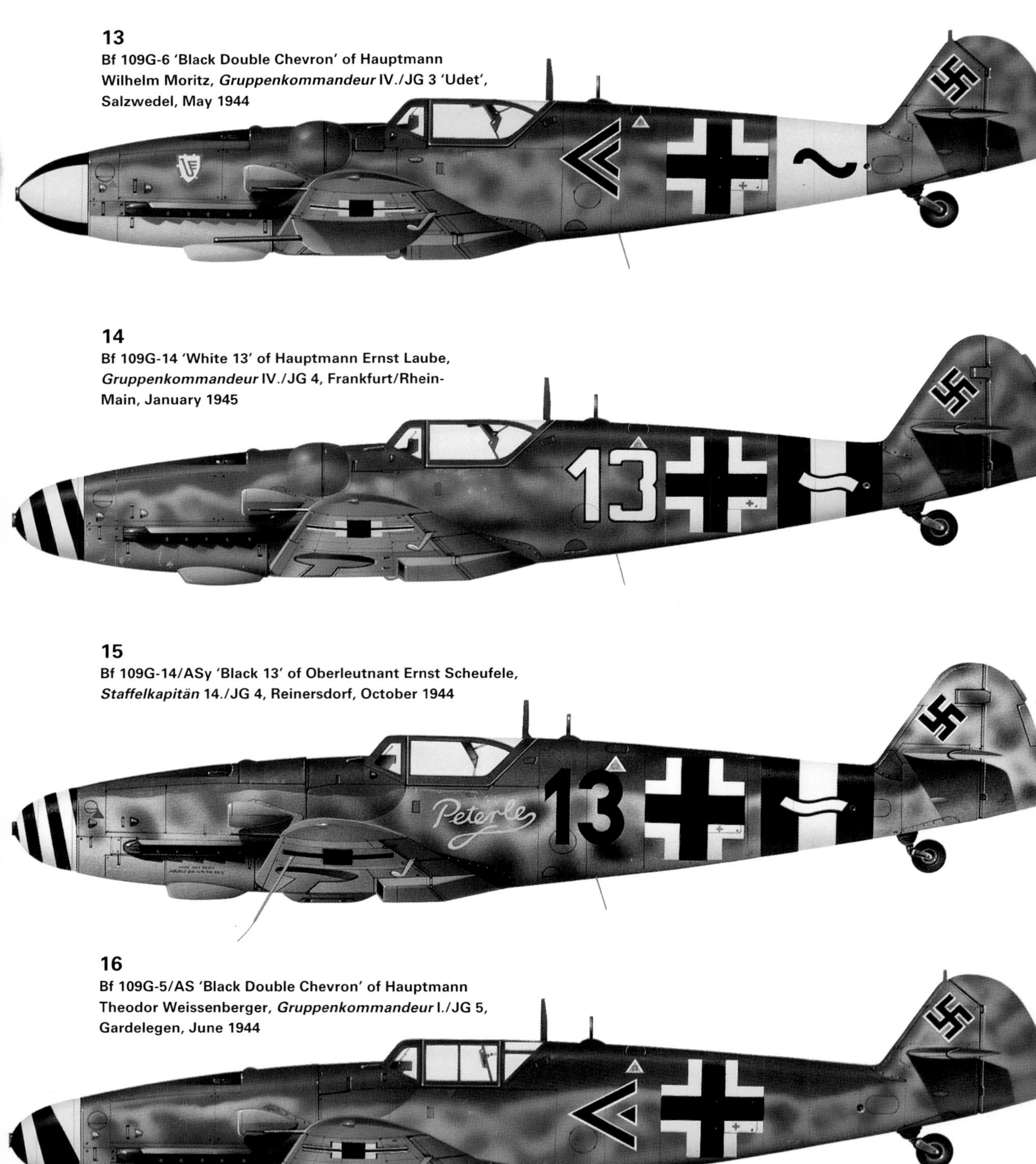

13

Bf 109G-6 'Black Double Chevron' of Hauptmann Wilhelm Moritz, *Gruppenkommandeur* IV./JG 3 'Udet', Salzwedel, May 1944

14

Bf 109G-14 'White 13' of Hauptmann Ernst Laube, *Gruppenkommandeur* IV./JG 4, Frankfurt/Rhein-Main, January 1945

15

Bf 109G-14/ASy 'Black 13' of Oberleutnant Ernst Scheufele, *Staffelkapitän* 14./JG 4, Reinersdorf, October 1944

16

Bf 109G-5/AS 'Black Double Chevron' of Hauptmann Theodor Weissenberger, *Gruppenkommandeur* I./JG 5, Gardelegen, June 1944

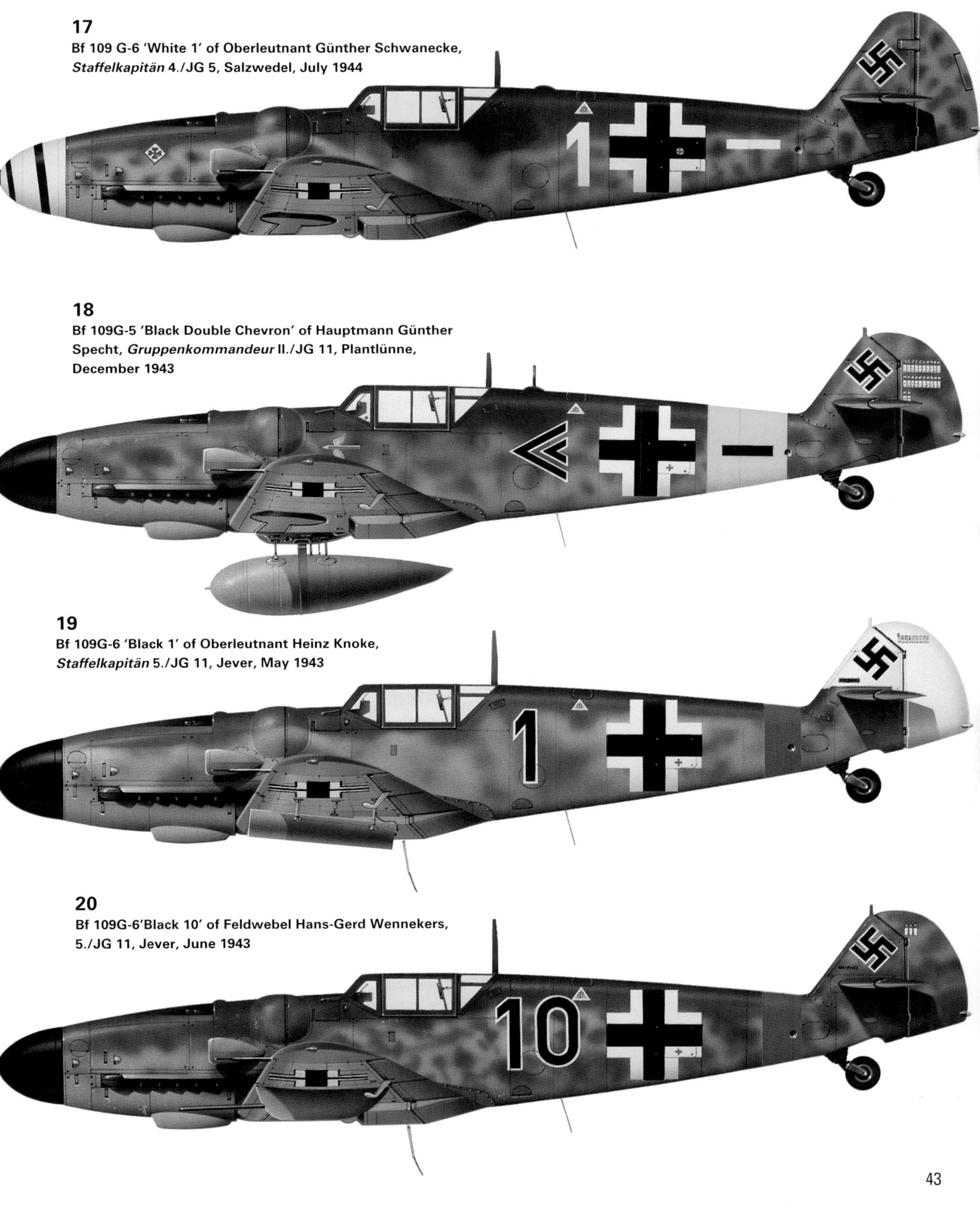

17

Bf 109 G-6 'White 1' of Oberleutnant Günther Schwanecke, *Staffelkapitän* 4./JG 5, Salzwedel, July 1944

18

Bf 109G-5 'Black Double Chevron' of Hauptmann Günther Specht, *Gruppenkommandeur* II./JG 11, Plantlünne, December 1943

19

Bf 109G-6 'Black 1' of Oberleutnant Heinz Knoke, *Staffelkapitän* 5./JG 11, Jever, May 1943

20

Bf 109G-6'Black 10' of Feldwebel Hans-Gerd Wennekers, 5./JG 11, Jever, June 1943

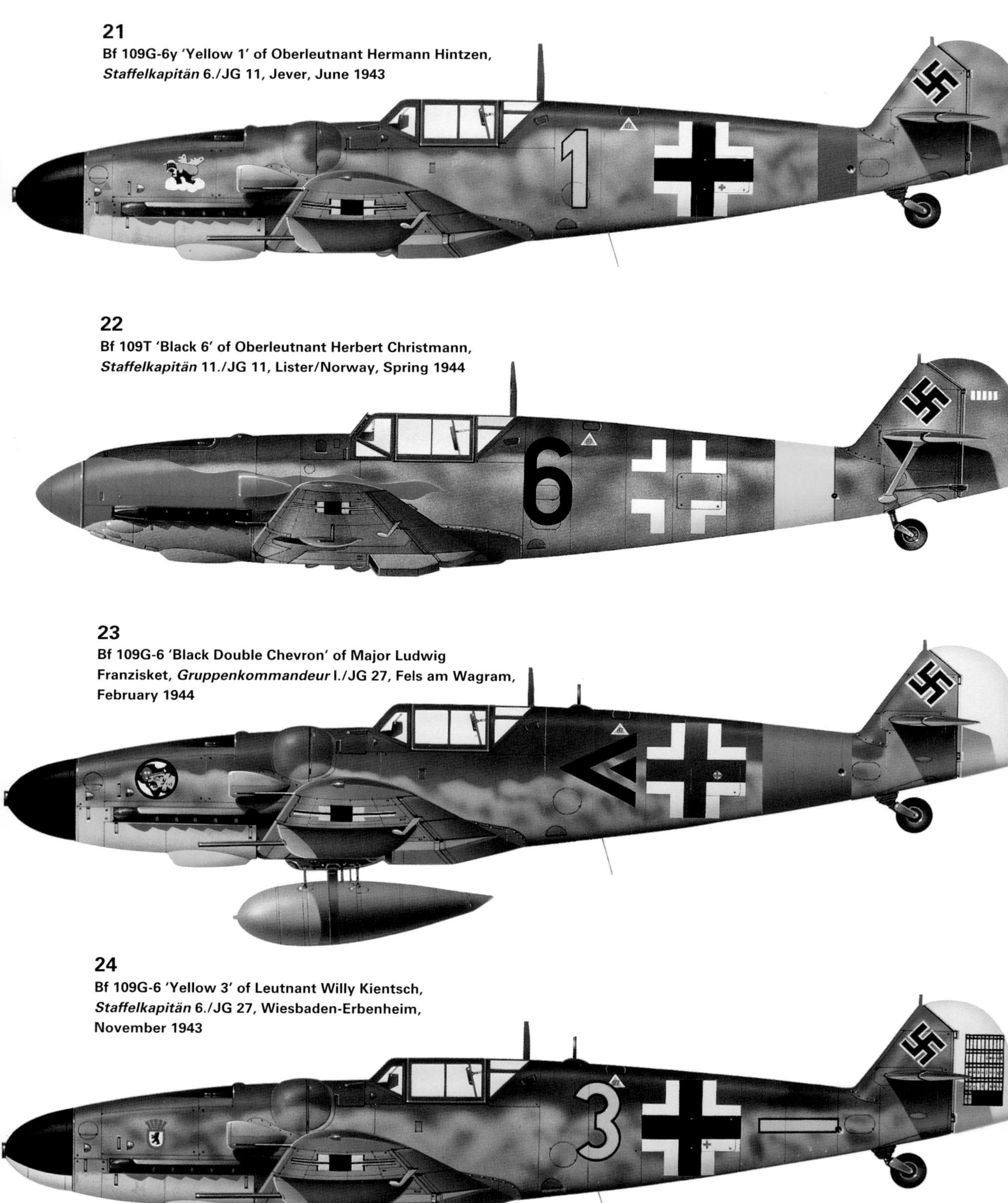

21

Bf 109G-6y 'Yellow 1' of Oberleutnant Hermann Hintzen, *Staffelkapitän* 6./JG 11, Jever, June 1943

22

Bf 109T 'Black 6' of Oberleutnant Herbert Christmann, *Staffelkapitän* 11./JG 11, Lister/Norway, Spring 1944

23

Bf 109G-6 'Black Double Chevron' of Major Ludwig Franzisket, *Gruppenkommandeur* I./JG 27, Fels am Wagram, February 1944

24

Bf 109G-6 'Yellow 3' of Leutnant Willy Kientsch, *Staffelkapitän* 6./JG 27, Wiesbaden-Erbenheim, November 1943

25

Bf 109G-6 'Yellow 1' of Leutnant Dr Peter Werfft, *Staffelkapitän* 9./JG 27, Vienna-Seyring, March 1944

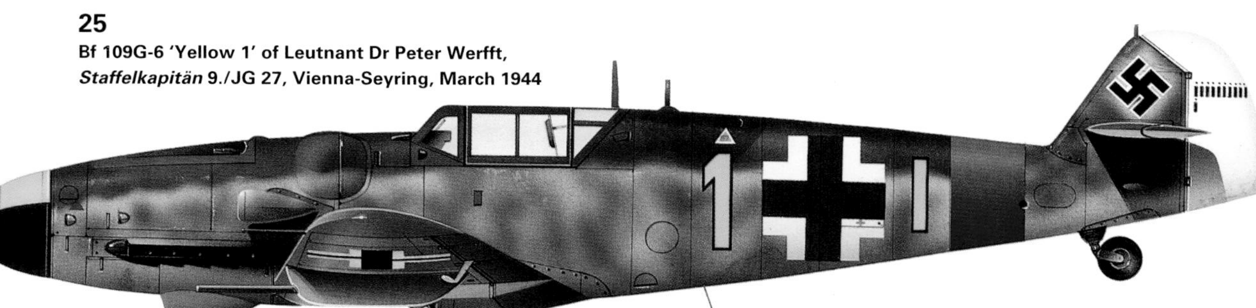

26

Bf 109G-6 'Black Double Chevron' of Hauptmann Otto Meyer, *Gruppenkommandeur* IV./JG 27, Graz, March 1944

27

Bf 109G-6 'White 10' of Oberleutnant Alfred Grislawski, *Staffelkapitän* 1./JGr 50, Wiesbaden-Erbenheim, September 1943

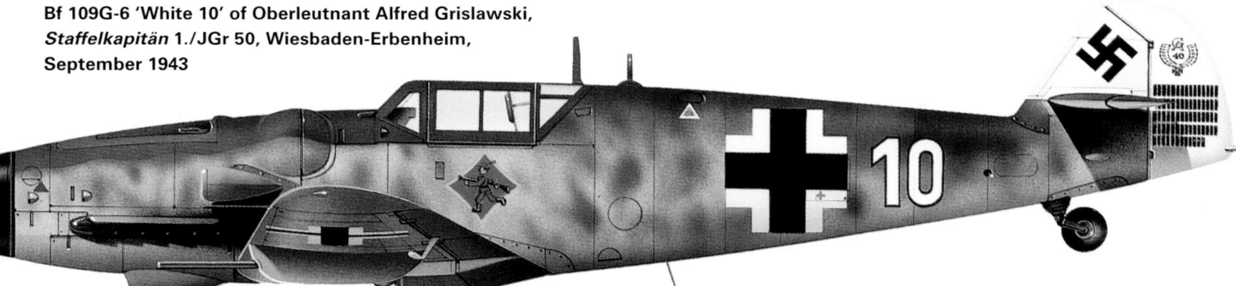

28

Bf 109G-6 'Yellow 1' of Leutnant Alfred Hammer, *Staffelkapitän* 6./JG 53 'Pik-As', Vienna-Seyring, February 1944

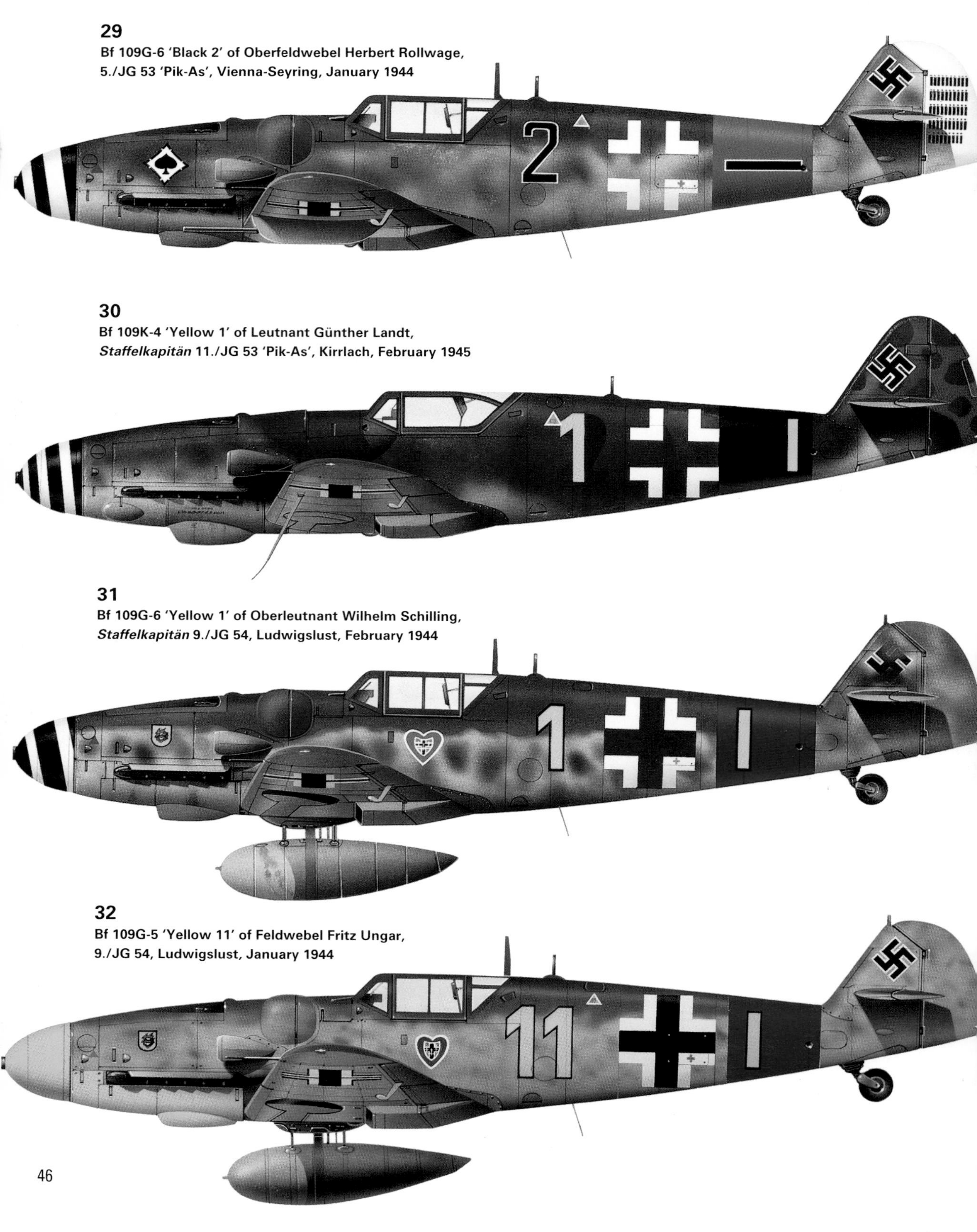

29

Bf 109G-6 'Black 2' of Oberfeldwebel Herbert Rollwage, 5./JG 53 'Pik-As', Vienna-Seyring, January 1944

30

Bf 109K-4 'Yellow 1' of Leutnant Günther Landt, *Staffelkapitän* 11./JG 53 'Pik-As', Kirrlach, February 1945

31

Bf 109G-6 'Yellow 1' of Oberleutnant Wilhelm Schilling, *Staffelkapitän* 9./JG 54, Ludwigslust, February 1944

32

Bf 109G-5 'Yellow 11' of Feldwebel Fritz Ungar, 9./JG 54, Ludwigslust, January 1944

33

Bf 109K-4 'White 1' of Hauptmann Menzel, *Staffelkapitän* 9./JG 77, Lohausen, December 1944

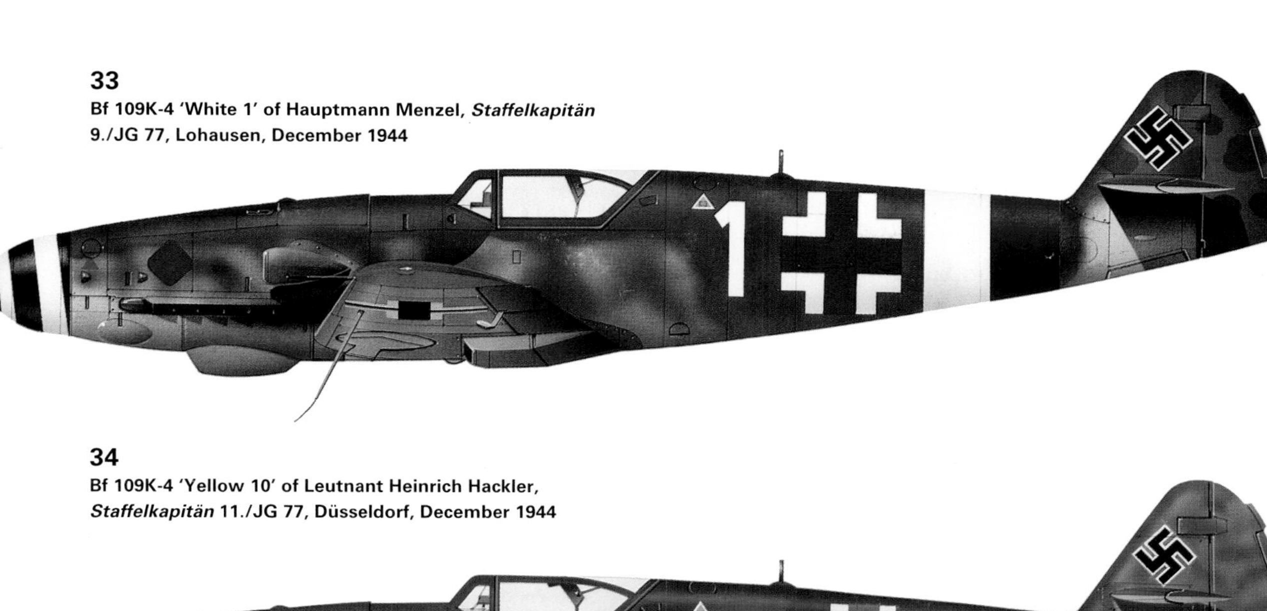

34

Bf 109K-4 'Yellow 10' of Leutnant Heinrich Hackler, *Staffelkapitän* 11./JG 77, Düsseldorf, December 1944

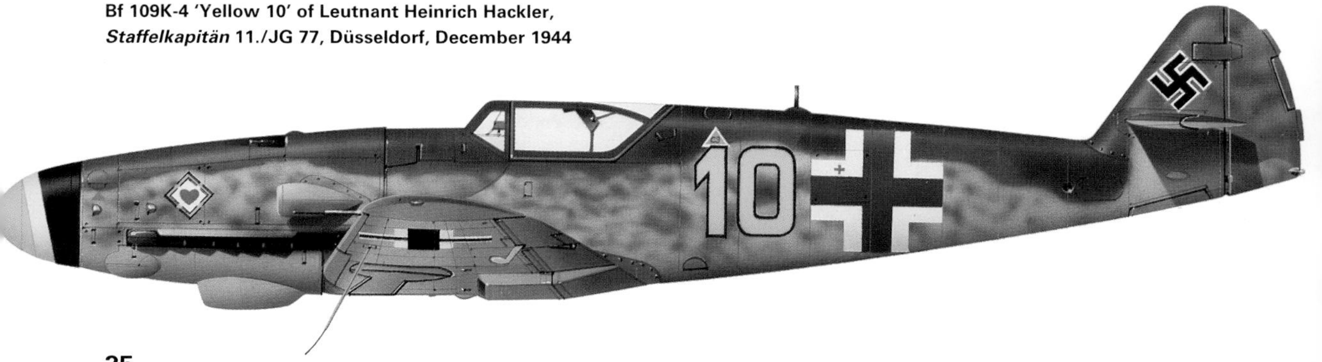

35

Bf 109G-10 'Red 2' of Feldwebel Eberhard Gzik, 2./JG 300, Borkheide, September 1944

36

Bf 109G-6 'White 6' of Unteroffizier Willi Reschke, 1./JG 302, Götzendorf, July 1944

CHAPTER THREE

IN THE BALANCE

During the lull that followed Schweinfurt, VIII Bomber Command underwent reorganisation. The B-17s of 1st and 4th Bomb Wings now operated as the 1st and 3rd Bomb Divisions, while the B-24s – recently returned from their temporary deployment to North Africa and participation in the historic raid on the Rumanian oilfields at Ploesti – became the 2nd Bomb Division.

All three formations were involved in the next incursion into Germany on 6 September. While the Liberators carried out a diversionary sweep over the North Sea, the two Flying Fortress divisions attempted to reach Stuttgart 'via the side door' by flying down the length of France. The former prompted no reaction whatsoever. The latter has been described as 'one of the most costly fiascos in Eighth Air Force history'. Heavy clouds in the target area caused many groups to become separated. Forty-five B-17s failed to return, nearly half of them (predominantly from the 1st BD) crash-landing or ditching through shortage of fuel. Bombers came down in Switzerland, France, the Channel and the North Sea!

While VIII Bomber Command had been reorganising, the Luftwaffe had been strengthening. In August three more Bf 109 *Gruppen* had been returned to the Reich from other fronts – II./JG 3 from Russia and IV./JG 3 and II./JG 27 from Italy. The two JG 3 *Gruppen* were not yet operational, but the Stuttgart 'fiasco' of 6 September provided II./JG 27 with its baptism of fire in the Defence of the Reich.

Hauptmann Werner Schroer and his pilots were no strangers to US heavy bombers. They had already downed nearly 50 B-17s and B-24s during their previous six months service in the Mediterranean. Schroer himself had accounted for a dozen of them. Now they scrambled from their new base at Eschborn, on the outskirts of Frankfurt, to take on the UK-based Flying Fortresses of VIII Bomber Command for the first time.

Despite the abysmal conditions, they found and attacked a large formation of B-17s in the Stuttgart area. The 20 *Gustavs* kept up their assault for the best part of half-an-hour, by the end of which time they had claimed nine Flying Fortresses. A treble for the *Gruppenkommandeur* took Schroer's personal score to 88. Two of his *Staffelkapitäne* were also successful, 6./JG 27's Leutnant Willy Kientsch getting two and Hauptmann Otto Meyer of 4./JG 27 one.

It had been an impressive debut – one the unit would equal, but never surpass, throughout the remainder of its Defence of the Reich career. The day was marred only by the loss of *Gruppen-Adjutant* Oberleutnant Dankward *Freiherr* von Maltzahn.

Hauptmann Werner Schroer, Mediterranean *Experte* and *Gruppenkommandeur* of II./JG 27, would claim his first three Defence of the Reich victories – a trio of Flying Fortresses – during the 6 September 1943 raid on Stuttgart

The most successful *Gruppe* in action against the 6 September 1943 Stuttgart raiders was III./JG 3. Oberfeldwebel Alfred Surau of 9. *Staffel*, seen here perched on the wheel of his 'Yellow 6', was credited with two of the *Gruppe's* ten victories. Note 9./JG 3's striking yellow, black and white 'eye' emblem adorning the *Beule*

Another unit in action over Stuttgart was JGr 50, up from Wiesbaden-Erbenheim. Hermann Graf and Alfred Grislawski each claimed a B-17 close to the target area, with Graf adding a second 18 minutes later some distance to the south over the Black Forest.

A more unlikely claimant on this date was the *Geschwader-Adjutant* of JG 3, Oberleutnant Hermann *Freiherr* von Kap-herr. The *Stab* (HQ) of JG 3 had been recalled from the Russian front back in the late spring and had since been stationed – minus aircraft – at München-Gladbach. On the very day of the attack on Stuttgart, it was scheduled to transfer to Rheinberg, on the western fringes of the Ruhr, where it would receive its new Bf 109G-6s the following month. Unless he happened to be visiting one of JG 3's component *Gruppen* – all four of which were now back in Germany – on this date, it is difficult to know how, and from whom, Oberleutnant von Kap-herr managed to 'borrow' the machine that enabled him to take off and claim his first four-engined bomber!

It was one of JG 3's *Gruppen* that was credited with the highest number of kills against the Stuttgart B-17s. As if to make up for their disappointing performance during the Schweinfurt-Regensburg raid, the pilots of III./JG 3 downed no fewer than ten Flying Fortresses in an engagement that lasted for more than 30 minutes, and took them from Stuttgart, across the Rhine and westwards into France.

Gruppenkommandeur Hauptmann Walther Dahl claimed his first two 'heavies' to add to his Russian front total of 51. Another double went to 9. *Staffel's* Oberfeldwebel Alfred Surau (who thus remained ten behind his *Kommandeur* with 43), while two of the *Gruppe's* most successful eastern front *Experten,* Hauptmann Wilhelm Lemke and Leutnant Hans Schleef, each claimed one to bring their scores to 128 and 96 respectively.

Exactly three weeks later, September's only other incursion into Reich airspace took VIII Bomber Command's B-17s back over very familiar territory indeed. But the 27 September attack on the North Sea port of Emden broke new ground in other ways. Four of the Fortresses were equipped with British H2S radar. Although three of the sets promptly malfunctioned, this was the first step down an electronic road that would eventually allow the US bombers to hit targets through solid cloud.

Another milestone was the introduction of new 108-gallon 'paper' drop tanks which – for the first time ever – permitted relays of P-47s to escort the bombers all the way to a target inside the Reich.

7./JG 3's 'comet' emblem makes an equally distinctive backdrop as Feldwebel Kurt Gräf (left) gets his point across to two fellow NCO pilots at Bad Wörishofen in October 1943

The unexpected appearance of the Thunderbolts was a huge shock to the resident JG 11, which had long regarded Germany's North Sea coastline as its own. II./JG 11 had scrambled from Jever as usual. Within minutes the bombers were in sight, curving in towards Emden from the south. But then Feldwebel Hans-Gerd Wennekers spotted a large number of fighters high above the bomber formation. As they had radial engines, he at first took them to be Fw 190s. But there was something distinctly odd about them – and why weren't they attacking? Wennekers and his wingman decided to go up and have a closer look.

A pair of unidentified high-altitude Bf 109G-5s taxi out for another mission in defence of the homeland in the late summer of 1943

As soon as the pair began to climb, the 'Focke-Wulfs' immediately dived down towards them. Wennekers only realised he was under attack when he heard his wingman's excited shout over the RT. 'Look out! They're trying to shoot you down!' The two *Gustavs* stood on their wingtips and pointed their noses earthwards. It was an unwise move. Luftwaffe pilots would quickly learn that the one thing you did *not* do was try to out-dive a seven-ton Thunderbolt. This time, however, Wennekers got away with it. But his rapid descent had taken him out of the frying pan into the fire. As he pulled out of his dive, he found himself in the middle of a formation of B-17s, staring at the dorsal hatch gunner of the nearest bomber less than 65 ft away. No doubt equally shocked by this sudden apparition, the gunner promptly ducked back inside the fuselage!

By this time other pilots of the rocket-equipped 5. *Staffel* had made their first pass at the bombers. Two Fortresses had gone down, one claimed by Heinz Knoke, when 'suddenly four odd-looking single-engined fighters dived past me. They have white bands on their wingtips. *Verdammt!* They must be Thunderbolts!'

Despite the US fighters' intervention, II./JG 11 was credited with bringing down another six Flying Fortresses, plus two of the escorting P-47s. But the *Gruppe* paid an unprecedented price for their victories – ten pilots killed or missing, plus another four wounded. The air battle for the Reich had suddenly entered a whole new dimension.

The only other Bf 109 *Gruppe* to claim against the Emden force was II./JG 3. From their new base at Amsterdam-Schiphol, the unit's eastern front veterans attacked the bombers during both their approach and withdrawal. In the light of II./JG 11's experiences closer to the target area, the *Gruppe's* first foray into Defence of the Reich operations proved remarkably successful – six B-17s downed for one

Hauptmann Anton Hackl, *Gruppenkommandeur* of III./JG 11, poses arms akimbo in front of his 'Black Double Chevron'. The seemingly odd two-tone appearance of the machine is accounted for by the fact that the area of fuselage visible between 'Toni' Hackl and Leutnant Gerhard Oppermann on his right displays JG 11's new yellow Defence of the Reich band, while the fin and rudder (on which part of Hackl's score can just be made out in the original print) are both white as befits a formation leader

pilot killed and two wounded. It should perhaps be pointed out, however, that of the 15 bombers claimed, less than half were actually lost.

On 2 October the Flying Fortresses returned to Emden, again escorted by Thunderbolts. This time the Bf 109 opposition was provided by II./JG 3 and III./JG 11. One of the latter's trio of B-17 kills was victory 127 for their new *Gruppenkommandeur*, Hauptmann Anton Hackl. Already wearing the Oak Leaves (awarded while serving with JG 77), this was 'Toni' Hackl's third Defence of the Reich Flying Fortress, the first two having been claimed during more recent operations with JG 11's *Geschwaderstab*. He would go on to add 29 more heavy bombers (including at least one daylight RAF Lancaster) to his final score of 192, ending the war as the *Geschwaderkommodore* of JG 11, and one of the Luftwaffe's leading *Viermot-Töter* (four-engined bomber killers).

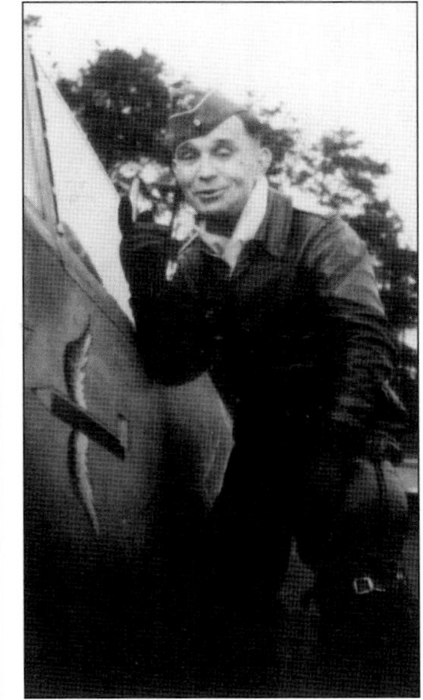

Hauptmann Günther Specht on the wing of one of the many *Gustavs* he flew – a high-altitude Bf 109G-5, adorned with his own personal 'winged pencil' emblem

The newcomers of II./JG 3 also numbered several highly decorated and high-scoring eastern front *Experten* among their ranks. One such was Hans-Joachim Kirschner, the *Kapitän* of 5. *Staffel*. His B-17 – one of four credited to the *Gruppe* on this date – took his tally to 173. Unlike Hackl, however, Kirschner would add only one more heavy bomber to his score and be killed before the year was out.

Kirschner's second, and last, B-17 was to be claimed just 48 hours after the first. On 4 October, VIII Bomber Command's Flying Fortresses targeted Frankfurt and the Saarland region. But, firstly, two groups of B-24s 'trailed their coats' in a diversionary sweep across the North Sea in another attempt to split the Luftwaffe's defences. This time it achieved the desired result. Among the units scrambled against the Liberators was II./JG 11 (plus the attached *Jasta* Helgoland, which was now on the mainland sharing the *Gruppe's* Jever base).

Hauptmann Specht's pilots intercepted the B-24s to the north of Heligoland. Their six claims included one apiece for Günther Specht, Heinz Knoke and Oberleutnant Hans-Heinrich Koenig, the new *Kapitän* of *Jasta* Helgoland. 5. *Staffel's* Feldwebel Hans-Gerd Wennekers scored a double. Flying a *Gustav* armed with 30 mm cannon, he hit one of the Liberators so hard that it reared up into the machine above and both went down into the North Sea (thereby taking his heavy bomber total to five). The *Gruppe's* six successes would have been a fair approximation of the B-24's four admitted losses, had the Fw 190 pilots not submitted claims for another five!

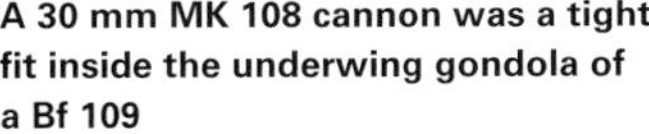

A 30 mm MK 108 cannon was a tight fit inside the underwing gondola of a Bf 109

Meanwhile, the B-17s were heading across the Low Countries and eastern France towards their assigned targets. Things did not go entirely to plan for either attackers or defenders, however. The bomber leaders were 100 miles off course, and the Luftwaffe controllers, unable to forecast the enemy's intentions, failed to take the proper countermeasures. Only two Bf 109 *Gruppen*, II./JG 3 and II./JG 27, made contact with the Flying

The hands of Oberleutnant Joachim Kirschner, the long-serving *Staffelkapitän* of 5./JG 3, are just a blur as he re-lives and describes in vivid detail a recent action

Fortress formations, but they were prevented from carrying out effective attacks by the bombers' escorting Thunderbolts. The *Gruppen* succeeded in downing just two B-17s each, one of II./JG 3's pair being credited to Joachim Kirschner.

Frankfurt suffered severe damage in the 4 October raid. This prompted the furious local *Gauleiter* (regional political leader) to complain in person to Hitler about the Luftwaffe's 'failure' to protect the city. The Führer passed on his displeasure to *Reichsmarschall* Göring who, in turn, vented his spleen on his subordinates at a meeting of Luftwaffe leaders three days later. Charges of 'lack of aggressive spirit' and worse were levelled. Göring demanded that drastic steps be taken to improve his flyers' performance.

All Defence of the Reich fighters were to be fitted with barographs to prove that every pilot had climbed to the altitude at which the bombers usually operated, and gun-cameras to ensure that he then closed with the enemy. Serious consideration was even given to the employment of 'aerial commissars' – officers who would accompany the fighters aloft, but then stand off from the action to monitor the pilots' performance!

The upshot was a three-point 'order' sent in the *Reichsmarschall's* name to every unit involved in Defence of the Reich operations:

1: There are no weather conditions that will prevent fighter units from taking off!

2: Every fighter pilot who returns without victory and with his machine undamaged will face court-martial!

3: If a fighter pilot is short of ammunition, or if his weapons malfunction, he is to ram the enemy bomber!

Hitherto, Göring had expressed nothing but praise for his units' performance in defence of the homeland. But his decree opened up a rift between the *Reichsmarschall* and his pilots that grew ever wider, culminating in the dismissal of Adolf Galland, Göring's *General der Jagdflieger*, in January 1945 and near mutiny by many of Galland's peers.

A series of four heavy raids in the second week of October soon provided the Reich's Defence pilots with the perfect opportunity to respond to their Commander-in-Chief's ill-judged accusations. They grasped it with both hands. The four raids would cost VIII Bomber Command a total of very nearly 150 bombers. And the Bf 109 units played a major part in the defenders' success. They were credited with over 90 kills – a good 60 per cent of all victories claimed.

8 October took VIII Bomber Command back to Bremen and the nearby U-boat yards at Vegesack. It also brought them into contact with the North Sea's three 'old guard' *Gruppen* of II./JG 11, III./JG 11 and III./JG 1. Despite the presence of escorting Thunderbolts, the Bf 109s claimed a total of 11 heavy bombers.

The three *Gruppenkommandeure*, Hauptleute Specht, Hackl and Olejnik, were credited with one apiece (taking their respective scores to 18, 128 and 42). Two other familiar names among the claimants were Heinz Knoke and Hans-Gerd Wennekers, while the B-17 downed by Siegfried Zick at Talge, south of Quakenbrück, raised the latter's tally to five. Hauptmann Friedrich Eberle, the *Staffelkapitän* of 8./JG 1 who was to replace Robert Olejnik at the head of III. *Gruppe* the following day, was credited with the only P-47 kill.

I. and II./JG 3 were also involved in the action. From their base at Bönninghardt, I. *Gruppe* fell foul of the fighter escort before they could get to the bombers. Against a claim for one P-47 (by Hauptmann Detlev Rohwer, *Kapitän* of 2. *Staffel*), they lost three pilots killed or missing, plus two wounded. Up from Amsterdam-Schiphol, the pilots of Major Kurt Brändle's II./JG 3 fared much better – four B-17s, including a brace for Leutnant Franz Ruhl, and one P-47 for a single loss of their own.

Twenty-four hours after Bremen, VIII Bomber Command mounted its longest mission to date against several targets far along the Baltic coast, including Danzig and Gotenhafen (Gdynia). This would take the bombers well beyond the range of their escorting P-47s, but the US planners hoped that once they had broken through the North Sea 'crust', the unescorted 'heavies' would face little organised opposition as they headed further eastwards along the Baltic coastline. And so it proved.

Even the Bf 109 *Gruppen* of JGs 1 and 11 – despite many of their pilots going up against the enemy formations on both their outward and return flights – failed to match their previous day's total. III./JG 11, for example, claimed just one B-17. This fell to Oberleutnant Hugo Frey, the *Kapitän* of 7. *Staffel*, and was his ninth heavy bomber in as many months.

As they crossed the Schleswig-Holstein peninsula separating the North Sea from the Baltic, the bombers came under attack from an unexpected quarter. The Bf 109s of I./JG 5 had recently been transferred down from Norway for temporary deployment to Frederikshavn, in Denmark. It was from here that they took off to intercept the 'heavies', and they managed to down a B-17. South of the bombers' route III./JG 54, commanded now by ex-JG 2 Channel front veteran Hauptmann Siegfried 'Wumm' Schnell, was also scrambled to meet the raiders. Its pilots were credited with five destroyed against one of their own wounded.

On 10 October, for the third time in three days, VIII Bomber Command mounted a major mission. At one stage this raid on Münster seemed almost to surpass August's Schweinfurt action in ferocity, with reports of 30 bombers and 26 Luftwaffe fighters going down in less than 25 minutes. Although exaggerated, this gives some indication of the intensity of the battle

Between them, the six main participating Bf 109 *Gruppen* were credited with just 12 of the 47(!) bombers claimed. The two most successful units were III./JG 1 and III./JG 26, who brought down four B-17s each. Two of the claimants were *Staffelkapitäne* – 7./JG 11's Oberleutnant Heinrich Klöpper and 12./JG 26's Hauptmann Hermann Staiger. Coincidentally, both had previously served with JG 51 on the eastern front, where each had won the Knight's Cross. The two Münster Flying Fortresses took their totals to 87 and 34 respectively.

The three consecutive raids had cost the Americans 88 admitted bomber losses (plus almost 500 damaged), but worse was to come four days later when, incredibly, they were sent back to Schweinfurt!

Despite the losses off 17 August, such was the priority placed upon the need to destroy Germany's ball-bearing production capacity that a second strike against Schweinfurt was deemed essential. Like the combined Schweinfurt/Regensburg raid before it, VIII Bomber Command's Mission No 115 of 14 October would result in the loss of exactly 60 B-17s. It would also drive the final nail into the coffin of the

Leutnant Franz Ruhl of 4./JG 3, who claimed a brace of Flying Fortresses during the Bremen raid of 8 October 1943, would himself be reported missing in action against B-17s on 24 December 1944 when the 'Battle of the Bulge' was at its height

unescorted bomber formation concept. There would be no more deep penetration raids – however vital the target to the Allied was effort – until there were enough fighters with sufficient range to escort the bombers all the way to their objective and back.

Equally aware of the importance of Schweinfurt, the Luftwaffe put everything it had into the air in its defence – single and twin-engined fighters, nightfighters, fighter-bombers, school machines and local industrial defence *Staffeln*. Amongst this motley collection were at least a dozen Bf 109 *Gruppen*. Seven of the more peripheral units (such as those of JGs 1 and 11 up on the North Sea coast) did not contribute greatly to the battle, being credited with just 11 bombers between them, and losing seven pilots in the process.

The other five *Gruppen* together claimed no fewer than 52 B-17s, out of an overall Luftwaffe total of 148! Hermann Graf's JGr 50 got six, but suffered the only fatality among the five. II./JG 27 and II./JG 51 downed nine each. I./JG 27 went one better with ten, including a double for *Gruppenkommandeur* Hauptmann Ludwig Franzisket. But the highest score of *any Gruppe* involved in second Schweinfurt was the 18 claimed by Hauptmann Walther Dahl's III./JG 3. Like Franzisket, Dahl got two, as did Wilhelm Lemke and 7. *Staffel's* Unteroffizier Wolfgang Rentsch.

It had been an undisputed victory for the defenders. After such blood-letting, it is hardly surprising that the second half of October saw just one incursion into Reich airspace. The mission to Düren on 20 October saw just two B-17s downed by II./JG 3 – one providing victory 106 for Knight's Cross-wearer Oberleutnant Werner Lucas, *Kapitän* of 4. *Staffel*. His first heavy bomber, it also proved to be his last kill before he was himself brought down by Spitfires over Holland four days later.

The Düren mission also saw the first attempted use by the Americans of British 'Oboe' pathfinding equipment (which failed), and the first escort mission to Germany by twin-engined P-38 Lightning fighters. The original Lightning groups that had arrived in the UK in the summer of 1942 had been transferred to North Africa before the Defence of the Reich campaign had begun.

By the winter of 1943 that campaign had risen to new dimensions. What had started out as almost a private war between the guardians of the German Bight and the first half-dozen US heavy bomber groups had now developed into an impersonal test of strength as hundreds of bombers, and their attendant escorts, clashed against equal numbers, or more, of defending Luftwaffe fighters. The latter had, for example, put up an estimated 800 individual sorties during second Schweinfurt.

And although VIII Bomber Command was currently restricted in its choice of targets by the range of its escorting fighters, the battle for Germany's skies was expanding not

A new threat – B-17Gs of the Fifteenth Air Force, based in Italy, cross the Alps to attack the southern extremities of the Greater German Reich

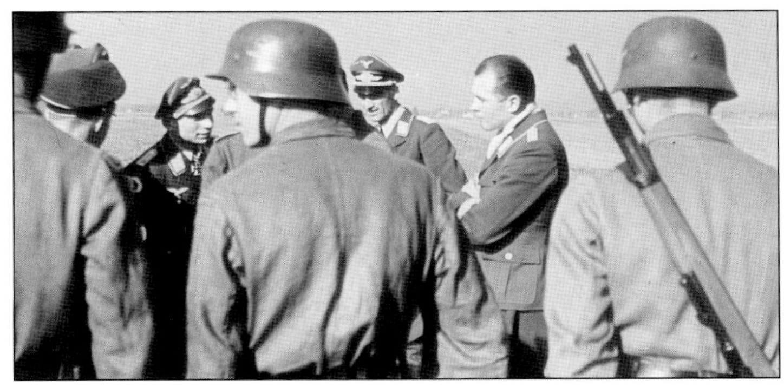

A bareheaded Hauptmann Karl Rammelt, *Gruppenkommandeur* of II./JG 51, is seen in deep discussion with a group of his pilots including, third from left, the Knight's Cross-wearing Oberleutnant Günther Rübell. The reason for the gathering, which obviously required the presence of armed Luftwaffe soldiers, is unfortunately not known. No fewer than 11 of Rammelt's final total of 46 victories would be heavy bombers, the majority of them Fifteenth Air Force machines

Pictured (right) during earlier service in the Mediterranean, Hauptmann, later Major, Gerhard Michalski, *Gruppenkommandeur* of II./JG 53 from July 1942 to April 1944, is seen here demonstrating fighter tactics to a young pilot with the aid of a model Bf 109 and Spitfire. The puppy stuffed in the aircraft's tropical filter appears not in the least bit interested! Some 13 heavy bombers would be included in Michalski's end-of-war tally of 73

just numerically, but also geographically. The successful invasion of Italy by Allied ground troops meant that their air forces would not be far behind. This would inevitably lay the southern ramparts of Hitler's so-called *Festung Europa* ('European Fortress') wide open to air attack.

From their bases in North Africa the 'heavies' of XII Bomber Command had already mounted one such assault – a double strike on 1 October against the Messerschmitt works at Augsburg, in southern Germany, and Wiener Neustadt, in Austria. It was to counter just such an eventuality that I./JG 27 had been transferred from Münster to Austria in August. Major Franzisket's *Gruppe* had intercepted the B-24s attacking Wiener Neustadt and shot down six of them (claims for a further five remained unconfirmed).

Meanwhile, III./JG 3 up from Bad Wörishofen, west of Munich, had found the B-17s of XII Bomber Command retiring from their abortive raid on Augsburg. They harried them back out across Lake Constance and, reportedly, well into Swiss airspace, claiming seven of their number.

The Luftwaffe had taken other measures to strengthen the Reich's vulnerable southern borders by withdrawing two more *Jagdgruppen* from the Italian front back to the homeland. Hauptmann Karl Rammelt's II./JG 51 had arrived at Munich-Neubiberg on 18 August – minus aircraft – to re-equip with new Bf 109G-6s. By mid-October the unit was sufficiently familiarised to participate in second Schweinfurt and claim the nine victories already mentioned. And it was two days after the Schweinfurt raid that the pilots of II./JG 53, commanded by Major Gerhard Michalski, were flown by Ju 52/3m into Wien (Vienna)-Seyring, also to receive new G-6s.

Both *Gruppen* were paraded in front of *Reichsmarschall* Göring and his entourage during the C-in-C's tour of inspection of Germany's southern defences in the latter half of October. Still smarting from the Führer's rebuke after the raid on Frankfurt, Göring's speeches of welcome upon the units' incorporation into the Defence of the Reich organisation lacked a certain warmth. At Neubiberg Karl Rammelt's pilots were told that they would have to display 'ruthless aggression' when attacking enemy bombers, 'not like some crafty brethren who just fly around aimlessly, using up fuel and writing-off machines to no purpose whatsoever'.

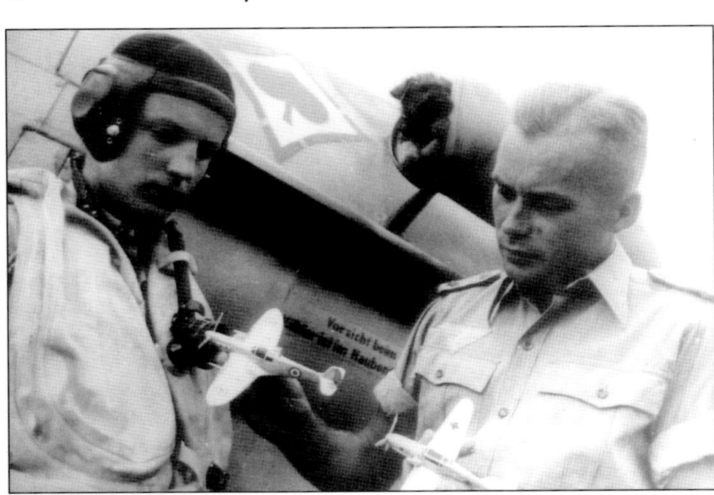

II./JG 53 had been ordered from Wien-Seyring to I./JG 27's base at nearby Fels am Wagram for the

Reichsmarschall's inspection. Here Göring was even more blunt;

'I'm not pointing the finger at any one *Gruppe* or *Staffel* in particular, but I promise you this. I will not have cowards in my Luftwaffe – these I will root out!'

Many pilots must have wondered what they were getting into.

A dissatisfied ***Reichsmarschall*** **'welcomes' newcomers to the Defence of the Reich organisation during his tour of southern airfields in October 1943. Among his entourage are** ***General der Jagdflieger*** **Adolf Galland (third from left in leather greatcoat) and Oberst Güther Lützow, Inspectorate of Fighters (West), who is almost entirely hidden behind his corpulent C-in-C, except for the top of his cap and the tip of his boot**

On 1 November the 'heavies' of XII Bomber Command were redesignated to become the nucleus of the new strategic Fifteenth Air Force. Twenty-four hours later its B-17s and B-24s launched a combined raid on the Bf 109 production plant at Wiener Neustadt. They were dealt with even more harshly than before (had the C-in-C's recent strictures been taken to heart?), this time by the *Gustavs* of I./JG 27, II./JG 51 and II./JG 53, who claimed six Flying Fortresses and 19 Liberators between them. US sources confirm the loss of six B-17s, but admit to only five B-24s. One of II./JG 53's four Flying Fortresses took *Gruppenkommandeur* Gerhard Michalski's score to 60. It was the first of 13 'heavies' he would be credited with. At the other end of the scale, exactly half of I./JG 27's 16(!) B-24s were awarded to first-time claimants.

With this raid on Wiener Neustadt, the pattern was set for the final weeks of 1943 and the first of 1944. From the UK, the Eighth Air Force – in ever-increasing numbers, but still without that essential fighter protection – would strike at familiar targets along Germany's northern coastline and across her western borders. From the south (where they would move from Africa to Italy in December), the 'heavies' of the Fifteenth Air Force would mount less frequent, but deeper penetration, raids against the Reich's 'soft underbelly'.

The campaign was now rapidly developing into a straightforward war of attrition. Given America's resources in men and *matériel,* the final outcome of any such contest was hardly in question. But it was not decided yet. Göring would continue to strip the other fighting fronts to bolster his Reich's Defence forces. And the *Jagdgruppen* protecting the homeland would continue to take a steady – at times heavy – toll of the enemy. But their own casualties were beginning to rise too, most worryingly among the experienced unit leaders.

On 3 November II./JG 3 claimed four of the P-47s escorting a raid on Wilhelmshaven. Two of them had fallen to *Gruppenkommandeur* Major Kurt Brändle. They were the first Defence of the Reich victories for the Oak Leaves-wearing Brändle, and raising his overall total to 172. That same afternoon, II./JG 3's own Amsterdam-Schiphol base came under attack from B-26 Marauders. The *Gruppe* scrambled just as the first bombs were falling. They chased the raiders back out to sea, becoming embroiled in a vicious dogfight with the medium bombers' Spitfire escort. For one RAF fighter downed, they lost five of their own – among them Kurt Brändle.

Major Kurt Brändle, ***Gruppenkommandeur*** **of II./JG 3, is seen here in pensive mood, despite the congratulatory bunch of greenery he is clutching. Brändle was another who would go down over the North Sea in late 1943**

It was the *Jagdgruppen* stationed in the Low Countries – the frontline of the Reich's Defence organisation, who were not only within easy range of the 'heavies'' escort fighters, but also subject to attack by the Allies' tactical air forces – that suffered some of the heaviest casualties.

During that same Wilhelmshaven raid on 3 November the three B-17s claimed by Leeuwarden-based III./JG 1, which included a pair for Oberleutnant Heinrich Klöpper, *Kapitän* of 7. *Staffel*, cost the lives of Klöpper's two fellow *Staffelkapitäne*, Hauptmann Alfred Faber of 8. and Oberleutnant Rainer Framm of 9./JG 1. The latters' predecessors, the eastern front 'turncoat saboteurs' Herwig Zuzic and Eugen Wintergerst, had both already been killed.

The Bf 109 *Jagdgruppen's* greatest November successes were achieved during the month's three raids on Bremen. Together, they were credited with over 50 enemy aircraft destroyed (out of a total 84 admitted US bomber and fighter losses). Many of the Bight's veterans, among them Günther Specht, Siegfried Zick and Hugo Frey, added to their growing scores. The last raid of the three, on 29 November, saw II./JG 3's Leutnant Leopold 'Poldi' Münster add a brace of P-38s to the five B-17s he had already claimed in defence of the Reich. 7./JG 1's Heinrich Klöpper also got a P-38 on that date. It was his 94th victory. But during their return to Leeuwarden Klöpper and his two wingmen were killed when they dived out of low cloud at high speed straight into the ground. III./JG 1 had lost all three of its *Staffelkapitäne* in the space of a month!

Apart from the ever worsening weather, December was very much a repetition of the month before. The 'heavies' of the Fifteenth Air Force made two more incursions from the south – against Innsbruck and Augsburg, while the *Jagdgruppen* along the northern and western borders of the Reich experienced the same combination of successes and losses.

It was the losses that were to dominate the first week of December, with two more highly successful eastern front veterans falling victim to the very different kind of war they found themselves fighting in the west. Both were brought down by P-47s over the Low Countries.

On 1 December Oberleutnant Herbert Schramm, *Staffelkapitän* of 5./JG 27, was killed in action over Belgium after tangling with fighters escorting a raid on targets to the northeast of Cologne. Schramm, who had claimed just three B-17s since commencing Defence of the Reich operations, would be honoured with posthumous Oak Leaves on 1 February 1945. Three days after Schramm's loss Hauptmann Wilhelm Lemke, the ex-*Staffelkapitän* of 9./JG 3 who had been brought in to replace the fallen Kurt Brändle as *Gruppenkommandeur* of II./JG 3, was shot down by Thunderbolts west of Nijmegen, in Holland. Awarded the Oak Leaves little more than a week earlier for the 125 victories he had achieved in Russia, Lemke had since added three B-17s and three P-47s in defence of the homeland.

It was the second of two raids on Bremen, on 20 December, that again led to the Eighth Air Force's heaviest losses for some time – 33 of their aircraft failed to return. The defending Bf 109s claimed a total of 30, 11 being credited to Siegfried Schnell's III./JG 54 alone. The B-24 downed by 6./JG 27's Oberleutnant Willy Kientsch northwest of the target area was his ninth heavy bomber of the Reich campaign (he had already been credited with nine over the Mediterranean). He was awarded the Knight's Cross on 22 November when his score was 43. Now it stood at exactly 50.

Not far away another Knight's Cross-wearing *Staffelkapitän*, Leutnant Ernst Süss of 9./JG 11, was far less fortunate. He had just brought down one of the bombers' escorting P-38s near Oldenburg (for victory 68) when his own G-5 was hit by a second Lightning. He managed to bail out, but was allegedly shot in his parachute. Oddly, US sources indicate that the P-38s reported neither a loss nor a claim on this date.

Ex-JG 52 eastern front veteran Oberfeldwebel Ernst Süss, seen here (left) with Major Hermann Graf, had been commissioned and appointed *Staffelkapitän* on 9./JG 11 by the time he was shot down by P-38s on 20 December 1943

Forty-eight hours later II./JG 11 also lost a *Staffelkapitän* when 6./JG 11's Hauptmann Egon Falkensamer was killed in action over the German-Dutch border by P-47s escorting bombers to Osnabrück. Recently returned to his *Staffel* after a six-month stint instructing, Falkensamer had two 'heavies' on his score sheet, both downed in May.

But December 1943 is worthy of mention for two other reasons. On 5 December the long-awaited P-51B Mustang made its operational debut. And on 13 December – for a combined strike against the northern ports of Bremen, Hamburg and Kiel – the Eighth Air Force, for the first time ever, put over 1000 aircraft into the air.

True, the P-51s were a group on loan from the tactical Ninth Air Force, and their mission took them only as far as France. And true, 'only' 637 bombers succeeded in attacking their primary targets on 13 December. But the writing was on the wall, and it did not bode well for 1944.

In fact, even before that, the borrowed Mustang group had already participated in all six of the last attacks to be mounted against the Reich in 1943. Due partly to the pilots' operational inexperience, however, this did not provide the immediate panacea that had – perhaps unfairly – been expected of the P-51B. Although the Mustangs claimed four kills, they lost eight of their own. The first had failed to return from the 11 December raid on Emden, the victim possibly of an attack by 9./JG 11's Oberfeldwebel Emil Schmelzinger over Holland. Four more went down during the Bremen operation on 20 December. Günther Specht and Hugo Frey of JG 11 were each credited with a P-51 on this date.

This Erla-canopied Bf 109G-6 of III./JG 1, sitting on a waterlogged dispersal at Volkel early in 1944, sports the new *Geschwader* badge – a winged red '1' – introduced by recently appointed *Kommodore* Oberst Walter Oesau. Less easy to spot is the aft fuselage red Defence of the Reich band with the white III. *Gruppe* vertical bar superimposed

In the first week of 1944, the Eighth Air Force returned twice to Kiel, and also struck at targets in the Rhineland. Then, on 11 January, the 'heavies' set out to attack a number of aircraft factories in central Germany. And here began what one German historian has been moved to describe as 'the slaughter of the Reich's Defence fighter units'.

THE TIDE TURNS

The Eighth Air Force's Mission No 182 of 11 January 1944, which saw over 650 bombers despatched against aircraft manufacturing and assembly plants at Oschersleben, Halberstadt and Brunswick, provoked the strongest Luftwaffe response since second Schweinfurt the previous October. In all, 19 single and twin-engined fighter *Gruppen*, several specialised smaller units, and elements from five nightfighter *Geschwader* were deployed against the attackers. The results were announced in an official bulletin the following day:

'136 North American aircraft, including 124 four-engined bombers, were shot down, the majority before reaching their targets.'

Although less than half the number quoted above, the Eighth Air Force's true losses of 60 downed (plus 184 damaged) were severe enough, equalling the cost of the two earlier Schweinfurt operations.

Between them, the eight Bf 109 *Jagdgruppen* in action on this day put in claims for 50 of the enemy. Although this figure is clearly over-optimistic, there is no doubt that the Bf 109s were heavily involved, with three units – the veteran II./JG 11, III./JG 11 and II./JG 27 – alone being credited with 30 victories. Several already well-known names added further to their growing scores. A Flying Fortress for 5./JG 11's Feldwebel Wennekers took his total to a round dozen. Anton Hackl, *Gruppenkommandeur* of III./JG 11, and one of his *Staffelkapitäne*, Hugo Frey (7./JG 11), each claimed a brace of B-17s, raising their respective tallies to 133 and 27. II./JG 27's ten victories included a pair each for *Gruppenkommandeur* Werner Schroer and Oberleutnant Karl-Heinz Bendert, *Kapitän* of 5. *Staffel*, taking their tallies to 95 and 47 respectively. And the B-24 downed by Oberleutnant Willy Kientsch, 6./JG 27's *Staffelkapitän*, was his 11th bomber in defence of the Reich.

Once again the Luftwaffe had dealt the Eighth Air Force an unquestionably heavy blow (although, given the numbers involved, the losses represented a casualty rate of less than ten per cent). But – and it was a big but – it had cost the defenders 32 pilots killed. That was the equivalent of an entire operational *Gruppe* lost in a single day! Taken to extremes, this meant that, in theory at least, the entire Defence of the Reich organisation could be wiped out in less than three weeks!

In reality, of course, the losses were immediately made good. But it was the start of a downward spiral from which the Reich's defenders would never recover. As their casualties climbed – which from now on they would continue to do, month by month, until the final collapse – those brought in to replace them were, in the main, either ex-bomber pilots lacking all fighter experience, or ever more inadequately-trained youngsters straight from fighter school. Inevitably, these newcomers would be even more vulnerable in combat and would, in their turn, soon need replacing. It was a vicious and accelerating circle.

And although they were in the vast majority, the tyros' names were not the only ones to appear on the casualty lists. Even those pilots who had succeeded in establishing themselves as *Experten* in the fraught arena of the Reich's Defence operations – and they were precious few – were beginning to be picked off one by one by the juggernaut of the Eighth Air Force as the enemy's numbers grew and his tactics were refined.

One major innovation introduced by the Americans at this juncture was in the use of their fighters. Gone were the days of the pioneering P-47 escorts who grimly stayed with the bombers as long as possible before their 'short legs' forced them to turn back. Now, VIII Fighter Command had enough fighters with sufficient range – the very prerequisites stipulated earlier – to introduce 'area patrols'.

This system involved assigning groups of fighters to adjoining areas all along the bombers' route to the target. Each group was then responsible in turn for protecting the entire bomber stream as it passed through its own particular area. In addition, other fighters ranged far ahead, and to either side, of the bombers' path in order to disrupt the Luftwaffe's efforts to concentrate its forces for a concerted attack. As yet still in their infancy, these tactics, involving ever-increasing numbers of fighters, would present the defenders with near insurmountable problems in the months ahead as they tried to fight their way through to the bombers.

For the present, leaving aside the Luftwaffe's technical advances in ground-to-air communications and control, the defenders tried to respond to the enemy's inexorable build-up of strength in kind by adding to their own numbers. And a pool of experienced fighter pilots was close to hand.

Back in the summer of 1943 an ex-bomber pilot, Major Hajo Herrmann, had come up with an idea for a new form of nightfighting. The '*Wilde Sau*' ('Wild Boar') method, as it was known, employed single-engined fighters sent up, independent of radar, to search for RAF night bombers by visual means alone (see *Osprey Aircraft of the Aces 20*).

The first *Wilde Sau Geschwader*, JG 300, had been established under Herrmann's command at the end of July 1943. Initially, each of its three component *Gruppen* was 'twinned' with an existing day *Jagdgruppe*, sharing both the latter's base and aircraft (III./JG 11 at Oldenburg, for example, played host to III./JG 300). This over-utilisation proved expensive, however, and by year-end III./JG 300 had lost over 30 of III./JG 11's *Gustavs* on nocturnal operations, many of them written off in accidents.

Although not unduly high in the overall scheme of things, this attrition affected host and guest unit alike, and impaired the combat efficiency of both. It was this factor, coupled with a decline in *Wilde Sau* victories – plus, above all, the demands being made upon the daylight defenders of the Reich – that brought about a change of policy. Henceforth, JG 300's nocturnal role would be secondary (and soon cease altogether). From bases – and with machines – of its own, the unit's pilots, trained in blind-flying, would be an invaluable asset to daytime operations which, as now in the depths of winter, often had to be flown under the worst possible weather conditions.

Two more intended *Wilde Sau Geschwader* – JGs 301 and 302, each commanded by ex-Stuka pilots – which had been activated in the interim were likewise reassigned predominantly to daylight defence duties at the turn of the year. Among the three units there would subsequently be a bewildering and inexplicable series of redesignations. But the important fact is that, with their change of role, the Defence of the Reich organisation had benefited to the tune of nine new *Jagdgruppen* at a single stroke. Six of the nine, incidentally, flew Bf 109s (the II. *Gruppe* of each *Wilde Sau Geschwader* was equipped with the Fw 190). And two had already been in action by day, I./JG 300 and I./JG 302 each having claimed a single victory during the Eighth Air Force's mission to Oschersleben on 11 January.

Early morning winter sunshine casts long shadows across I./JG 27's Fels am Wagram base as an oberleutnant pilot astride a motorcycle checks progress of work on the engine of his *Gustav*. In the background a crane mounted on a captured British six-wheeler lifts a replacement engine from its trailer

But for the next 18 days Germany was defended by her oldest and staunchest ally – the weather. A small force of Fifteenth Air Force B-17s attacked the Bf 109 components factory at Klagenfurt, in Austria, on 16 January, but the Eighth Air Force's intended strikes against Frankfurt of 24 January had to be aborted because of the atrocious weather conditions. Despite the weather having improved little in the meantime, the Eighth's 'heavies' tried again for Frankfurt five days later. This time they made it, but 29 of their number (plus 15 of their supporting fighters) failed to return.

One of the most successful of the defending *Jagdgruppen* on this occasion was Major Walther Dahl's III./JG 3. Its claims for 15 B-17s included another pair for the *Gruppenkommandeur*. The unit lost two of its own pilots, as did II./JG 27 up from nearby Wiesbaden-Erbenheim. One of the latter pair was the *Kapitän* of 6. *Staffel*, Oberleutnant Willy Kientsch, whose *Gustav* flew into high ground in the Hunsrück hills south of Koblenz while dogfighting in the low-level murk with P-38s. Willy Kientsch's final score of 53 included 20 heavy bombers – over half of them claimed in Defence of the Reich – which would earn him posthumous Oak Leaves.

Twenty-four hours later, still without a break in the weather, nearly 800 'heavies' were despatched against a Bf 110 production plant at Brunswick. Heavy cloud cover prevented the attack, but also greatly hampered the defenders. The eight Bf 109 *Jagdgruppen* that went up scored just seven victories between them, while losing 17 of their own pilots. I./JG 3's two fatalities occurred as a direct result of the appalling conditions when *Gruppenkommandeur* Major Klaus Quaet-Faslem and his wingman both flew into a hillside in thick cloud while trying to find a safe place to land. Göring's absurd dictum about there being 'no weather conditions that will prevent fighter units from taking off' was proving costly! The posthumous Knight's

Seen in happier times and sunnier climes, Leutnant Willy Kientsch (left) enjoys a hand of *Skat* 'somewhere in the Mediterranean', where he claimed his first 41 victories. He would add another 12 – all but one of them heavy bombers – in Defence of the Reich before losing his life in the murk of a northern European winter on 29 January 1944

Hauptmann Heinrich Wurzer was JG 302's top-scoring Bf 109 *Experte*, ending the war with 25 heavy bombers (and a single P-51) to his name

Cross awarded to Major Quaet-Faslem for his 49 victories, the last three of them B-17s, almost added insult to injury.

That same 30 January saw another future Reich's Defence *Experte* open his account against the Americans. Three of the eight *Gruppen* to engage the enemy on that date were *Wilde Sau* units. I./JG 302's sole victory was a B-17 credited to Hauptmann Heinrich Wurzer, the *Kapitän* of 1. *Staffel*. It was his third kill, the first two having been RAF night bombers. The little-known Wurzer would go on to add a further 22 US 'heavies' (plus a solitary P-51) to his score over the next five months.

January ended with another strike by the Fifteenth Air Force on Klagenfurt, and February opened on the third day of the month with the Eighth's returning to a very old haunt indeed – Wilhelmshaven. But the weather over the Bight was no better than that further inland, and the only three victories claimed – all for P-47s – went to III./JG 11's familiar triumvirate of Anton Hackl, Hugo Frey and Siegfried Zick. However, while remaining operational throughout, the *Gruppe* had just completed conversion on to the Fw 190. These were the trio's first kills on the new fighter, and mark their unit's disappearance from this present narrative.

JG 11's sole remaining Bf 109 *Gruppe*, Major Günther Specht's II./JG 11, would continue to fly its Messerschmitts until the end. On 10 February one of Specht's stalwarts, Oberleutnant Heinz Knoke, claimed a Flying Fortress for his 20th kill northeast of Osnabrück.

An even more famous name to claim a B-17 (his fourth in Defence of the Reich) on that same date was Oberstleutnant Hermann Graf. Since the disbandment of the quasi-experimental *Jagdgruppen* 25 and 50 back in the winter of 1943, many of their highly experienced pilots had been posted to other homeland defence units. After the briefest of stints as *Kommodore* of JG 1, Graf had replaced the long-serving Anton Mader at the head of JG 11 on 11 November.

But not even the likes of a Graf could reverse the growing trend in Reich's Defence operations of declining success rates bought at ever-higher costs. The seven Bf 109 *Gruppen* that opposed the Eighth's raid on Brunswick on that 10 February were credited with 16 victories, but suffered 14 of their own killed plus six wounded in return.

The same pattern was reflected the following day when the enemy again struck at Frankfurt. Eight Bf 109 *Gruppen* were scrambled, and they claimed eleven and lost nine. And so it would go on, with the outnumbered defenders slowly but surely losing the brutal war of attrition. But bald statistics such as these hide a wide range of individual fortunes within. On 11 February, for example, three of II./JG 3's four victories – all P-38s – had provided a treble for future eastern front Oak Leaves winner Feldwebel Gerd Thyben. IV./JG 3, on the other hand, lost their *Kommandeur* when Major Franz Beyer was killed in action south of Liège, in Belgium.

Having achieved numerical superiority – over 600 US fighters had supported the B-17 raid on Frankfurt – the enemy now produced his trump card. For 11 February also witnessed the operational debut of the Eighth's first Mustang group. True to form, this consisted of a cross-Channel sortie to the 'nursery slopes' of northern France. But before long Mustangs would be questing into the furthestmost recesses of the Reich and no corner of the Führer's domain would be immune from attack.

The heavyweight P-47 had performed sterling service, and would continue to do so right up until war's end. But it was the P-51 which undoubtedly tipped the scales in the daylight battle for Germany's skies.

That battle was not won yet, however, and on 20 February the Eighth Air Force launched Operation *Argument* – now better known as 'Big Week' – which was specially aimed at neutralising the Luftwaffe as part of the 'softening up' process prior to the Allied invasion of Normandy in the summer. A week-long series of daily heavy raids was to be mounted against Germany's airfields and aircraft manufacturing plants.

Not surprisingly, the Luftwaffe reacted fiercely to this onslaught on its own very being. But the 11 Bf 109 *Gruppen* involved on the opening day of the enemy's 'Big Week' put in a disappointing performance. They managed to claim only 15 bombers between them. Three of the fifteen were credited to one pilot, Leutnant Leopold Münster, *Staffelkapitän* of 5./JG 3, who succeeded in bringing down a trio of B-24s on their way to Brunswick.

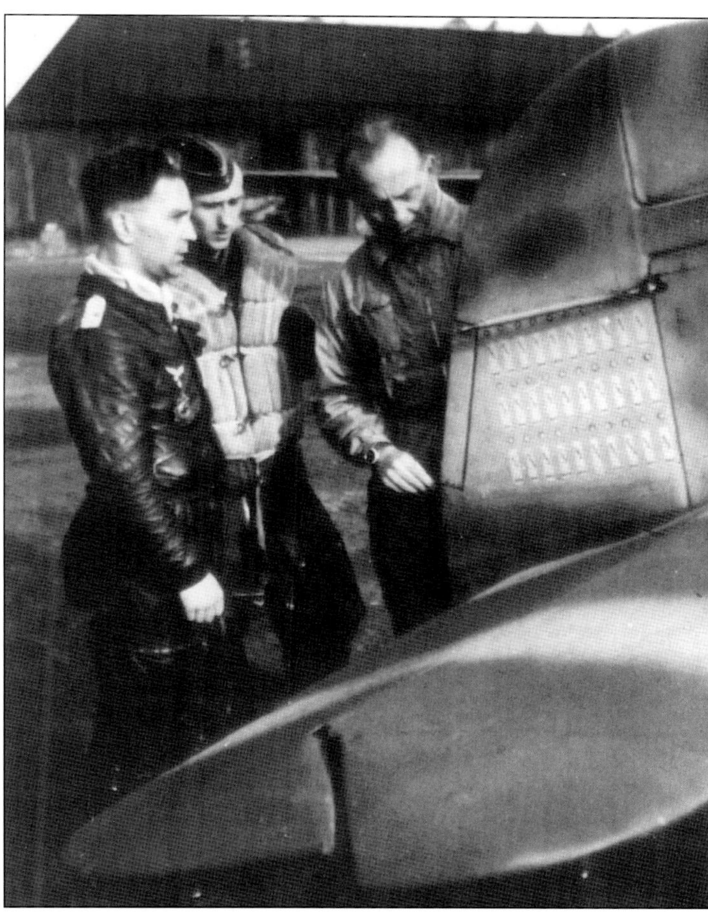

Professor Kurt Tank (right), designer of the Fw 190, admires the scoreboard on the rudder of Major Günther Specht's *Gustav* (possibly the same high-altitude machine as that seen on page 51 marked with the 'winged pencil' emblem). One more victory added to the 30 shown here would earn Specht the Knight's Cross on 8 April 1944

Brunswick was again among the targets for the following day when the eight Bf 109 *Gruppen* who engaged the raiders claimed ten kills for ten losses. On 22 February, the Eighth Air Force returned yet again to aircraft factories in the Brunswick-Halberstadt area, and on this occasion the defending Bf 109s achieved 26 victories for the loss of seven of their own. Among the claimants was II./JG 11's Günther Specht, whose two kills (a P-51 and a B-17 both brought down southwest of Hannover) took his total to 30. The *Gruppe's* two other victories, a Flying Fortress apiece for Heinz Knoke and Hans-Gerd Wennekers, put them on 21 and 13 respectively.

II./JG 11's score of four was equalled by a single *Staffel*. The ex-*Jasta* Helgoland, now redesignated 11./JG 11, but still operating semi-independently and still flying its venerable, long-span Bf 109Ts, was credited with the shooting down of four B-17s. One of these was credited to the unit's *Kapitän*, Oberleutnant Herbert Christmann.

22 February also saw the Italian-based Fifteenth Air Force make its first contribution to 'Big Week' with a raid on several Messerschmitt plants around Regensburg. This strike had originally been planned for the opening day of the offensive, but had had to be aborted due to severe icing conditions at high altitude over the Alps. Among the *Gruppen* scrambled

against this incursion from the south were I./JG 27 at Fels am Wagram and II./JG 53 from Wien-Seyring. The defenders' kill-loss ratio was much more favourable against the smaller, less well-protected Fifteenth Air Force formations, the *Gruppen* claiming a total of 11 bombers for three pilots killed.

Oberleutnant Herbert Christmann, the last *Kapitän* of the *Jasta* Helgoland who oversaw the unit's redesignation as 11./JG 11, is seen here wearing his flying helmet and standing behind the wing of his flamboyantly decorated Bf 109T (see colour profile 22). The figure standing *on* the wing beside the cockpit is Christmann's mechanic in his regulation black overalls

Among II./JG 53's successful pilots were two veteran Oberfeldwebels. Stefan Litjen's three B-17s were his first Defence of the Reich victories, and they took his overall total to 35. Herbert Rollwage, who had already been credited with two of the 15(!) P-38s claimed by the *Gruppe* in a 40-minute dogfight south of Vienna on 7 January, now added a single Liberator, which gave him his half-century.

Twenty-four hours later, with the Eighth Air Force anchored to its East Anglian bases by solid overcast, the Fifteenth struck at aircraft and ball-bearing factories at Steyr, in Austria. The defending Bf 109s reportedly had a field day, with I./JG 27 submitting claims for 16 kills and III./JG 3 – up from Leipheim – for no fewer than 20 (these totals included seven P-38s). The enemy's admitted bomber losses, all B-24s, were 17. I./JG 27's claims included a pair for Hauptmann Hans Remmer, *Kapitän* of 1. *Staffel*, taking his score to 22.

The *Gruppenkommandeur* of III./JG 3, Major Walther Dahl, likewise added a B-24 and a P-38 to his score (kills 60 and 61), while the Liberator credited to Hauptmann Emil Bitsch, *Staffelkapitän* of 8./JG 3, was not only the fourth heavy bomber of his Defence of the Reich career, but would also prove to be the last of his 108 victories.

On each of the next two days, 24 and 25 February, the Reich's aircraft industry would be attacked from both north and south. The Eighth Air Force's raids on targets in northern and central Germany on the 24th resulted in its heaviest losses of 'Big Week' with 49 bombers failing to return. The nine defending Bf 109 *Gruppen* claimed 23 kills.

To the south, where the Fifteenth Air Force struck for the second day running at Steyr, the three Bf 109 *Gruppen* that were scrambled almost equalled their northern counterparts' total. They were credited with 22 US aircraft destroyed (and for fewer losses). Two of the latter units' *Kommandeure* added to their scores, Walther Dahl claiming a brace of B-17s and a P-38 this time, and II./JG 53's Major Gerhard Michalski downing a single Flying Fortress.

On 25 February the Eighth and Fifteenth Air Forces combined forces to target aircraft plants and Luftwaffe airfields in central southern Germany. No fewer than 32 *Gruppen* – both single- and twin-engined, from as far afield as the English Channel coast to northern Italy – were sent up to oppose them. Among the 13 Defence of the Reich Bf 109 *Gruppen* to see action this day was a newcomer.

Since its brief appearance over Denmark the previous autumn, I./JG 5 had been stationed in Rumania and Bulgaria protecting the Ploesti oilfields. Now under its recently-appointed *Kommandeur*, Major Erich Gerlitz, the *Gruppe* had been returned to the homeland for re-equipment with rocket-armed Bf 109G-6s and assignment to Reich's defence duties. The unit had already claimed its first B-17 near Straubing three days earlier, but on 25 February its own airfield at Obertraubling, south of Regensburg, was on the list of targets. The *Gruppe* was able to scramble just in time to bring down three bombers, but lost two of its own pilots, including a *Staffelkapitän*.

With a number of aircraft destroyed or damaged on the ground, and their base resembling 'a moonscape, one crater next to the other', Gerlitz and his pilots were quickly transferred to Herzogenaurach – not the most auspicious of introductions to their new theatre of operations.

Thus ended (a day prematurely) 'Big Week'. The offensive had failed in one of its primary stated aims – to disrupt Germany's aircraft manufacturing capacity. Fighter production would continue to rise in the six months ahead before peaking in September. But 'Big Week' had laid waste to many of the Luftwaffe's operational airfields. And it was also responsible for the greater proportion of the Defence of the Reich's overall losses for February 1944 – 240 pilots killed and 146 wounded.

If February had been dominated by 'Big Week', then March can be encapsulated in one word – Berlin! The first three raids of the month had provided the usual mix of individual successes offset by steady losses. Among the former, the 3 March attack on Wilhelmshaven (chosen as an alternative target after the planned first ever daylight heavy bomber raid on Berlin had to be aborted due to the deteriorating weather) resulted in a Mustang each for the 'old firm' of Knoke and Wennekers.

III./JG 11's *Kommandeur*, Günther Specht, was not flying on this day, and it was Heinz Knoke who led the *Gruppe's* 18 *Gustavs* out of the sun in a classic bounce on some 60 P-51s high over Hamburg. Twenty minutes later, and nearly 110 miles (180 km) to the southwest, one of a pair of P-38s claimed by II./JG 27 near Magdeburg left *Gruppenkommandeur* Werner Schroer just one short of his century.

On 4 March the Eighth Air Force set out again for Berlin, only to be thwarted once more by severe weather conditions. Most of the bombers turned back before reaching the Ruhr to seek targets of opportunity along the Rhine. But one combat wing of 30 B-17s, together with their Mustang escort, pressed on to drop their bombs on the southwestern outskirts of the city – the first USAAF bombers to attack the German capital. They paid for their determination by suffering a third of the day's total bomber losses. Among the *Jagdgruppen* to engage them over the target area was II./JG 3 up from nearby Gardelegen. A B-17 over Döberitz, followed by a P-51 shortly afterwards, were victories 90 and 91 for Leutnant Leopold Münster, *Kapitän* of 5. *Staffel*.

Forty-eight hours later, the Eighth's Mission No 250 of 6 March finally took it all the way to Berlin. Although the weather was still not good, nearly 700 heavy bombers attacked targets in and around the capital through breaks in the heavy cloud. Having signalled their intentions by their two previous attempts to attack the city – or 'Big B' as the American crews had already dubbed it – it is not surprising that they encountered ferocious opposition. Twenty-five fighter *Gruppen* of every type, plus a number of specialised smaller units, were hurled against the attackers,

A Flying Fortress of the 452nd BG cruises over Berlin, with aircraft just visible on the distinctive curved apron of Tempelhof airport in the top left-hand corner of the photograph. This shot was reportedly taken during the raid of 29 April 1944

inflicting upon them their highest single day's loss of the entire war – 69 bombers downed and over 350 damaged. The claims by the defenders (excluding flak) were nearly double that figure. They were credited with 121 aircraft destroyed, of which the 11 participating Bf 109 *Gruppen* were responsible for 35.

From their base at Wunstorf, south of the bombers' approach route, III./JG 11 was ordered to take off and gain height over the nearby Steinhuder Lake. This was the assembly point for six *Jagdgruppen* – a mixed force of nearly 120 Fw 190s and Bf 109s in all – preparing to mount a concerted attack on the enemy formations which had just been reported crossing the Dutch border into German airspace. The *Gefechtsverband* (battle group) headed northwestwards and sighted the bombers near Quakenbrück.

Flying top cover, Günther Specht led the 15 *Gustavs* of II./JG 11 into action against a group of escorting Thunderbolts. 5./JG 11's Unteroffizier Wilhelm Fest got the first, but then the *Staffel* was in trouble. Hans-Gerd Wennekers managed to shoot another P-47 off the trail of Kapitän Oberleutnant Heinz Knoke, only to be hit himself by a third enemy fighter. With his machine damaged and a bullet clean through his left wrist, Wennekers bailed out. Another pilot also had to take to his parachute, and two others were killed in the engagement.

Heinz Knoke went on to claim a B-17 a quarter of an hour later (one of three credited to the *Gruppe* in the space of five minutes), but his 'Black 1' was struck by return fire and he had to force-land back at Wunstorf. Even for the veterans of II./JG 11, the Defence of the Reich campaign was becoming an almost daily struggle for existence.

The *Gefechtsverband* included another Bf 109 *Gruppe* highly experienced in homeland defence operations. Since being withdrawn from the Low Countries, III./JG 54 had been stationed at various bases in northern Germany, including Schwerin, Ludwigslust and Lüneburg. It was from Lüneburg that its 20 fighters, led by *Gruppenkommandeur* Hauptmann Rudi Sinner, took off in defence of the capital. Over the past months the *Gruppe* had extracted a steady toll of Eighth Air Force bombers and fighters (24 during 'Big Week' alone), and today was to be no exception. But it paid an unaccustomedly heavy price for its ten kills.

Tall-tailed Bf 109G-6 'gunboat' 'Yellow 9' served with 9./JG 54 in early 1944 possibly at Lüneburg. It boasts a full set of markings for this period, including a rear fuselage blue Defence of the Reich band

Rudi Sinner had taken command only days earlier. Previously the *Kommandeur* of IV./JG 54 on the eastern front, he had exchanged places with Hauptmann Siegfried Schnell at the end of February. Perhaps inexperience with the enemy in the west led him in too close as he tried to pick off a straggling B-17 south of Bremen, but he was seriously wounded by return fire and fortunate to be able to extricate himself from his wildly spinning *Gustav*.

The *Kapitän* of his 8. *Staffel*, Oberleutnant Gerhard Loos, was not so lucky. The ex-eastern front *Experte*, who had been awarded the Knight's Cross only the month before, was caught by Mustangs during a second sortie against the bombers' withdrawal some two hours later. He too managed to bail out – at 2000 ft – but accounts differ as to what happened next. His opponent reported that 'as his parachute opened the harness came apart and he fell to his death'. A German source states that, at a height of 200 ft Loos realised he was drifting into high-tension cables and deliberately chose to release his parachute harness.

III./JG 54 suffered three other pilots killed and two wounded in what was to be their last major engagement flying Bf 109s in defence of the Reich. In April, under their new *Kommandeur*, Hauptmann Werner Schroer (ex-II./JG 27), the surviving pilots transferred down to Illesheim, west of Nuremberg, to convert on to the Fw 190.

The most successful Bf 109 *Gruppe* in action on 6 March, however, was IV./JG 3, which was credited with 13 victories without loss to themselves. Also being led by a relatively new *Kommandeur* – Major Friedrich-Karl Müller, brought in from I./JG 53 in Italy to replace the fallen Franz Beyer – IV./JG 3 formed part of a second *Gefechtsverband* (including a number of twin-engined *Zerstörergruppen*) which engaged the US bombers to the east of Brunswick. The Oak Leaves-wearing Müller quickly claimed his first Defence of the Reich victories – a brace of B-17s that took his overall total to 119. Future Knight's Cross winner Leutnant Hans Weik, *Staffelkapitän* of 10./JG 3, also downed two Flying Fortresses, putting him on 19 – exactly a century behind his high-scoring *Kommandeur*.

But the most highly decorated and highest scoring pilot of all to take to the air in defence of the capital on this day was Oberstleutnant Hermann Graf, now the *Kommodore* of JG 11. Flying at the head of his *Stabsschwarm* Graf engaged a formation of B-24s to the west of Berlin. The Liberator he claimed there provided him with victory 209.

The 6 March 'Battle of Berlin' was a watershed in the Defence of the Reich campaign. Heinz Knoke himself later described it as 'the most exhausting day's fighting I ever experienced'. It had been costly too. For their (inflated) claims of 121 enemy aircraft destroyed, the defenders had paid with 36 killed and 27 wounded. And while they would never hit the Americans as hard again (although they would come close on two future occasions), their own casualty list was a stark warning of what they could expect over the months ahead as the enemy's strength and pressure grew.

Nor would the price to be paid be evenly distributed, for by now the Reich's defenders fell into three distinct categories. Most at risk were the

Oberleutnant Gerhard Loos, *Staffelkapitän* of 8./JG 54, lost his life in action against Mustangs south of Bremen during the bombers' return from Berlin on 6 March 1944

The B-17 credited to 5./JG 27's *Staffelkapitän* Oberleutnant Karl-Heinz Bendert on 8 March 1944 was his fifth Defence of the Reich heavy bomber victory

Mid-March 1944 at Leipheim, and the last traces of winter snow are still on the ground as III./JG 3's machines are readied for their next mission. The *Gustavs* – each now bearing JG 3's new rear fuselage white Defence of the Reich band – are sharing the tarmac with several Me 323 transports (the port wing of one of these six-engined giants can just be made out in the background at left)

youngsters, fresh out of fighter school, inadequately prepared and completely lacking in combat experience. Many did not survive their first mission. Those that did – and returned from the next three or four after that – might then begin to score. But these scores seldom reached double figures before they were brought down. These were the unsung heroes of the campaign who, by their very numbers, were responsible for by far the greater proportion of the successes – and the casualties – during its closing stages.

Next came those pilots whose units had been transferred in from other fronts. Many were highly experienced and had already amassed large scores. But that was no guarantee of survival in Defence of the Reich. Some successfully made the transition, continuing to add to their existing totals (although rarely at the same rate). Many did not.

Lastly came the *alte Hasen* ('old hares') of Reich's Defence, the veterans of the early days of the German Bight who had matured and grown in stature as the campaign itself had developed. But not even they were immune now.

There was no time for introspection, however. Just 48 hours after their first attack on Berlin, the enemy's bombers were back over the capital. The 8 March raid cost the Eighth Air Force another 37 of its 'heavies'. Many of these must have fallen to the 11 defending Bf 109 *Gruppen*, who numbered 31 *Viermots* (four-engined bombers) among their total of 40 claims. Some pilots repeated, or even improved upon, their performance of two days earlier. Hermann Graf got a Mustang (his first) near Celle.

IV./JG 3 was again credited with 13 victories, but this time at the expense of one killed and two wounded. Among those claiming were *Kommandeur* Friedrich-Karl Müller (three bombers) and Hans Weik (a B-17 and a P-51). I./JG 302's Hauptmann Heinrich Wurzer downed a pair of B-24s over Magdeburg to add to his two B-17s from the previous raid, thereby taking his rapidly lengthening Defence of the Reich bomber score sheet to nine.

Neither I./JG 3 nor II./JG 27 had been successful on 6 March. They now made good the omission with seven victories between them, but lost two pilots each. I./JG 3's experiences reflected the knife-edge nature of

the campaign at this crucial stage. The 44-victory *Kapitän* of 1. *Staffel*, Leutnant Hans Frese, was killed in action, while Oberleutnant Hans Schleef, *Kapitän* of 3./JG 3, claimed a single P-51 to take his score to 98. Meanwhile, one of II./JG 27's four B-17s had given Oberleutnant Karl-Heinz Bendert, the *Staffelkapitän* of 5./JG 27, his half-century.

The remainder of the month was marked by the growing number of casualties among the ranks of the experienced, high-scoring formation leaders – just the sort of pilots the Defence of the Reich could least afford to lose.

Exactly a week after the second attack on Berlin, III./JG 3 became entangled with a large group of P-47s escorting bombers back from a raid on Brunswick. In a furious dogfight above the Dutch border the unit lost Knight's Cross-holder Hauptmann Emil Bitsch, *Kapitän* of 8. *Staffel*. Bitsch had spent his entire operational career with III./JG 3, the last four of his 108 victories having been heavy bombers downed over the Reich. Twenty-four hours later, on 16 March, Major Erich Gerlitz, *Gruppenkommandeur* of I./JG 5, also fell victim to P-47s east of Ulm.

Two days after that III./JG 3 was again in action, with Leutnant Ekkehard Tichy, *Kapitän* of 9. *Staffel*, claiming a Mustang northwest of Stuttgart. It was Tichy's eighth Defence of the Reich kill. But when he went after a Flying Fortress minutes later his own cockpit was shattered by enemy fire. He managed to bail out of his stricken *Gustav* but lost the sight of one eye. After recuperating, Tichy volunteered for duty as a *Sturm* pilot, flying the Fw 190 (see *Osprey Aviation Elite Units 20*).

It was towards the end of the month that the Reich's Defence lost two of its most senior *Geschwaderkommodores*. Oberstleutnant Wolf-Dietrich Wilcke had headed JG 3 since the autumn of 1942. After being awarded the Swords for 155 victories at the end of that year, he had been banned from further operational flying. Although he observed the ban while in the east, six months into *Stab* JG 3's Defence of the Reich duties, its *Kommodore* was back in the air – albeit without specific official permission. A P-38 downed on 10 February had been quickly followed by three heavy bombers. On 23 March he led his *Stabsschwarm* in an attack on a formation of B-17s near Brunswick. After claiming a bomber and one of the escorting P-51s, Oberstleutnant Wilcke was set upon by the other Mustangs and was last seen going down to the southeast of the city.

Oberstleutnant Hermann Graf had likewise been banned from combat flying after reaching his double century in Russia. But he too had long been back in action in Defence of the Reich, first at the head of JGr 50 and latterly as *Kommodore* of JG 11. On 29 March Graf and his *Stabsschwarm* attacked a group of Flying Fortresses retiring south of Bremen. Oberstleutnant Graf downed one of the bombers' Mustang escorts and then rammed (or collided with?) a second. Seriously wounded, he nevertheless managed to take to his parachute, surviving to return after a long convalescence to his operational roots in the east, where he commanded his old unit, JG 52, until the final surrender.

March had also seen the addition of two more Bf 109 *Gruppen* to the Defence of the Reich order of battle. Both were used to shore up Austria's southern ramparts. Major Ernst Düllberg's III./JG 27 was brought back up from the Aegean area to Wien-Seyring, while IV./JG 27, under Hauptmann Otto Meyer, flew in to Graz-Thalerhof from Yugoslavia.

Portrayed here as an Oberfeldwebel, the later Leutnant Ekkehard Tichy claimed seven heavy bombers in defence of the homeland while serving with III./JG 3. After recuperating from severe wounds, including the loss of one eye, he would add four more as a *Sturm* pilot flying Fw 190s

Pictured earlier on the eastern front with a cigar-chomping Major Wolfgang Ewald (left), Oberstleutnant Wolf-Dietrich Wilcke of JG 3 was one of the small band of highly experienced, high-scoring *Geschwaderkommodores* to be killed on Defence of the Reich operations. Shot down by Mustangs on 23 March 1944, *'Fürst'* ('Prince') Wilcke's final score of 162 kills included four heavy bombers

What a difference a few weeks make. In this still from a German newsreel shown throughout Germany in late March 1944, a pair of I./JG 27's 'gunboats' kick up slush at Fels am Wagram as they run up their engines ready for take-off . . .

. . . in fact, outside the newsreel cinemas spring had already arrived by that time. His arm resting nonchalantly on the starting handle of a I./JG 27 *Gustav*, this 'black man' (mechanic) enjoys a quiet moment in Fels am Wagram's late morning sun. Note the modified *Afrika* badge of 3./JG 27, the 'Staffel Marseille' (see *Aviation Elite Units 12*)

The newcomers were thus on hand to back up I./JG 27's opposition to the Fifteenth Air Force's attacks on Klagenfurt and Graz on 19 March. Between them, the three *Gruppen* claimed a slightly optimistic 25 B-24s shot down – 13 by III./JG 27 alone. The Fifteenth admitted the loss of 18 of its bombers.

Successes such as this would continue for several weeks more in the south. But the Eighth Air Force's UK-based offensive, which had begun 15 months earlier by lapping at Germany's North Sea defences, was now regularly breaching the Reich's western walls, if not yet with impunity, then certainly with ever-increasing strength and confidence. Despite the lingering bad weather, the Eighth would mount 13 attacks on the Reich in April (and the Fifteenth Air Force four). The second of them, against Luftwaffe airfields in the Brunswick area on 8 April, was opposed by a dozen Bf 109 *Gruppen* whose combined claims totalled 'only' 25 kills – 19 of them bombers. One of the B-24s lost had fallen victim to Major Friedrich-Karl Müller. It was victory 123 for Müller, and his first since replacing Wolf-Dietrich Wilcke as *Kommodore* of JG 3.

Three days later 11 of those same 12 Bf 109 *Gruppen* more than redressed the balance when they were credited with 51 enemy aircraft

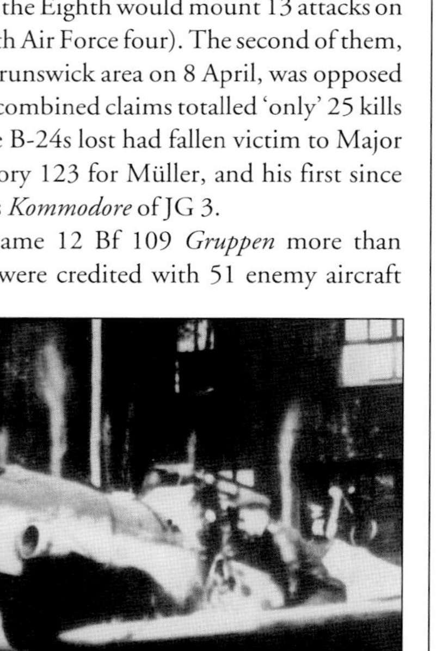

An unfortunately rather blurred shot of Major Günther Specht's high-altitude Bf 109G-5/AS, its spinner decorated with greenery and with a large cut-out Knight's Cross draped across its cowling in celebration of Specht's winning the award on 8 April 1944 for his 31 victories in the west. Although not apparent here, this machine sports JG 11's new *Geschwader* badge beneath the cockpit

destroyed. IV./JG 3 made the biggest contribution with claims for no fewer than 25. The 11 April strikes on aircraft factories and airfields in central and northern Germany cost the Eighth Air Force 64 'heavies'.

Among IV./JG 3's claimants was Oberleutnant Otto Wessling, *Kapitän* of 11. *Staffel*, whose trio of B-17s took his score to 80. He would add three more Flying Fortresses to his total before he was himself shot down by P-51s near Kassel on 19 April. Although he managed to crash-land and escape from his blazing *Gustav*, Wessling was strafed on the ground by the Mustangs as he sought cover. Having been awarded the Knight's Cross as an NCO on the eastern front, Otto Wessling would be honoured with posthumous Oak Leaves on 20 July.

IV./JG 3 was by far the most successful Bf 109 *Gruppe* in April, having made claims for another 19 B-17s (including Wessling's last) on 18 April and a further 16 on 24 April. But on the latter date I./JG 3 also lost a *Staffelkapitän* in similar circumstances to Wessling's. Another ex-eastern front NCO who had won the Knight's Cross, Leutnant Franz Schwaiger had since risen to become *Kapitän* of 1./JG 3 in place of the recently fallen Hans Frese. After an inconclusive dogfight with Mustangs to the north of Augsburg, Schwaiger made a successful belly-landing in a large open field – one source states he had run out of fuel – but then he too was attacked on the ground by strafing P-51s before he could reach cover.

Another of the 12 JG 3 pilots to be killed on 24 April was Hauptmann *Freiherr* von Kap-herr, the *Kommandeur* of III. *Gruppe*. Kap-herr, who had been in office only three days (having been transferred in from III./JG 3), was flying at the head of his new command for the first time when he was shot down over Neuburg an der Donau (Neuburg-on-Danube) close to where Schwaiger had belly-landed. He was the fourth *Kommandeur* of III./JG 3 to be killed since the *Gruppe* had commenced Defence of the Reich operations.

On 29 April the Eighth Air Force's Mission No 327 took it back to Berlin. Sixty-three of its bombers would fail to return (the last time in the war that the 'Mighty Eighth' would suffer 60+ combat casualties in a single day). IV./JG 3, now commanded by Major Wilhelm Moritz, was again in the thick of the action, and the most successful, with claims for 14 bombers against a single fatality of its own. II./JG 11 was also back in the fray after having spent the past few weeks re-equipping with a special high-altitude variant of the Bf 109. But despite a dozen kills, this was not the II./JG 11 of old. It not only had new aircraft, but many new pilots – mostly green youngsters – *and* a new *Gruppenkommandeur*.

With Günther Specht about to take over as *Kommodore* of JG 11 in place of the wounded Hermann Graf, Major Günther Rall of JG 52 was brought in from the eastern front to head II./JG 11. Wearing the Swords, Rall was the third-highest scoring fighter pilot in the entire Luftwaffe. Although almost all of his operational career to date had been against the Red Air Force at low to medium level, the new *Kommandeur* now claimed his first Defence of the Reich kill – a P-38 to the north of Hannover, at an altitude of 26,000 ft. It was victory 274 for Rall.

Another of the *Gruppe's* 12 claimants was Oberleutnant Heinz Knoke, who downed a P-51, only to fall foul of a group of Thunderbolts himself shortly afterwards. He survived a nasty crash landing near Brunswick, but a fractured skull would keep him off flying for nearly four months. Knoke

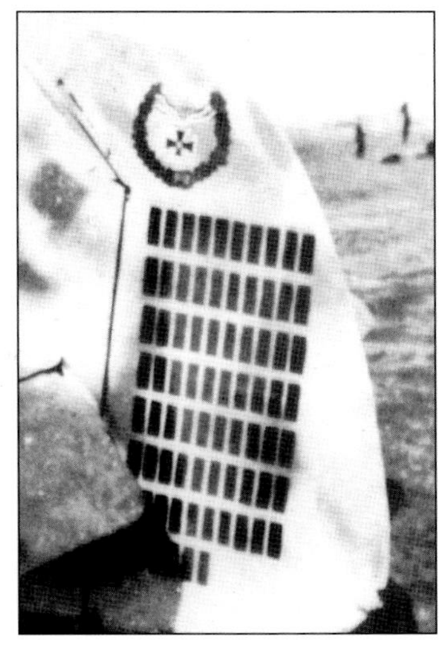

Although a complete novice in Defence of the Reich when compared to Günther Specht, IV./JG 27's top scorer, Feldwebel Heinrich Bartels, had 73 victories to his credit when the *Gruppe* flew in to Graz-Thalerhof from the Aegean at the end of March 1944. Bartels had already added several more kills by the time this shot of his rudder tally was taken the following month. His final score of 99 included 26 in defence of the homeland – all fighters – before he himself fell victim to P-47s on 23 December 1944

would assume command of III./JG 1 in August, but then sustained further injuries a few weeks later.

The Eighth Air Force returned to Berlin on 7 and 8 May, and the defending Bf 109 *Gruppen* again suffered varied fortunes. On the latter date IV./JG 3 was credited with an astonishing 24 heavy bombers (although a third of these had been downed by the Fw 190s of the newly attached 11. *Staffel*). The *Gruppe's* most successful pilots, *Kommandeur* Wilhelm Moritz and Hans Weik, the *Kapitän* of 10./JG 3, added a double and a treble respectively to their existing scores, bringing them to 37 and 31.

II./JG 3's more modest nine victories cost it two killed, one of them the *Gruppe's* top scorer. Leutnant Leopold Münster had already claimed a B-17 west of Brunswick before going after a formation of B-24s sighted over Hildesheim. But the highly experienced *Kapitän* of 5. *Staffel* must have misjudged his pass for he collided with his chosen victim. The Liberator exploded in mid-air, sending its assailant down too. 'Poldi' Münster was another who would be awarded posthumous Oak Leaves (on 12 May). His final score totalled 95, with the last 19 having been claimed in Defence of the Reich – all but four of them heavy bombers.

Another 'near centurion', Leutnant Leopold Münster of II./JG 3 claimed 15 'heavies' destroyed in his tally of 19 Defence of the Reich victories. His last bomber (kill 95 overall) cost 'Poldi' Münster his own life when he collided with the B-24 southeast of Hildesheim on 8 May 1944

On 10 May the Fifteenth Air Force put in its first appearance of the month over the Reich. Between them, IV./JG 27 and II./JG 302 were credited with 13 of the enemy, who were attacking targets in the Wiener Neustadt area. Among II./JG 302's seven victories was a pair of B-24s for Hauptmann Heinrich Wurzer.

The next day another *Geschwaderkommodore* was lost. With service dating back to before the Spanish civil war, where he had scored his first eight kills as a member of the *Legion Condor*, Oberst Walter Oesau had since risen to become one of the Luftwaffe's foremost aces. He had been *Kommodore* of JG 2 on the Channel coast for almost two years. Then, after a brief period of office as *Jafü Bretagne* (Fighter-Leader Brittany), he had been appointed *Kommodore* of JG 1 on 12 November 1943.

Putting his Channel front experience to good use, 'Gulle' Oesau had claimed nine heavy bombers while leading JG 1, the last of them being brought down during the 6 March 'Battle of Berlin'. But on 11 May 1944 it was Oberst Oesau who was to fall, downed by P-38s at the end of a vicious 20-minute dogfight as he tried to belly-land his damaged *Gustav* near the Belgian town of St Vith. In his honour, the *Geschwader* was subsequently awarded the official title JG 1 'Oesau'.

Oesau's loss may have been a bitter blow, but it was the raids launched by the Eighth Air Force 24 hours later that heralded the beginning of the end for the defenders of the Reich. Mission No 353 of 12 May saw nearly 900 bombers sent to bomb six major oil refineries – five in eastern Germany and one in Czechoslovakia. This first attack by

Another high-ranking *Geschwaderkommodore* to fall victim to US fighters while defending the homeland was Oberst Walter Oesau of JG 1. Seen here (left) on the Channel front with Hauptmann Siegfried Schnell, Oesau was flying 'Green 13' when he was downed by P-38s near St Vith, in the Ardennes, on 11 May 1944

the Eighth on the Reich's oil industry had long been feared by Germany's military and industrial leaders alike. And with good reason. What 'Big Week' had signally failed to do – curb Luftwaffe operations by targeting aircraft manufacturing plants and airfields – the sustained oil offensive that was now beginning would achieve beyond all expectations. Luftwaffe activity would not merely be curbed, it would be crippled.

Fighter production was still rising, and the schools were still turning out enough pilots to fly the machines being produced, after a fashion. But the rapidly worsening fuel situation, which in the months ahead would go from critical to catastrophic, soon rendered all such efforts meaningless.

The defenders reacted violently to this initial assault on their lifeblood. The 11 Bf 109 *Gruppen* sent up in opposition claimed a total of 89 aircraft destroyed (nearly double actual US losses). Several experienced formation leaders added to their already considerable scores. A brace of B-17s downed within five minutes took Major Friedrich-Karl Müller, *Kommodore* of JG 3, to 140. Major Günther Rall led his high-altitude II./JG 11 down on to a large formation of P-47s and claimed one of them, before he and all three other members of his *Stabsschwarm* were shot down in the dogfight that followed. Rall bailed out, but his left thumb had been severed. He was phlegmatic about his injury – 'Who needs two thumbs anyway?' – but although he would be appointed *Kommodore* of JG 300 in the closing days of the war, the P-47 downed over Nassau had been the last of Günther Rall's 275 victories.

Another *Gruppenkommandeur* wounded on this date was I./JG 27's Major Ludwig Franzisket, who was hit by return fire from a B-17 he was attacking near Frankfurt-on-Main. At least two experienced *Staffelkapitäne* were killed. Hauptmann Gerhard Sommer of 4./JG 11 was brought down by US fighters south of Bielefeld.

Having been on Defence of the Reich operations from the outset, 15 of Sommer's 20 victories had been heavy bombers, making him one of the campaign's foremost *Viermot-Töter* (four-engined bomber killers). He would be awarded a posthumous Knight's Cross on 19 August. Further to the south, Leutnant Jürgen Hoerschelmann, *Kapitän* of 7./JG 3, fell prey to Mustangs near Fulda. The few remaining *Experten* engaged in homeland defence were getting steadily fewer!

A revealing indication as to the make up of the Reich's Defence strength by this stage of the hostilities is provided by the two most successful *Gruppen* in action on 12 May. Of II./JG 3's 12 claims, all but one were made by pilots with three victories or fewer. And 16 of the 20 kills credited to IV./JG 3 went to pilots with scores in single figures. In fact, this was to be one of IV./JG 3's last major successes flying Bf 109s in Defence of the Reich.

Having operated for the last two months in conjunction with *Sturmstaffel* 1 (the experimental Fw 190 unit now incorporated into the *Gruppe* as 11./JG 3), and no doubt influenced in no small measure by their consistently high scores of late, Maj Wilhelm Moritz's IV./JG 3 was the first *Jagdgruppe* to be selected for the specialist *Sturm* role. Before the month was out it had converted onto heavily armed and armoured Fw 190s (see *Osprey Aviation Elite Units 20*).

Meanwhile, the Bf 109 *Gruppen* soldiered on. Against a series of four US raids in the middle weeks of May, their (mainly young) pilots claimed

The operational career of Hauptmann Ernst Boerngen, *Gruppenkommandeur* of I./JG 27, came to an end when he rammed a Liberator – his 24th heavy bomber victory – near Helmstedt on 19 May 1944

a total of 69 kills. The biggest success of any one day was the eight victories credited to I./JG 27 in the Brunswick area on 19 May. These included a pair of B-24s for Hauptmann Ernst Boerngen, who had succeeded the wounded Ludwig Franzisket as *Kommandeur* just six days earlier. Boerngen's first victim was brought down by cannon fire and the second he rammed. Bailing out with severe wounds, Boerngen was rushed to hospital, but surgeons were unable to save his right arm.

On 24 May I./JG 27 (whose pilots seemed to be waging their own personal two-front war!) was back in action against the next Fifteenth Air Force incursion up from Italy. It claimed a dozen of the raiders attacking airfields in Austria. I./JG 302 went one better, being credited with 13 enemy aircraft brought down to the south and west of Vienna. Eight of the thirteen consisted of doubles, including another brace of B-24s for Heinrich Wurzer.

Oberstleutnant Theodor Weissenberger of 7./JG 5 indicates victory 112 – an Airacobra of the Red Air Force, downed on 25 July 1943 – that won him the Oak Leaves while serving on the Arctic front. He would later head I./JG 5 in Normandy and Defence of the Reich, before converting to the Me 262 in November 1944

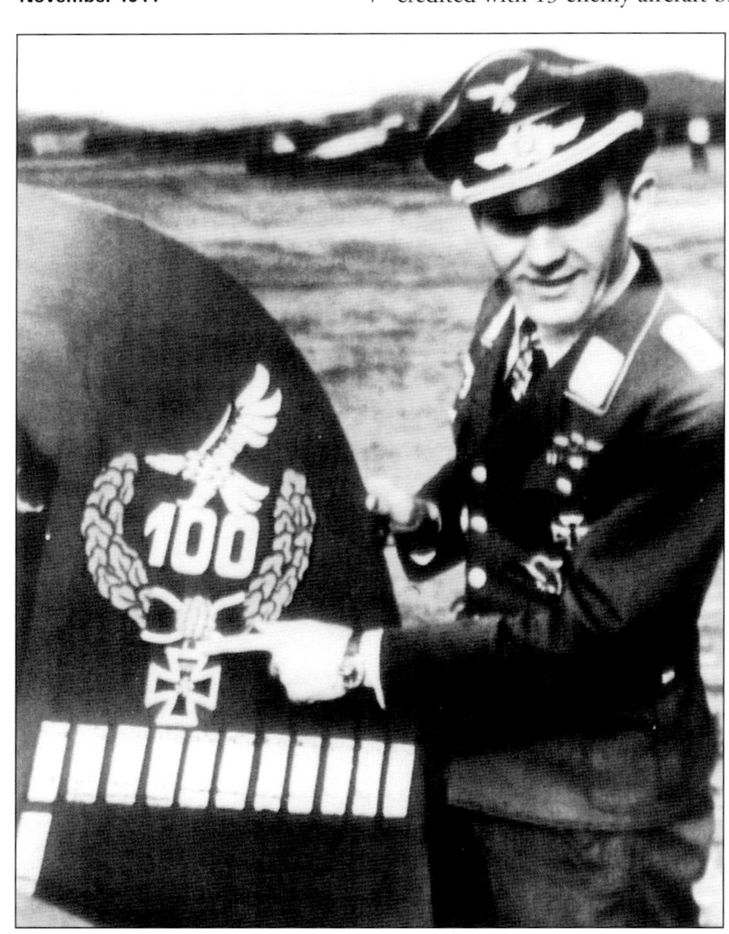

But it was the Eighth Air Force that was doing the damage. Mission No 373 of 27 May, aimed at marshalling yards in western Germany, was the first time it had despatched more than 1000 bombers against the Reich. And although this gave veteran NCO, and recent Knight's Cross winner, Oberfeldwebel Herbert Rollwage of II./JG 53 the opportunity to claim his 11th Defence of the Reich heavy bomber, it also cost the Herzogenaurach-based I./JG 5 seven killed and five wounded. Among the former was the *Gruppenkommandeur*. After attacking a formation of bombers heading back across the French border, Major Horst Carganico lost his life when he attempted to force-land his damaged *Gustav* and crashed into high-tension cables.

Horst Carganico had been in command of I./JG 5 for only two months. Prior to that he had been the long-serving *Kommandeur* of II./JG 5 in the Arctic. And it was this unit, led now by the Oak Leaves-wearing Oberleutnant Theodor Weissenberger, that was to be the last complete *Gruppe* to be added to the Defence of the Reich's order of battle. After a brief stop-over in the Baltic states (where Weissenberger had downed a trio of Soviet fighters on 18 May to take his total to 175), II./JG 5 would arrive at Gardelegen, northwest of Brunswick, at the end of the month.

Seen here (left) as a Fahnenjunker-Oberfeldwebel (NCO Officer Candidate) during II./JG 3's early days in Defence of the Reich, Leutnant Hans Grünberg had replaced the fallen Leopold Münster as *Staffelkapitän* of 5./JG 3 on 9 May 1944. His 21 victories in the west included 14 heavy bombers before he too, like Weissenberger above, transitioned onto the Me 262 in November 1944

In the meantime, the Eighth Air Force had struck twice more at the Reich's oil. On 28 May the defending Bf 109s were credited with 33 enemy aircraft destroyed, 13 by III./JG 27 alone. The following day their combined total was just 20, with II. and III./JG 3 claiming six and seven respectively. As was the norm by now, most of these victories went to single-figure pilots, one of the few exceptions being the B-24 brought down near Pölitz on the 29th by Leutnant Hans Grünberg of 5./JG 3. This was Grünberg's seventh Reich's Defence bomber. It took his overall total to 70, for which he would subsequently receive the Knight's Cross on 8 July.

But 29 May was overshadowed by the loss of yet another veteran *Geschwaderkommodore*. Since taking over JG 3 from Wolf-Dietrich Wilcke two months earlier, Major Friedrich-Karl Müller had claimed 18 Defence of the Reich victories, all but one of them heavy bombers. Having been operational without a break since the beginning of the war (his first eight victories had been gained with III./JG 53 during the Battle of France), it has been suggested that complete exhaustion – exacerbated by his recent command responsibilities – was a contributing factor to 'Tutti' Müller's losing control of his machine and crashing upon landing back at Salzwedel after aborting this day's mission.

29 May also saw the Fifteenth Air Force return to Wiener Neustadt. The Bf 109 opposition, which included *Stab*, I., III. and IV./JG 27 and I./JG 302, downed 23 enemy aircraft between them. I./JG 302 got seven (only one B-24 for Heinrich Wurzer this time). Of the other claimants, the *Kommodore* of JG 27, Oberstleutnant Gustav Rödel, and two of his *Gruppenkommandeure*, Major Wolfgang Redlich (I.) and Major Ernst Düllberg (III.), were each credited with a B-24 apiece (taking their individual totals to 94, 37 and 33 respectively).

But perhaps the highest scorer in action against the Fifteenth Air Force on this date was the Oak Leaves-wearing Leutnant Ernst-Wilhelm Reinert, ex-JG 77 and now *Staffelkapitän* of 12./JG 27. The P-51 he downed near St Pölten – the second of his new Defence of the Reich career – provided Reinert with victory 168.

Although the *Experten* in the south were still adding to their totals, there was a price to pay here too. After claiming his B-24, Wolfgang Redlich had himself been hit by fire from the other bombers in the formation. Like Reinert's Mustang above, Redlich's *Gustav* crashed not

Another *Geschwaderkommodore* to lose his life in defence of the homeland was Wolf-Dietrich Wilcke's successor at the head of JG 3, Major Friedrich-Karl Müller. Some sources have suggested that complete physical and mental exhaustion contributed in no small measure to his fatal crash at Salzwedel on 29 May 1944

Shown wearing the Oak Leaves awarded for his 103 victories on the eastern front as a Feldwebel with JG 77 in 1942, Hauptmann Ernst-Wilhelm Reinert rose to become IV./JG 27's final *Kommandeur* of the war, and one of only two pilots to win the Swords while flying Bf 109s in the Defence of the Reich

Having spent two-and-a-half years on General Staff and training duties since his earlier service with I./JG 27 in North Africa, Major Wolfgang Redlich's 11-day stint as the unit's *Gruppenkommandeur* in May 1944 netted him just one heavy bomber to add to his 36 victories of 1940-41

Hauptmann Karl-Heinz Langer, *Kommandeur* of III./JG 3, claimed two of the seven B-17s credited to his *Gruppe* on 30 May 1944. Subsequently promoted to Major (as seen here in April 1945), Karl-Heinz Langer's final Defence of the Reich total numbered ten – four of them heavy bombers

far from St Pölten, west of Vienna. Major Redlich was the third *Gruppenkommandeur* to be lost by I./JG 27 in little more than a fortnight.

On 30 May the Reich was again subject to a combined assault from both north and south, the Eighth Air Force targeting aircraft plants and depots in central Germany and the Fifteenth aiming for one last knock-out blow against the Wiener Neustadt complex. The performance of the Bf 109 *Gruppen* opposing these strikes was not overly impressive, the only exception being Hauptmann Karl-Heinz Langer's III./JG 3, whose seven claims – all for B-17s attacking the Junkers aircraft and engine plant at Dessau – accounted for a third of the day's Bf 109 victories.

Part of III./JG 3's success may have been due to II./JG 11, whose pilots were performing their usual role as top cover on this day, claiming three P-51s in the Dessau-Magdeburg area in the process. Two of the Mustangs were credited to II./JG 11's new *Kommandeur*. Another ex-JG 52 eastern front veteran, Oberleutnant Walter Krupinski had recently been awarded the Oak Leaves (for his 177 victories against the Red Air Force) before being posted to Defence of the Reich duties. Having served briefly as *Staffelkapitän* of 1./JG 5, Krupinski had now replaced the wounded Günther Rall at the head of II./JG 11. The two Mustangs had raised his total to 190. In complete contrast – and much more typical of the times – the other P-51 credited to the *Gruppe* was a first for Unteroffizier Karl Keil.

On the following day, 31 May, the Eighth Air Force was back over the Reich, this time targeting marshalling yards. The pressure, it seemed, was both relentless and unremitting.

But then – suddenly – the skies of Germany were empty of USAAF heavy bomber streams, and their ever present fighter escorts.

THE LAST ACT

During the late spring and early summer on 1944, the Eighth Air Force had been dividing its time and energies between the Reich and targets in northwestern occupied Europe. But in the first week of June the US bombers were to concentrate solely on cross-Channel strikes as part of the final run-up to the Allied invasion of Normandy. The Luftwaffe had contingency plans in place to counter this long-awaited event. They included the immediate despatch of almost every single Reich's Defence *Jagdgruppe* to the threatened area to reinforce the resident JGs 2 and 26.

Thus, in the space of a few hours in the aftermath of the Normandy landings of 6 June, the carefully structured edifice of the Defence of the Reich organisation – so painstakingly put together over the course of the past 18 months – was torn apart.

More used to heavy bombers at high altitude, the *Gruppen* sent to France suffered appalling casualties in medium to low-level operations against the invading forces. As summer turned to autumn, the survivors would be withdrawn to the homeland. Here, their losses were made good, and most *Gruppen* would then return to Defence of the Reich duties at near full strength in terms of men and equipment.

But those duties bore little resemblance to the Reich's Defence of old. Each *Gruppe* was now four *Staffeln* strong (the majority having been reinforced by additional *Staffeln* culled from the ranks of the *Jagdgruppen* operating on the eastern front). And in an attempt to preserve his few remaining experienced formation leaders, *Reichsmarschall* Göring had laid down specific criteria for their protection. A *Staffelkapitän* could only fly a sortie if accompanied by at least five other aircraft. A *Gruppenkommandeur* needed at least 15 friendly fighters with him in order to participate in a combat mission, and a *Geschwaderkommodore* required a force of 44 before he could be risked operationally!

The biggest change of all, however, was in the nature of the enemy. As they withdrew from France back to the homeland, the depleted *Jagdgruppen* had been harried all the way by aircraft of the Allied tactical air forces, which had, by this time, gained a firm foothold on the continent. Defence of the Reich was thus no longer just a straightforward battle against high-flying US bomber formations (as well as increasingly frequent daylight incursions by the 'heavies' of RAF Bomber Command). The homeland now also had to be defended against medium bomber raids and the hordes of enemy fighter-bombers that were beginning to roam almost at will over her western provinces.

The Luftwaffe leadership tried to draw a distinction between these two forms of enemy onslaught. Those *Jagdgruppen* opposing the Allies' tactical air forces would be placed under the direct control of *Luftwaffenkommando West* (the redesignated *Luftflotte* 3 – the command previously responsible for all units in France and the Low Countries prior to the recent retreat). The *Gruppen* engaged in the strategic defence of the homeland would remain, as before, part of *Luftflotte Reich*.

Such administrative niceties had little relevance in the confusion of day-by-day operations, however. Tactical units would be ordered up against high-altitude bomber formations as and when the occasion demanded, and the strategic *Gruppen* would often find themselves committed to action against medium level bombers and fighter-bombers in defence of their own bases or other nearby targets.

Every *Jagdgeschwader* engaged in defending the homeland – whether officially part of *Lw.Kdo. West* or *Lfl.Reich* – was therefore allotted its own distinctive coloured fuselage markings, the so-called 'Reich's Defence Bands', to aid recognition in the air. For further details of Bf 109 operations in Normandy and during the months that followed see *Osprey Aircraft of the Aces 29.*

But to return to the first week of June 1944, and those empty skies over Germany. With the vast bulk of the Reich's Defence units having decamped westwards, the onus of protecting the homeland was resting almost entirely on the shoulders of two of the ex-*Wilde Sau Geschwader* – JGs 300 and 302 (JG 301's *Gruppen* were currently divided between Normandy (I.) and the defence of Rumania and Bulgaria).

Unaffected by the historic battle of the Normandy beachheads in the north – now in its fourth day – the first US heavy bombers to reappear over the Reich were those of the Fifteenth Air Force flying up from Italy. On 9 June nearly 500 B-17s and B-24s attacked targets in the Munich area. The defending I./JG 302 claimed 16 Liberators, and a single P-51, without loss to themselves.

2. *Staffel's* Oberfeldwebel Artur Gross was credited with a trio of B-24s. Four other pilots got doubles. Among the latter was Heinrich Wurzer, whose two B-24s downed south of Landshut took his daylight bomber total to 19. Another of the four was Oberfeldwebel Anton Benning. An ex-transport pilot (who had flown supplies into beleaguered Stalingrad) before joining *Wilde Sau*, Benning ended the war as a leutnant with the Knight's Cross and seven daylight heavy bombers among his final total of 14.

While operations in the south would continue to take a regular, if declining, toll of Fifteenth Air Force machines – I./JG 302, for example, was never able to repeat its performance of 9 June – it was to be a very different story in the north when the Eighth Air Force, relieved of its immediate commitments over Normandy, resumed its attacks on the Reich.

Pictured in tropical uniform and wearing the Knight's Cross he won as a bomber pilot in 1942, Hauptmann Iro Ilk (left) later commanded III./JG 300 in both *Wilde Sau* and daylight Defence of the Reich operations. He was shot down and killed by RAF Spitfires near Duisburg on 25 September 1944

The first of these took place on 18 June when over 1200 bombers flew in across an eerily quiet North Sea, where once they would have faced the combined opposition of JGs 1 and 11, to attack oil and other targets in northwest Germany.

Forty-eight hours later a similar number of bombers mounted major strikes on oil installations further inland. The two defending Bf 109 *Gruppen*, I. and III./JG 300 were virtually powerless against such overwhelming force. III./JG 300 was vectored northwards from its Jüterborg base against a large formation of B-24s over the Baltic coast. Although the 2nd Bomb Division lost 34 of its Liberators on this date (18 of which sought sanctuary in neutral Sweden), much of the damage they suffered was reportedly inflicted by twin-engined, rocket-firing Me 410s. III./JG 300 lost five dead and an equal number wounded. *Gruppenkommandeur* Hauptmann Iro Ilk – who had won his Knight's Cross as a bomber pilot in 1942 – was among the latter, being forced to bail out west of Anklam.

And so it would go on for the remainder of the month, with the Eighth Air Force targeting the Reich's oil on three more occasions, and the two *Gruppen* sustaining further losses for very little return. The only 'success' as far as Bf 109 operations was concerned (and serving to highlight yet again the very different conditions existing on the Reich's northern and southern flanks) was I./JG 302's bringing down seven B-24s and a trio of P-51s out of the Fifteenth Air Force formations – altogether nearly 1000 strong – attacking oil installations near Vienna on 26 June. But even this was little more than a pinprick, and had cost the *Gruppe* three killed.

At the end of June the first *Gruppe* to be returned from Normandy resumed Defence of the Reich operations. II./JG 5's sojourn in the west had been brief, and it had suffered fairly low casualty figures by invasion front standards – eight killed or missing, plus one wounded. Also supplementing the homeland's order of battle in July were II./JG 27, newly re-equipped with high-altitude Bf 109G-6/AS fighters, and III./JG 53, recently flown in from Italy.

But the veterans among these latest additions were too few to halt the downward spiral of the Bf 109s' declining fortunes. The post-Normandy Defence of the Reich campaign would be built around the three new Fw 190-equipped *Sturmgruppen*. Each of these would form the nucleus of a *Gefechtsverband* (battle group), with Bf 109 units being used primarily as escorts and top cover for the armoured Focke-Wulfs. The *Sturmgruppen's* task was to find and attack the US bomber formations. The Bf 109s' function was to protect them against enemy fighters while they did so.

Just what this division of labour meant in practice was vividly demonstrated on 18 July when more than 500 bombers of the Fifteenth Air Force specifically targeted one of the *Sturmgruppen's* own airfields at Memmingen, in southern Germany. The Focke-Wulfs claimed a staggering 47 heavy bombers. The Bf 109s of I./JG 300 downed two P-51s, those of II./JG 27 got one and III./JG 300 none at all – at a combined a cost of nine pilots killed and five wounded!

On the following day, 19 July, both the Eighth and Fifteenth Air Forces were despatched against targets in the southwest of Germany and Munich areas. The two attacks, some 90 minutes apart, were carried out by close on 1500 heavily escorted bombers. The five opposing Bf 109 *Gruppen* were credited with a total of 14 enemy bombers and two fighters. The most successful was again I./JG 302, whose score of ten Flying Fortresses was higher than that of either of the two *Sturmgruppen* involved on this date.

One of the ten B-17s had been claimed by 1./JG 302's Unteroffizier Willi Reschke. It was his third daylight Defence of the Reich heavy

Another ex-bomber pilot Knight's Cross recipient, Hauptmann (later Major) Gerhard Stamp was *Gruppenkommandeur* of I./JG 300, whose high-altitude Bf 109s provided top cover for the *Geschwader's* II.(*Sturm*) *Gruppe* during homeland defence. Stamp's own victories included at least four heavy bombers (two by night). In November 1944 he set up the Me 262-equipped *Sonderkommando* Stamp to investigate air-to-air bombing techniques (shades of Heinz Knoke!)

Willi Reschke's 27 victories were almost equally divided between his time as an Unteroffizier with 1./JG 302 flying Bf 109s and his service as a feldwebel (later oberfeldwebel) with 9. *Staffel* and the *Geschwaderstab* of JG 301, where he flew the Fw 190 and, latterly, the Ta 152

bomber victory (although he already had four others downed beyond the Reich's eastern borders, and a single P-51, under his belt). Reschke, in fact, would end the war as the *Gruppe's* highest scorer, just exceeding Hauptmann Heinrich Wurzer's overall total of 26. Wurzer, however, who had been severely wounded after claiming his last brace of B-24s over Vienna on 8 July, had achieved all his victories (including his opening pair of RAF 'heavies' by night) while flying the Bf 109, whereas nearly half of Reschke's final tally of 27 would be gained *after* I./JG 302's redesignation as III./JG 301 and conversion to the Fw 190.

But such emphasis on the successes of the (very) few is misleading. The closing months of the Defence of the Reich campaign were dominated by the ever-lengthening casualty lists. And, despite Göring's restrictions, veteran – if not always high-scoring – formation leaders continued to feature upon them.

II./JG 5's experiences were not atypical. This *Gruppe* had lost its recently appointed *Kommandeur*, Oberleutnant Hans Tetzner, during the engagements around Munich on 19 July. The following day, Oberleutnant Lorenz Andresen, *Staffelkapitän* of the attached 9./JG 5, was shot down by US fighters over central Germany. And a little over a month later, on 25 August, Tetzner's replacement at the head of the *Gruppe*, Oberstleutnant Kurt Kettner, would be killed in action against a major raid by the Eighth Air Force on aircraft component plants along the Baltic coast. The locations of these three losses, from Munich in the south to the Baltic in the north, also give an indication of just how thinly stretched the Defence of the Reich's forces now were.

The embattled Bf 109 *Gruppen* were still managing to claim victories, however. On 24 August, for example, the newcomers of III./JG 53 were credited with what was to be the highest score of their homeland defence career – eight B-17s downed over Luneburg Heath. One fell to the unit's long-serving *Kommandeur*, Major Franz Götz. It was *'Altvater'* ('Old Father') Götz's second heavy bomber over the Reich. He would add two more before being appointed *Kommodore* of JG 26 in January 1945.

But individual achievements counted for little against the repeated hammer blows of the Eighth and Fifteenth Air Forces – particularly those still being directed against the Reich's battered oil industry. At the end of August Hitler's armaments minister, Professor Albert Speer, was bemoaning the fact that, after the latest bombing raids, the production of aviation fuel in September would amount to little more than ten per cent of the total figure forecast just two weeks earlier. Speer went on to demand action from the Luftwaffe. What was needed, he said – and by mid-September at the latest – was one final mass attack against the enemy's bomber formations. He called for 'the best units, the most successful fighter pilots and at least 1200 fighter aircraft' to be made available at once.

It was just this kind of action that *General der Jagdflieger* Adolf Galland was already planning, although not within Speer's strict time limitations. Galland's 'Big Blow', as he termed it, was intended to inflict such swingeing losses upon the Americans that they would be forced to call a temporary halt to their bombing offensive – rather as they had done in the wake of the disastrous Schweinfurt-Regensburg raids a year earlier. Only this time, it was hoped, the breathing space would be even longer,

These Bf 109Ks of III./JG 77 were photographed at Neuruppin, northwest of Berlin, in 1944. Note the *Geschwader's Herz-As* (Ace of Hearts) badge on the cowling

allowing time for the new wonder weapons – primarily the Me 262 jet fighter – to be put into service in decisive numbers.

To this end August and September saw further units returned, or added, to the Defence of the Reich commands. Among them were no fewer than ten Bf 109 *Gruppen* – I. and II./JG 3, III./JG 4, II./JG 11, III./JG 27, II./JG 53, I./JG 76 and all three *Gruppen* of JG 77. In October another two units would join them, III./JG 3 and I./JG 27, and in November yet two more, III./JG 1 and IV./JG 27. But Galland's attempts to mount his planned 'Big Blow' against the Eighth Air Force would be thwarted and his carefully husbanded Reich's Defence units hijacked by the Führer for another purpose entirely.

Meanwhile, the Bf 109 *Gruppen* remained in the unenviable position of having to protect Germany's industrial complexes from further damage on the one hand, and themselves from the Allies' overwhelming air superiority on the other. It was a battle they were losing on both fronts. Of the 20 major strikes launched by the Eighth and Fifteenth Air Forces in September, all but seven were directed principally against oil targets. The most costly to the enemy were the Eighth's raids on 11 and 12 September, from which a total of 75 bombers failed to return.

And the highest scorers among the defending Bf 109 *Gruppen* on these dates were, somewhat surprisingly, two of the newest additions to the ranks of Reich's Defence. III./JG 4 and I./JG 76 were both ex-*Zerstörergruppen* now converted to single-seaters and based on airfields to the south of Berlin. On 11 September III./JG 4 was vectored down from Alteno towards the B-17 formations attacking targets in the Chemnitz and Czech border areas, where they were credited with a dozen of the bombers and two P-51s. The twenty *Gustavs* of I./JG 76 were directed almost due west from nearby Gahro to intercept another bomber stream, only to be pounced upon near Kassel by two groups of Mustangs. In a protracted dogfight they claimed five of the superior enemy force.

The validity of some of these victories may be open to serious question, for the obvious inexperience of the two *Gruppen* is clearly reflected in their casualty figures. Each lost 14 pilots – over three quarters of their strength! III./JG 4 suffered nine killed and five wounded, while I./JG 76's casualties were equally divided. Despite these appalling losses, both were in action again the following day. Although ostensibly providing cover for the Fw 190s of II.(*Sturm*)/JG 4, each *Gruppe* nonetheless submitted claims for another seven Flying Fortresses apiece (which cost them a further 12 pilots killed and three wounded).

Also in action on that 12 September was a very 'old hare' indeed – in experience, if not in age. Alfred Grislawski had been a long-serving member of Hermann Graf's famous 9. *'Karaya' Staffel* of JG 52 on the eastern front. He had then joined his erstwhile *Staffelkapitän* back in the homeland, serving under him first in JGr 50 and then, briefly, in JG 1. Recently transferred to III./JG 53 as *Kapitän* of 11. *Staffel*, Hauptmann Grislawski was credited with a brace of B-17s shot down in the Berlin area. These took his final score to 132, the last 23 of which – including 17 heavy bombers – had been claimed in Defence of the Reich.

Oddly, Grislawski would receive official credit for a further victory when he downed a P-38 on 26 September. Although this was the date on which he was himself wounded in a dogfight with Lightnings over Münster, he has denied submitting any such claim.

The above instances may be the extremes, but they accurately reflect the daily lot of the 19 Bf 109 *Jagdgruppen* flying in Defence of the Reich during the closing weeks of 1944. Most were composed of poorly trained youngsters, fighting against impossible odds. They were being killed or wounded in their hundreds and their names are now all-but forgotten. But among them were a few remaining veterans – the *Experten* who were trying to lead by example, and who were still adding to their totals, albeit with far less frequency than in their high-scoring heydays.

On 2 November the Eighth sustained its last major losses of the ongoing oil offensive when 40 of the nearly 1200 bombers despatched against Merseburg and other refineries in central Germany failed to return. But in the brutal war of attrition the defenders fared far worse, losing almost fifty per cent of the 305 fighters that engaged the enemy! And of the 73 pilots killed, nearly half came from the ranks of three Bf 109 *Gruppen* alone. II./JG 3 suffered most, sacrificing 12 for no known victories. I./JG 27 claimed two P-51s against 11 pilots lost, and IV./JG 27's four P-51s cost it ten killed.

Hauptmann Julius Meimberg, *Gruppenkommandeur* of II./JG 53, is awarded the Knight's Cross by Oberst Karl Hentschel at Malmsheim in October 1944. Meimberg ended the war with 59 victories to his credit, four of these being heavy bombers

The Luftwaffe's poor performance and catastrophic losses on 2 November were the subject of heated debate between Hitler and Luftwaffe Chief of General Staff *Generalmajor* Eckhard Christian four days later. Out of favour with his Führer for very obvious reasons, *Reichsmarschall* Göring was by now keeping a very low profile.

Hitler had been informed that 80 enemy aircraft had been shot down, including 30 by the two *Sturmgruppen* and 30 by flak;

'So the remaining 260 fighters in action managed to claim 20 between them. And they lost?'

'Ninety, *Mein Führer.*'

'Right – in 260 sorties they shoot down 20 and lose 90.'

'One other thing', Christian pointed out, 'The *Sturmgruppe* (sic) had another *Gruppe* flying solely as escort.'

'I don't give a damn about that. As far as I'm concerned, the escort *Gruppe* is supposed to shoot too. Enemy fighters were shot down as well, not just bombers?'

'Of course.'

'There you are then. The result is totally unsatisfactory.'

Christian tried to explain the difficulties the *Jagdgruppen* were operating under, but the Führer was having none of it;

'I'm saying nothing against the pilots – just the results obtained. Taking these figures, it would mean that if 2600 fighters went up I could expect them to achieve 200 victories. In other words, any hope of decimating the enemy by a massed attack is simply not there. It is therefore ridiculous to keep producing fighter aircraft just so that the Luftwaffe can operate in large numbers!'

It was the end of Galland's plans for a 'Big Blow'. Hitler would use the bulk of the western *Jagdgruppen* to support his own surprise counter-offensive in the Ardennes the following month. But before becoming involved in the Battle of the Bulge, as Hitler's last-ditch venture in the west is now commonly known, two of the Bf 109 *Gruppen* were to be credited with one final major success against Allied heavy bombers.

On 12 December 140 Lancasters of RAF Bomber Command mounted a daylight attack on steelworks in the Ruhr. Catching the British 'heavies' devoid of fighter cover, I./JG 3's *Gustavs* claimed 13 of them. Following close on their heels, IV./JG 27 added a further eight. But it appears that the bogey of over-optimistic claiming persisted right up until the end. Just seven Lancasters were in fact lost, with an eighth crash-landing at an Allied airfield in Belgium and another ditching in the North Sea (the two latter without aircrew casualties).

By the closing weeks of 1944 hundreds of Allied fighters and fighter-bombers, such as these P-47s of the Ninth Air Force's 404th FG, were roaming at will over Germany, shooting up anything that grabbed their attention either in the air or on the round. Note the lead aircraft – a razorback D-model that has had its dorsal spine painted black to simulate a bubble canopy

At the other end of the spectrum, Oberleutnant Ernst-Wilhelm Reinert – ex-JG 77 veteran of the Russian and Mediterranean campaigns, and now *Staffelkapitän* of 14./JG 27 – was credited with the last of his 174 kills at the height of the Battle of the Bulge. His victim, about as far removed from a high-altitude heavy bomber as it was possible to get, was a humble Auster AOP aircraft. Reinert sent it down on 27 December near Eupen, south of Aachen – ironically, the very area where the Eighth's P-47 escort fighters had originally been forced to turn back for home.

Now the bubble-canopied successors to those early razorback Thunderbolts were the scourge of the skies above the Ardennes battlefield and beyond. Just four days earlier, on 24 December, they had accounted for one of the highest scoring Bf 109 *Experten* to be lost during the Ardennes fighting. Oberfeldwebel Heinrich Bartels of IV./JG 27 was just one short of his century when he was shot down south of Bonn.

Although they were utilised primarily for the same sort of medium to low-level missions as they had flown in Normandy, the Bf 109 *Gruppen* over the Ardennes did not suffer the same crippling losses. It was the ill-conceived operation of New Year's Day 1945 that would finally break the back of the *Jagdwaffe* in the west.

Operation *Bodenplatte* ('Baseplate') was a travesty of Galland's cherished 'Big Blow'. No fewer than 33 *Jagdgruppen*, plus a number of other units, were assembled for a mass attack – not against one of the Eighth Air Force's bomber streams as the *General der Jagdflieger* had envisaged, but against a selected number of airfields occupied by the Allies' tactical air forces in the Low Countries and France.

For very little return, the *Jagdwaffe* lost over 200 pilots killed, missing or captured during *Bodenplatte*. Among these appalling casualties figures were two *Geschwaderkommodores*. One of them was JG 11's Major Günther Specht, who disappeared without trace near Maastricht, in Holland. Although *Stab* JG 11 had by this time converted to Fw 190s, Specht's loss – he remains missing to this day – broke one of the final links in the chain dating back to the beginnings of the Defence of the Reich.

The *Jagdwaffe* in the west never recovered from the slaughter of 1 January 1945 (as well as the two *Kommodores*, it had also lost six *Gruppenkommandeure* and nine *Staffelkapitäne* – experienced formation leaders that it was now impossible to replace). It was nevertheless sent up again just a fortnight later against yet another major raid by the Eighth Air Force on the Reich's already shattered oil industry. 25 *Jagdgruppen* were scrambled in response, 13 of them flying Bf 109s.

But rather than dealing the enemy a big blow, the defenders delivered their last gasp. The Americans lost just seven B-17s. They cost the *Jagdwaffe* a further 107 pilots killed (including 43 from the Bf 109 *Gruppen*). Among the hardest hit were III. and IV./JG 300 (the latter

Despite the critical situation there were still smiles to be seen, as here outside III./JG 77's ops building at Düsseldorf in late December 1944. The pilots are, from left to right, Leutnant Hans-Werner Renzow (*StaKa* 10./JG 77, half-hidden), *Gruppenkommandeur* Hauptmann Armin Köhler, Leutnant Heinrich Hackler (*StaKa* 11./JG 77, who would go down during *Bodenplatte* – see profile 34) and Unteroffizier Hasso Fröhlich (wounded on 23 December 1944)

A Bf 109G-14 of III./JG 53 runs up its engine in a snowy dispersal among the trees at Kirrlach on 13 January 1945. This *Gruppe* did not participate in the next day's last major aerial battle in Defence of the Reich, but instead supported German ground troops on the west bank of the Rhine. JG 53 would continue in its tactical support role until the end in the west . . .

the ex-I./JG 76) – *Gruppen* that had not participated in *Bodenplatte* – who between them suffered 22 killed and four wounded.

It was the effective end of the Defence of the Reich campaign. Leaving just a skeleton force behind, most units were transferred eastwards during the next few days to oppose what was perceived to be a far greater and more immediate threat to the homeland than high flying bombers – the flood-tide of the Red Army already engulfing her eastern provinces.

And when the Eighth Air Force launched Mission No 968 – its final heavy bomber raid of the war – on airfields and marshalling yards in southeast Germany and Czechoslovakia on 25 April 1945, not one of the six Flying Fortresses that failed to return had fallen victim to a Luftwaffe fighter.

Die Schicksalsfrage:

Wo ist die Luftwaffe?

Das ist die Frage, die eure Soldaten an der Ostfront und in Italien immer wieder gestellt haben.

„Die Luftwaffe verteidigt die Heimat", sagte man ihnen.

JETZT AM HELLEN TAGE

fliegen amerikanische Bomber in Massen über Berlin. Heute waren sie zum 5. Male über der Reichshauptstadt. Natürlich fragt auch ihr jetzt:

„Wo ist die Luftwaffe?"

FRAGT GÖRING!
FRAGT HITLER!

USG 31

. . . and that end would not be long in coming. Although this US propaganda leaflet was dropped over Germany a year earlier, its message was even more apt by the spring of 1945. Its heading asks, 'Where is the Luftwaffe?' It then goes on to say, 'That is the question your soldiers on the eastern front and in Italy are always asking. They are being told; "The Luftwaffe is defending the homeland". It closes with, 'And now of course you are also asking "Where is the Luftwaffe?" Ask Göring! Ask Hitler!'

The answer was that what was left of it was lying scattered around, either singly or in dumps like this, without fuel and partially stripped of arms and equipment. Note the black-white-black Defence of the Reich bands on the IV./JG 4 machine second in the line-up – and the 'Plumed knight's helmet' *Geschwader* badge on the cowling. The battle – while not always as chivalrous as the latter might suggest – was, however, finally over

APPENDICES

AWARDS*

SWORDS

		Unit	Score at time of award	Final total/ Four-engined
1/2/45	Hptm Ernst-Wilhelm Reinert	JG 27	174	174/2
16/4/45	Maj Werner Schroer	JG 3	108	114/26

OAK LEAVES

20/6/43	Maj Gustav Rödel	JG 27	78	98/13
2/8/43	Olt Joachim Kirschner	JG 3	170	188/4
2/8/43	Hptm Werner Schroer	JG 27	84	114/26
25/11/43	Hptm Wilhelm Lemke	JG 3	130	131/3
2/3/44	Olt Walter Krupinski	JG 5	177	197/1
11/4/44	Hptm Walter Grislawski	JG 1	114	133/18
12/5/44	Lt Leopold Münster(†)	JG 3	95	95/15
20/7/44	Olt Willy Kientsch	JG 27	53	53/20
20/7/44	Olt Otto Wessling(†)	JG 3	83	83/11
25/11/44	Maj Gerhard Michalski	JG 4	?	73/13
21/1/45	Lt Herbert Rollwage	JG 53	70	71/14
1/2/45	Hptm Herbert Schramm(†)	JG 27	42	42/3
14/2/45	Maj Jürgen Harder	JG 11	64	64/9

KNIGHT'S CROSS

29/8/43	Hptm Emil Bitsch	JG 3	105	108/4
22/11/43	Lt Willy Kientsch	JG 27	43	53/20
5/2/44	Hptm Gustav Frielinghaus	JG 3	74	74/0
5/2/44	Olt Gerhard Loos	JG 54	85	92/2
11/3/44	Maj Walther Dahl	JG 3	64	128/36
6/4/44	Ofw Rudolf Ehrenberger(†)	JG 53	49	49/6
6/4/44	Ofw Herbert Rollwage	JG 53	53	102/14
8/4/44	Obstlt Günther Specht	JG 11	30	34/15
9/6/44	Hptm Josef Haiböck	JG 3	77	77/0
9/6/44	Maj Klaus Quaet-Faslem(†)	JG 3	49	49/3
24/6/44	Olt Georg-Peter Eder	JG 1	49	72/36
24/6/44	Hptm Hans Remmer(†)	JG 27	26	26/8
8/7/44	Olt Hans Grünberg	JG 3	70	82/14
20/7/44	Maj Ernst Düllberg	JG 27	37	50/10
27/7/44	Olt Franz Ruhl	JG 3	34	37/?
3/8/44	Maj Ernst Boerngen	JG 27	38	38/24
19/8/44	Hptm Gerhard Sommer(†)	JG 11	20	20/14
24/10/44	Hptm Horst Haase	JG 3	56	56/10
24/10/44	Maj Julius Meimberg	JG 53	48	59/4
24/10/44	Lt August Mors(†)	JG 5	?	?/?
29/1044	Lt Oskar Zimmermann	JG 3	28	30/?
6/12/44	Hptm Franz Barten	JG 53	52	52/?
14/1/45	Ofw Eduard Isken	JG 53	50	56/17

28/1/45	Lt Fritz Gromotka	JG 27	29	29/10
2/2/45	Hptm Peter Jenne	JG 300	17	17/12
7/2/45	Maj Armin Köhler	JG 77	?	69/13
22/2/45	Maj Dr Peter Werfft	JG 27	26	26/14
28/3/45	Maj Wilhelm Steinmann	JG 4	43	44/6
20/4/45	Maj Karl-Heinz Langer	JG 3	29	30/4
27/4/45	Hptm Heinz Knoke	JG 1	33	33/19

Key

(*) The above lists are based upon the names of pilots known to have been flying the Bf 109 in Defence of the Reich at the time of their awards. Many will have been decorated for victories previously scored either partly, or wholly, on other fronts. The figures quoted are overall totals, and do not refer specifically to claims made in Defence of the Reich

(†) Indicates that the award was conferred posthumously

ORDERS OF BATTLE

Bf 109 UNITS IN DEFENCE OF THE REICH

A: May 1943 – *Luftwaffenbefehlshaber Mitte**

Unit	*CO*	*Base*	*Est-Serv*
I./JG 1	Maj Fritz Losigkeit	Deelen (re-equipping)	
Stab JG 3	Oberst Wolf-Dietrich Wilcke	München-Gladbach	3 - 3
I./JG 3	Maj Klaus Quaet-Faslem	München-Gladbach	40 - 17
I./JG 11	Hptm Günther Specht	Jever	54 - 27
III./JG 11	Hptm Ernst Günther Heinze	Neumünster (forming)	
I./JG 27	Hptm Erich Hohagen	Poix/Leeuwarden	37 - 24
III./JG 54	Hptm Siegfried Schnell	Oldenburg	45 - 41
Totals			**179 - 112**

(*) Luftwaffe GOC Central, re-designated *Luftflotte Reich* on 3/2/44

B: May 1944 – *Luftflotte Reich*

III./JG 1	Maj Hartmann Grasser	Paderborn	48 - 21
Stab JG 3	Maj Friedrich-Karl Müller	Salzwedel	4 - 2
I./JG 3	Hptm Hellmut Mertens	Burg bei Magdeburg	26 - 9
II./JG 3	Hptm Gustav Frielinghaus	Gardelegen	29 - 23
III./JG 3	Maj Walther Dahl	Bad Wörishofen	31 - 9
I./JG 5	Maj Horst Carganico	Herzogenaurach	43 - 36
II./JG 5	Hptm Theo Weissenberger	Gardelegen	44 - 36
Stab JG 11	Maj Günther Specht	Oldenburg	4 - 3
II./JG 11	Hptm Walter Krupinski	Hustedt	31 - 14
Stab JG 27	Oberst Gustav Rödel	Wien-Seyring	4 - 4
I./JG 27	Maj Karl-Wolfgang Redlich	Fels am Wagram	44 - 34
II./JG 27	Hptm Fritz Keller	Wiesbaden-Erbenheim	24 - 12
III./JG 27	Hptm Ernst Düllberg	Götzendorf	26 - 20

IV./JG 27	Hptm Otto Meyer	Steinamanger (Hung.)	22 - 16
II./JG 53	Hptm Julius Meimberg	Frankfurt-Eschborn	31 - 14
I./JG 300	Maj Gerhard Stamp	Merzhausen	29 - 19
III./JG 300	Maj Iro Ilk	Wiesbaden-Erbenheim	27 - 25
I./JG 301	Hptm Richard Kamp	Neubiberg	25 - 21
I./JG 302	Hptm Richard Lewens	Wien-Seyring	27 - 11
Totals			**519 - 329**

C: 30 June 1944 – *Luftflotte Reich* (Post-Normandy Restructuring: No figures available)

II./JG 5	Olt Hans Tetzner	Salzwedel
I./JG 300	Maj Gerhard Stamp	Bad Wörrishofen
III./JG 300	Maj Iro Ilk	Jüterbog
I./JG 302	Hptm Heinrich Wurzer	Götzendorf

(Re-forming and/or re-equipping)

I./JG 3	Hptm Helmut Mertens	Wunstorf
II./JG 27	Hptm Fritz Keller	Fels am Wagram
III./JG 53	Maj Franz Götz	Bad Lippspringe

5 September 1944 (Post-Normandy Restructuring)

Stab JG 3	Maj Heinz Bär	Königsberg/Neumark	12 - 5
I./JG 3	Hptm Ernst Laube	Borkheide	18 - 14
III./JG 4	Hptm Friedrich Eberle	Alteno	68 - 58
II./JG 5	Hptm Franz Wienhusen	Reinsdorf	24 - 9
III./JG 300	Maj Iro Ilk	Jüterbog	20 - 18
Stab JG 11	Maj Günther Specht	Finsterwalde	? - ?
II./JG 27	Hptm Fritz Keller	Finsterwalde	45 - 23
III./JG 53	Maj Franz Götz	Mörtitz	52 - 36
I./JG 76	?	Gahro	62 - 50
I./JG 302	Hptm Heinrich Wurzer	Schafstädt	25 - 13
Stab JG 300	Oberst Walther Dahl	Erfurt-Bindesleben	5 - 3
I./JG 300	Maj Gerhard Stamp	Esperstedt	30 - 23
JGr 10	?	Parchim	17 - 14
Totals			**378 - 266**

(Re-forming and/or re-equipping)

III./JG 1	Hptm Heinz Knoke	Burbach
II./JG 3	Hptm Herbert Kutscha	Ziegenhain
I./JG 5	Hptm Theo Weissenberger	Wunstorf
I./JG 27	Hptm Rudolf Sinner	Rotenburg
IV./JG 27	Hptm Hanns-Heinz Dudeck	Hustedt
I./JG 53	Maj Jürgen Harder	Wien-Seyring
IV./JG 53	Hptm Hans Morr	Oldenburg

D: January 1945 – *Luftflotte Reich*

I./JG 300	Hptm Herbert Schob	Borkheide	57 - 37
III./JG 300	Hptm Herbert Nölter	Jüterbog	44 - 38
IV./JG 300	Hptm Heiner Ofterdinger	Wittstock	53 - 39
Totals			**154 - 114**

Lw.Kdo.West

I./JG 3	Olt Alfred Seidl	Paderborn	31 - 22
III./JG 3	Maj Karl-Heinz Langer	Bad Lippspringe	32 - 26
I./JG 4	Hptm Wilhem Steinmann	Darmstadt	41 - 33
III./JG 4	Hptm Gerhard Strasen	Griesheim	13 - 10
IV./JG 4	Hptm Ernst Laube	Frankfurt/Rhein-Main	26 - 17
II./JG 11	Hptm Karl Leonhard	Zellhausen	37 - 31
Stab JG 27	Maj Ludwig Franzisket	Rheine	2 - 2
I./JG 27	Hptm Eberhard Schade	Rheine	33 - 24
II./JG 27	Hptm Herbert Kutscha	Rheine/Hopsten	25 - 20
III./JG 27	Hptm Dr Peter Werfft	Hesepe	28 - 23
IV./JG 27	Hptm Ernst-Wilhelm Reinert	Achmer	24 - 22
Stab JG 53	Obstlt Helmut Bennemann	Echterdingen	4 - 1
II./JG 53	Hptm Julius Meimberg	Malmshein	46 - 29
III./JG 53	Maj Franz Götz	Kirrlach	39 - 25
IV./JG 53	Hptm Alfred Hammer	Echterdingen	46 - 34
Stab JG 77	Obstlt Erich Leie	Dortmund	2 - 1
I./JG 77	Hptm Joachim Deicke	Dortmund	43 - 24
II./JG 77	Maj Siegfried Freytag	Bönninghardt	32 - 20
III./JG 77	Maj Armin Köhler	Dortmund	10 - 7
Totals			**514 - 371**

E: April 1945 – *Luftflotte Reich*

III./JG 4	Hptm Gerhard Strasen	Jüterbog-Altdamm	61 - 56
I./JG 27	Hptm Emil Clade	Salzwedel	29 - 13
II./JG 27	Hptm Fritz Keller	Schwerin	48 - 27
III./JG 27	Hptm Dr Peter Werfft	Grossenhain	19 - 15
Totals			**157 - 111**

LW.Kdo.West

Stab JG 53	Obstlt Helmut Bennemann	Erbenschwang	1 - 1
II./JG 53	Maj Julius Meimberg	Ulm-Risstissen	39 - 24
III./JG 53	Hptm Siegfried Luckenbach	Kreuzstrasse	40 - 24
IV./JG 53	Hptm Alfred Hammer	Reichenbach	54 - 27
Totals			**134 - 76**

Colour Plates

1

Bf 109G-1/R2y 'Black 3' of Leutnant Heinz Knoke, 2./JG 1, Jever, February 1943

The only distinguishing marks on the otherwise standard finish of this high-altitude pressurised Bf 109G-1 are the victory bars on the rudder recording two of the pilot's kills. The first is topped by an RAF roundel (although, confusingly, Knoke already had *two* British machines to his credit by this stage in his frontline career). The second, surmounted by an American star, is for the B-24 claimed by Heinz Knoke on 16 February 1943. A real stalwart of the daylight Defence of the Reich campaign from the beginning, Knoke would, fittingly, be the very last of its *Experten* to be awarded a much coveted Knight's Cross.

2

Bf 109G-6 'White Double Chevron' of Hauptmann Friedrich Eberle, *Gruppenkommandeur* III./JG 1, Leeuwarden, October 1943

The heavily dappled, Erla-canopied *Gustav* 'gunboat' flown by the III./JG 1 *Gruppenkommandeur* displays the tightly spiralled spinner markings common to the unit's machines of the period. Note that the fighter is devoid of the regulation III. *Gruppe* vertical bar behind the fuselage *Balkenkreuz,* but that it does wear the white vertical tail surfaces indicative of a formation leader.

3

Bf 109G-6 'White 20' of Hauptmann Friedrich Eberle, *Gruppenkommandeur* III./JG 1, München-Gladbach, March 1944

When compared with the previous profile, this Bf 109G-6 offers a complete change of markings for one of the *Kommandeur's* later machines. Although the spinner spirals and white tail are now gone, the aircraft does boast a telltale III. *Gruppe* bar superimposed on the rear fuselage red Defence of the Reich band. It also features two further late war marking innovations – the command chevrons have been replaced by the number '20' (a common practice among JG 1's *Gruppe* CO's) and the new 'Winged 1' *Geschwader* emblem is displayed. This was not Eberle's first 'White 20', as he had bailed out of an earlier one after tangling with P-47s over Holland two months previously.

4

Bf 109G-6 'Black 1' of Oberleutnant Herwig Zuzic, *Staffelkapitän* 8./JG 1, Leeuwarden, June 1943

A wealth of unique markings adorn this Bf 109G, which was assigned to Oberleutnant Zuzic, the first *Staffelkapitän* of the newly reconstituted 8./JG 1. These markings are, from left to right, the *Staffel's* somewhat tongue-in-cheek emblem (a dachshund cocking its leg against Uncle Sam's top hat), the pilot's own red heart insignia below the cockpit, and his nickname (*Lauser*, which is German for ragamuffin). Finally, the fighter's rudder features the 13 kills Zuzic had brought with him from the eastern front (see page 27 for details). He would add just one B-17 victory in Defence of the Reich before being killed in a mid-air collision on 19 August 1943.

5

Bf 109G-6 'Black 5' of Feldwebel Alfred Miksch, 8./JG 1, Leeuwarden, July 1943

Also assigned to Zuzic's 8. *Staffel*, Miksch arrived from service on the eastern front (where he had been assigned to III./JG 3) with an even higher tally – 37 – of enemy aircraft destroyed. A brace of Mustangs and a Flying Fortress subsequently took Miksch's score to the 40 shown here on the rudder of his Bf 109G-6 'Black 5'. He would duly claim two more Flying Fortresses and a Lightning destroyed before being killed in action near Nijmegen, in Holland, on 1 December 1943.

6

Bf 109G-4 'Black Double Chevron 1' of Hauptmann Klaus Quaet-Faslem, *Gruppenkommandeur* I./JG 3 'Udet', München-Gladbach, circa May 1943

The command markings displayed by Hauptmann Quaet-Faslem's rather darkly segmented Bf 109G-4 are reportedly a combination of standard *Gruppenkommandeur's* chevrons, plus a 'Black 1' referring back to the pilot's previous command as *Staffelkapitän* of 2./JG 53. The longest serving of all I./JG 3's ten *Kommandeure*, Major Quaet-Faslem lost his life when he crashed in bad weather on 30 January 1944. He had claimed just three B-17s on Defence of the Reich operations.

7

Bf 109G-6/AS 'Black 14' of Unteroffizier Horst Petzschler, 2./JG 3 'Udet', Burg bei Magdeburg, May 1944

An example of the low-visibility overall light blue-grey finish briefly adopted by several of the Reich's Defence specialised high-altitude Bf 109 *Gruppen*, 'Black 14' was lost in action against P-51s near Madgeburg on 30 May 1944 while being flown by another pilot. Petzschler himself scored four kills – two fighters and two heavy bombers – in defence of the homeland before being wounded. He subsequently returned to his original unit, JG 51, surviving the war with a total of 27 victories.

8

Bf 109G-6 'Double Chevron' of Major Kurt Brändle, *Gruppenkommandeur* II./JG 3 'Udet', Schiphol, October 1943

Major Brändle's heavily dappled *Gustav* sports non-standard markings in the style peculiar to many of II. *Gruppe's* machines of this period. These include the 'mirror image' rearward-flying 'Winged U' *Geschwader* emblem (which would be correctly facing forward on the starboard cowling – the unit painter presumably always used the same side of the stencil for both left and right-hand badges!), the unexplained large red dot below the emblem and the outline-only fuselage symbols. Recent research suggests that only the last two of Kurt Brändle's 172 victories were actually claimed in Defence of the Reich. These were a brace of Thunderbolts brought down during a mission on 3 November 1943. Brändle himself failed to return from a second operation flown by II./JG 3 later that same day.

9

Bf 109G-6 'White 10' of Leutnant Franz Ruhl, *Staffelkapitän* 4./JG 3 'Udet', Rotenburg, February 1944

Franz Ruhl's rather tired looking Bf 109G-6 'White 10' also sports the back-to-front 'Winged U' synonymous with aircraft flown by the 'Udet' *Geschwader*. Note, however, the solid fuselage markings – white individual numeral combined with black horizontal *Gruppe* bar. Another unique feature of this aircraft is the partial white band forward of the tailplane, although the fuselage spine was left camouflaged possibly to reduce the risk of being spotted from the air. Leutnant Ruhl's numerous Defence of the Reich victories included at last 14 heavy bombers destroyed before he was reported missing in action on 24 December 1944 at the height of the Battle of the Bulge.

10

Bf 109G-6 'Black 1' of Hauptmann Joachim Kirschner, *Staffelkapitän* 5./JG 3 'Udet', Schiphol, October 1943

His machine bearing similar markings to Kurt Brändle's (profile 8), Joachim Kirschner was credited with four Flying Fortresses and a single fighter – victories 171-175 – during his brief stint on homeland defence duties. On 18 October 1943 he was appointed *Gruppenkommandeur* of IV./JG 27, then operating in the Aegean/Balkan areas, where he would be shot down by Spitfires on 17 December 1943.

11

Bf 109G-6y 'White 1' of Hauptmann Karl-Heinz Langer, *Staffelkapitän* 7./JG 3 'Udet', Bad Wörishofen, Autumn 1943

The most distinctive feature of Karl-Heinz Langer's 'White 1' is undoubtedly the white shooting star adorning the *Beule* (the bulge housing the breeches of the Bf 109G-6's MG 131 heavy machine guns). This marking was carried by virtually all 7. *Staffel* machines, and is said to have been inspired by the underwing rockets with which the unit had previously been equipped. Major Langer served as *Gruppenkommandeur* of III./JG 3 for the final year of the war, and during this time his final score reached 30, which included four Flying Fortresses in Defence of the Reich.

12

Bf 109G-6 'Yellow 7' of Hauptmann Wilhelm Lemke, *Staffelkapitän* 9./JG 3 'Udet', Bad Wörishofen, Autumn 1943

One of Langer's fellow *Staffelkapitäne* at Bad Wörishofen in the autumn of 1943 was Wilhelm Lemke of 9./JG 3. Unfortunately, his machine does not sport that unit's equally striking marking – a large yellow, black and white eye painted on the *Beule* (see photograph on page 49). Newly appointed as *Kommandeur* of II./JG 3, Lemke was awarded the Oak Leaves on 25 November 1943 for his 130 victories. The final five in this impressive tally were two P-47s and three B-17s in Defence of the Reich. Lemke himself then fell victim to P-47s over Holland just nine days later.

13

Bf 109G-6 'Black Double Chevron' of Hauptmann Wilhelm Moritz, *Gruppenkommandeur* IV./JG 3 'Udet', Salzwedel, May 1944

Oberleutnant Moritz had been *Staffelkapitän* of the original II./JG 1 for the greater part of 1942 before being posted to JG 51 on the eastern front. Now *Gruppenkommandeur* of IV./JG 3, and flying the Bf 109G-6 'gunboat' depicted here on Defence of the Reich duties, Moritz already had 39 victories under his belt. But it was his leadership of the unit after its imminent conversion to the Fw 190, and subsequent daring operations in the *Sturm* role (see *Osprey Aviation Elite Units 20*) that would be Moritz's finest hour.

14

Bf 109G-14 'White 13' of Hauptmann Ernst Laube, *Gruppenkommandeur* IV./JG 4, Frankfurt/Rhein-Main, January 1945

Typical of the many long-serving leaders – possessing a wealth of operational experience, if not necessarily very high scores – who commanded Defence of the Reich *Gruppen* during the closing weeks of the campaign, Ernst Laube had claimed his first victory over Malta in the spring of 1941 as a member of Joachim Müncheberg's famous 7./JG 26. Since then he had served with various units, latterly as the *Kommandeur* of I./JG 3 with whom his score had risen to 18. Laube is known to have added at least three more, all US fighters, after assuming command of IV./JG 4 on 19 December 1944.

15

Bf 109G-14/ASy 'Black 13' of Oberleutnant Ernst Scheufele, *Staffelkapitän* 14./JG 4, Reinersdorf, October 1944

Wearing identical Defence of the Reich aft fuselage markings as Laube's Bf 109G-14 above (a combination of JG 4's distinctive black-white-black bands with IV. *Gruppe's* shallow wavy bar superimposed), Scheufele's machine also carries an individual name below the cockpit. It would appear that the number '13' was regarded as a particularly lucky one by JG 4's formation leaders. Fortune certainly deserted Ernst Scheufele when he was brought down by anti-aircraft fire southeast of Aachen on 3 December 1944 . . . at the controls of another pilot's 'Black 2'! The ace's final tally of 18 victories included three heavy bombers.

16

Bf 109G-5/AS 'Black Double Chevron' of Hauptmann Theodor Weissenberger, *Gruppenkommandeur* I./JG 5, Gardelegen, June 1944

Wearing a textbook set of *Kommandeur's* markings, this is reportedly the machine that newly appointed Theo Weissenberger took to the Normandy front. He was flying this aircraft on 12 June when he clashed with P-47s near St André and shot three of them down, although he returned to base wounded. Weissenberger was back in action the following month, however, attaining his double century when he shot down a Spitfire southeast of Rouen on 25 July. Returning to Defence of the Reich duties, he finally left the *Gruppe* in November 1944 (after its redesignation as III./JG 6) to convert to Me 262 jet fighters.

17

Bf 109G-6 'White 1' of Oberleutnant Günther Schwanecke, *Staffelkapitän* 4./JG 5, Salzwedel, July 1944

Depicted immediately after II./JG 5's return from the Normandy front, the pristine condition of Günther Schwanecke's Bf 109G-6 'White 1' suggests that it is a replacement machine. Note the small *Gruppe* badge on the cowling. II./JG 5 was also redesignated in November 1944 when it became IV./JG 4. Schwanecke then served briefly as the *Staffelkapitän* of 13./JG 4, before joining his new unit's *Geschwaderstab*. He added several more confirmed kills to the ten victories that he had previously scored with II./JG 5, the last of them in the Berlin area during the closing days of the war.

18

Bf 109G-5 'Black Double Chevron' of Hauptmann Günther Specht, *Gruppenkommandeur* II./JG 11, Plantlünne, December 1943

This *Kommandeur's* machine bears its pilot's personal insignia of a winged pencil. It is not known for certain what this was intended to represent. Most are of the opinion that it was the irrepressible Specht's way of waving goodbye to paperwork – the hated 'bumph' that is the bane of every unit CO the world over. Surely he could not have harboured a secret desire to pilot a Do 17 'Flying Pencil'? Whatever the truth, it was soon to give way to JG 11's official (but much more bombastic) unit badge. Note here the *Geschwader's* yellow Defence of the Reich aft fuselage band, and Specht's victory tally on the rudder – six British and 16 American aircraft destroyed – which pinpoint the date as early December 1943. Number 22 was a P-47 downed near Oldenburg on 29 November.

19

Bf 109G-6 ' Black 1' of Oberleutnant Heinz Knoke, *Staffelkapitän* 5./JG 11, Jever, May 1943

Heinz Knoke's new Bf 109G-6 is seen here in post-'aerial bomber' mode, equipped with the appreciably more effective underwing rocket tubes. It has yet to exchange the thin red aft fuselage band for the broad yellow of Specht's machine above, but it *is* sporting white vertical tail surfaces as befits Knoke's present position as a formation leader. Seven more US victory bars have since been added to the score shown on the rudder of the Bf 109G-1 depicted in profile 1. This also helps to confirm the date, for Oberleutnant Knoke's ninth victim was a Flying Fortress shot down *en route* to Kiel on 19 May 1943.

20

Bf 109G-6'Black 10' of Feldwebel Hans-Gerd Wennekers, 5./JG 11, Jever, June 1943

Feldwebel Wennekers often flew as Knoke's *Katschmarek*, or wingman. His 'Black 10' also wears the narrow rear fuselage red band, but has forsaken the rocket-launching tubes in accordance with the newly issued instructions that all Bf 109 *Gruppen* operating against American heavy bombers were to be armed with underwing cannon. One of the diminishing number of veteran non-commissioned officers who formed the back-bone of JG 11 throughout the remainder of the war, Wennekers was actually an officer candidate (fahnenjunker-oberfeldwebel) at the time of his 20th, and final, victory – a Soviet Pe-2 twin-engined bomber downed east of Berlin on 16 April 1945.

21

Bf 109G-6y 'Yellow 1' of Oberleutnant Hermann Hintzen, *Staffelkapitän* 6./JG 11, Jever, June 1943

This *Gustav* of 6./JG 11 displays the *Staffel's* short-lived emblem on its cowling. Called the *Boeing-Klau* (Boeing-pincher) it consisted of a villainous figure with a sack of Boeings draped over its shoulder, and was based on the 'coal-pincher' propaganda character used throughout the war to encourage the German population to save energy. Hermann Hintzen out-lived his unit's comic badge by a long margin. Previously the *Kapitän* of *Jasta* Helgoland, he left 6./JG 11 in December 1943 to take up the first of a series of training appointments, during which time he added at least three more victories to the four he had achieved while flying frontline ops.

22

Bf 109T 'Black 6' of Oberleutnant Herbert Christmann, *Staffelkapitän* 11./JG 11, Lister/Norway, Spring 1944

Hermann Hintzen had been *Jasta* Helgoland's first *Kapitän*. Herbert Christmann (ex-JGr 50) was its last, continuing in command after the *Staffel's* redesignation as 11./JG 11 and until his posting to 1./JG 11 on the Normandy front in August 1944. His flamboyantly decorated *Toni* is seen here during 11./JG 11's secondment to *Luftflotte 5* in Scandinavia. Christmann's final score prior to his being killed in action over France on 20 August is not known for certain. It numbered at least six, and included two B-17s, one downed on the third day of 'Big Week'.

23

Bf 109G-6 'Black Double Chevron' of Major Ludwig Franzisket, *Gruppenkommandeur* I./JG 27, Fels am Wagram, February 1944

This fighter features a set of standard *Kommandeur* symbols and the familiar formation leader's white tail, but combined this time with JG 27's sage green Defence of the Reich band and I *Gruppe's* now somewhat inappropriate *Afrika* badge. Ludwig Franzisket had commanded both 1. and 3. *Staffeln* in North Africa, where he had claimed 24 victories (plus another over Malta). In Defence of the Reich he would add four B-17s to take his overall wartime total to 43.

24

Bf 109G-6 'Yellow 3' of Leutnant Willy Kientsch, *Staffelkapitän* 6./JG 27, Wiesbaden-Erbenheim, November 1943

Another ex-Africa veteran, Willy Kientsch had been one of II. *Gruppe's* most successful pilots in the desert and Mediterranean areas, where he scored his first 41 victories (including nine heavy bombers). The rudder tally of 43 shown here – the last two a pair of B-17s downed near Stuttgart on 6 September 1943 – would win him the Knight's Cross two months later (by which time he had added another Flying Fortress). At the time of his death on 29 January 1944, Kientsch's final total stood at 53, 20 of which were heavy bombers. Note the *Gruppe* badge on the cowling.

25

Bf 109G-6 'Yellow 1' of Leutnant Dr Peter Werfft, *Staffelkapitän* 9./JG 27, Vienna-Seyring, March 1944

Wearing an appreciably narrower aft fuselage band than Ludwig Franzisket's Bf 109G-6 (presumably to leave space for the vertical III. *Gruppe* bar?), Leutnant Dr Peter Werfft's *Gustav* is seen here displaying 11 victories on its white rudder. One of the Luftwaffe's oldest pilots, Dr Werfft would end the war, at the age of 40, as *Kommandeur* of III. *Gruppe*,

OSPREY AIRCRAFT OF THE ACES • 37

Bf 109 Aces of the Russian Front

SERIES EDITOR: TONY HOLMES

OSPREY AIRCRAFT OF THE ACES • 37

Bf 109 Aces of the Russian Front

John Weal

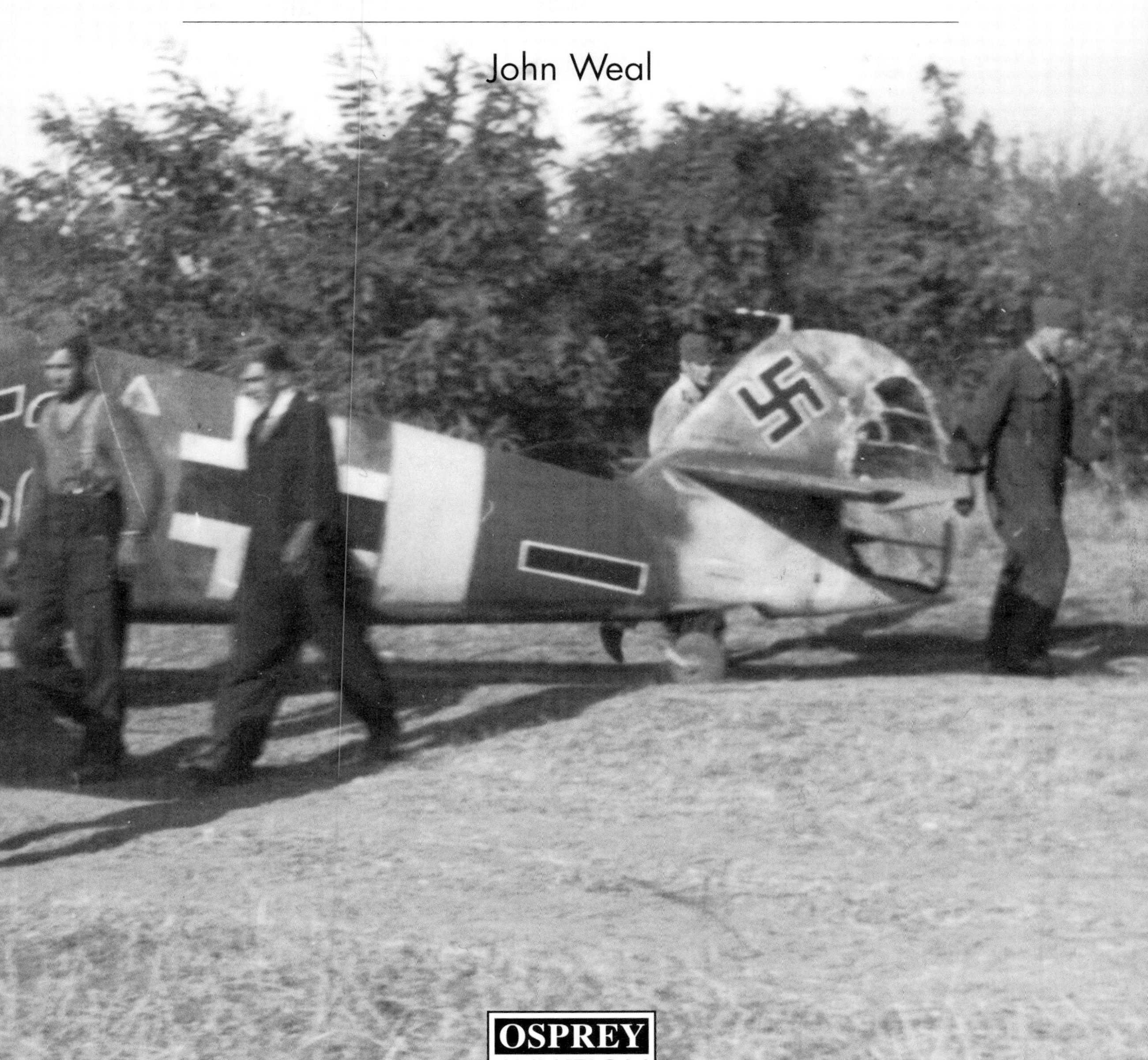

OSPREY AVIATION

Front cover
The 352 kills which made Erich Hartmann the most successful fighter pilot in the annals of aerial warfare were all scored with JG 52 – except one. For a few days early in February 1945, Hauptmann Erich Hartmann was appointed temporary acting *Kommandeur* of I./JG 53, a *Gruppe* which operated in close conjunction with JG 52 over Hungary in the closing weeks of the war.

During his brief tenure of office at the head of I. *Gruppe* of the famous 'Ace of Spades' *Geschwader*, Hartmann flew a winter-camouflaged *Gustav* bearing a simplified set of the same distinctive individual markings which had long adorned his JG 52 machines. Compare the truncated, unbordered 'tulip-leaf' nose decoration and plain red heart below the cockpit with those depicted in profile 22 in the colour section. Note, however, that the aircraft does wear the late-war Hungarian theatre marking of a yellow chevron below the port wing, its 'wraparound' ends just being visible on the leading-edge slot.

Here, Hartmann's tall-tailed G-6 pulls up and away from a smoking Airacobra, already *in extremis*, as he searches for more suitable prey. He would soon find it. One of a large gaggle of Yak-9 fighters escorting a formation of some 20 Soviet Air Force Douglas Bostons would provide 'Bubi' Hartmann with his 337th – and only non-JG 52 – victory of the war on 4 February 1945 (*Cover artwork by Iain Wyllie*)

First published in Great Britain in 2001 by Osprey Publishing
Elms Court, Chapel Way, Botley, Oxford, OX2 9LP
E-mail: info@ospreypublishing.com

ISBN 1 84176 084 6

Edited by Tony Holmes
Page design by Tony Truscott
Cover Artwork by Iain Wyllie
Aircraft Profiles by John Weal
Origination by Grasmere Digital Imaging, Leeds, UK
Printed through Bookbuilders, Hong Kong

01 02 03 04 05 10 9 8 7 6 5 4 3 2 1

EDITOR'S NOTE
To make this best-selling series as authoritative as possible, the Editor would be interested in hearing from any individual who may have relevant photographs, documentation or first-hand experiences relating to the elite pilots, and their aircraft, of the various theatres of war. Any material used will be credited to its original source. Please write to Tony Holmes at 10 Prospect Road, Sevenoaks, Kent, TN13 3UA, Great Britain, or by e-mail at: tony.holmes@osprey-jets.freeserve.co.uk

ACKNOWLEDGEMENTS
The author wishes to thank the following individuals for their invaluable help in providing photographs for this book – Michael Denley, Chris Goss, Michael Payne, Dr Alfred Price, Jerry Scutts, Robert Simpson and Herren Manfred Griehl, Walter Matthiesen and Holger Nauroth.

CONTENTS

BACKGROUND AND INTRODUCTION

The German invasion of the Soviet Union, code-named Operation *Barbarossa*, was a campaign unparalleled in both its scale and ferocity. Within weeks of its launch early on the morning of 22 June 1941, the frontline stretched a staggering 2780 miles (4480 km), linking the Arctic wastes of the Barents Sea in the north to the sub-tropical shores of the Black Sea in the south.

At first glance, the opposing armies appeared to be almost evenly matched. The Germans committed 120 divisions to the initial assault, holding a further 26 in immediate reserve, making a total of 146 divisions – some three million men in all. Facing them, the Soviet army had 149 divisions stationed in its westernmost military districts.

But the German and Russian divisions differed greatly in composition and strengths. Take the all-important tank, for example, which played such a crucial role throughout the campaign in the east. At the outset the Germans deployed 17 armoured divisions (plus a further two in reserve) against the Soviet's 36 – a seeming majority of two-to-one in favour of the Red Army. In reality, a Russian armoured division of 1941 numbered some 400 tanks, whereas its German counterpart varied between 150 and 200 . . . a fourfold advantage to the Soviets.

At the start of *Barbarossa* the sole single-engined fighter presence in the far north was provided by the ten Bf 109Es of the *Jagdstaffel* Kirkenes. This E-7 (complete with dust filter!) patrols the barren shores of the Arctic Ocean . . .

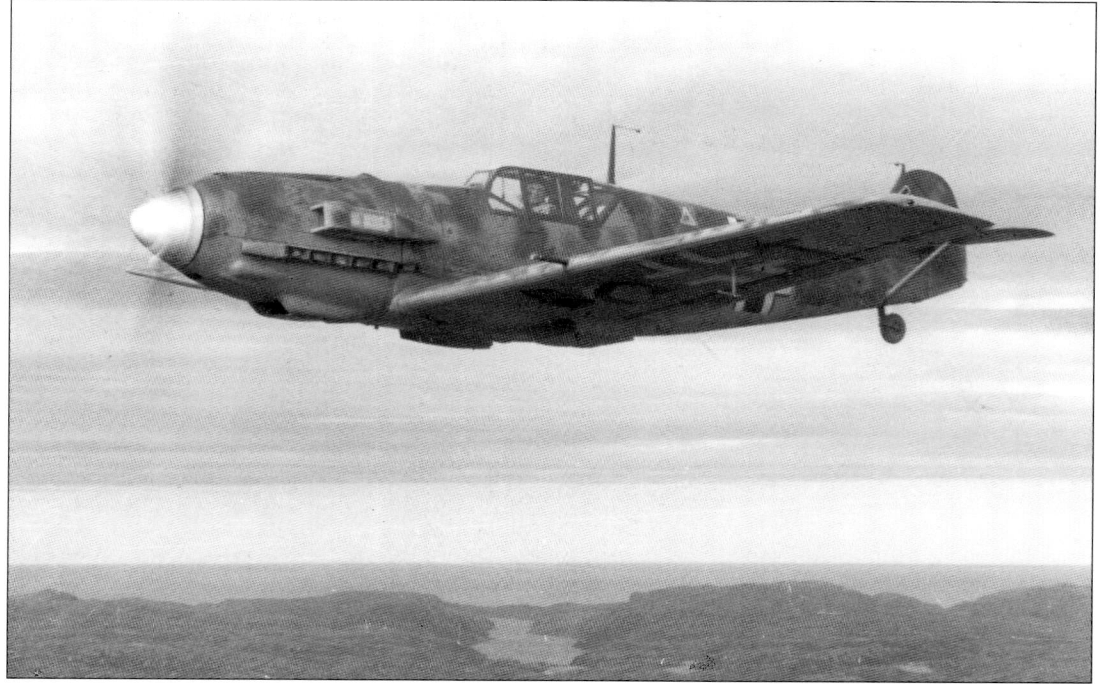

On paper, the Red Air Force enjoyed a similar numerical superiority. It is a little remarked fact that the Luftwaffe embarked upon *Barbarossa*, the Wehrmacht's most ambitious undertaking, with far fewer frontline aircraft (2598) than it had deployed either at the start of the *Blitzkrieg* in the west in May 1940 (3826) or at the height of the Battle of Britain some three months later (3705).

. . . whilst at the other end of the 2780-mile (4480-km) long front, this *Friedrich* rests between sorties safeguarding the Black Sea coast. Assigned to southernmost *Jagdgruppe*, III./JG 52, the aircraft was the mount of future Knight's Cross winner Obergefreiter Friedrich Wachowiak

In terms of single-engined fighters, the *Jagdwaffe* had exactly 619 serviceable machines (predominantly Bf 109Fs) ranged along the eastern front on the eve of the invasion. This was just over two-thirds (68 per cent) of the fighter arm's total available strength, the remaining third being deployed in the west, the homeland and the Mediterranean.

Yet it was in the east that Luftwaffe fighter pilots (understrength and overstretched as they were) would achieve the highest individual scores in the history of aerial warfare – scores that would be deemed impossible in other theatres and by other air forces.

Osprey's *Aircraft of the Aces* series has been based throughout on the accepted British and American definition of an 'ace' as being any fighter pilot with five or more aerial victories to his credit. Using this figure as a yardstick, a volume of this size dealing with the subject of the Bf 109 pilots on the eastern front would perforce consist of little more than a list of names. There are well over 5000 Luftwaffe fighter pilots in this category!

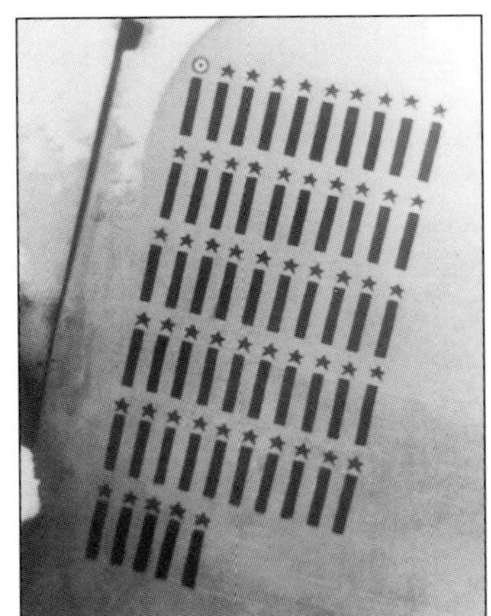

Indicative of the imbalance between the eastern and western fronts, the scoreboard on the rudder of this machine shows that its pilot, Oberfeldwebel Edmund Wagner of 9./JG 51, had claimed just one western victory prior to *Barbarossa*. With the first snows of the winter just starting to fall, Wagner has already added 54 Soviet kills. He would achieve two more before being killed in action against low-flying Pe-2s on 13 November 1941

In fact, the *Jagdwaffe* itself did not often use the dogmatic term *'As'* (ace) in relation to a specific number of victories. They preferred the more generic *'Experte'*, which was taken to mean any pilot of outstanding ability and achievement. The author has spoken to several Luftwaffe fighter pilots credited with 50 or more aerial victories – a far higher total than any western Allied ace – only to be told, in all seriousness, 'I was no great *Experte*. You really ought to talk to . . . ', and here would follow the name of some stellar individual with three or four times the number of the speaker's own kills.

Another of JG 51's NCO pilots, Oberfeldwebel – later Leutnant – Otto Gaiser is representative of the many hundreds of eastern front flyers who amassed scores in the high double figures, and yet who are practically unknown today. Gaiser had claimed 74 victories by the time he too was killed in a low-level encounter (this time with four Il-2 *Stormoviks*) early in 1944

In the history of aerial warfare, only two fighter pilots have achieved more than 300 victories – Hauptmann Erich Hartmann (left) and Major Gerhard Barkhorn (right), both of JG 52

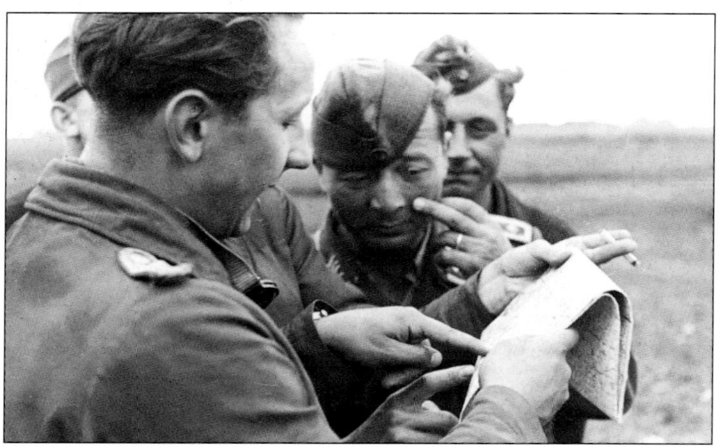

II./JG 3's Oberfeldwebel Ullmann points to an area on the map where he has just downed an enemy machine. The *Werkmeister* of 6. *Staffel* has reason to look doubtful, for the crash site could not subsequently be located, and the claim remained unconfirmed

The Luftwaffe hierarchy seems to have been taken almost unawares by the success of its own fighter pilots. In the opening months of the war 20 aerial victories would ensure the claimant the award of the Knight's Cross. Towards the close of hostilities some long-serving pilots would have amassed well over 100 kills in the east before they received this coveted decoration.

Oberleutnant Kurt Sochatzy, *Staffelkapitän* of 7./JG 3, was more fortunate. A witness on the ground took this telephoto shot of one of his victories – a Tupolev twin – as it headed down into the trees with no chance of recovery. Sochatzy claimed 38 Soviet kills (and a single No 603 Sqn Spitfire whilst on the Channel Front) before being rammed during a dogfight with an I-16 over Kiev on 12 August 1941. He would spend the next eight years in captivity in the USSR

Nothing better illustrated the yawning chasm between eastern and western front conditions than the prestigious 'century' of kills. Only a select handful of Luftwaffe fighter pilots topped the 100 mark in action solely against the western Allies. By contrast, over 70 pilots achieved this feat in the east. Eight claimed more than 200 victories, and two even surpassed the 300 figure!

In the light of post-war investigation, it is now conceded that overclaiming occurred in every air force. Mostly this was attributable to the heat and confusion of battle. Sometimes it was a case of genuine error – the trail of smoke emitted by a Bf 109 diving away at full throttle fooled many an Allied fighter pilot or air gunner into believing that his opponent was mortally hit. Only in very rare instances was it a matter of deliberate deceit. And any pilot suspected of falsifying his victory claims was given very short shrift by his peers.

Each of the combatant air forces tried to regulate claims by a strict set of conditions. None more so than the Luftwaffe, which required written confirmation of the kill by one or more aerial witnesses to the action, plus – if possible – back-up confirmation, also in writing, from an observer on the ground. Given the amount of paperwork this engendered back at OKL in Berlin, it is little wonder that it could sometimes take a year or more for a pilot's claim to receive official confirmation.

Major Gerhard Barkhorn is congratulated upon the completion of his 1000th operational sortie. The ribbons on the garland list the countries over which he has fought since joining II./JG 52 in August 1940 – (from bottom left) Denmark, Belgium, Soviet Union, France, England and Holland. By war's end Barkhorn would have flown no fewer than 1104 missions

Despite such bureaucratic safeguards, some of the more astronomical claims by Luftwaffe pilots on the eastern front still remain the subject of discussion, doubt and downright disbelief. So how were they achieved?

There is no simple answer, but rather a unique set of circumstances which was not replicated in any other campaign.

Firstly, it must be borne in mind that Luftwaffe pilots did not fly 'tours', with lengthy breaks in between, as was the practice in Allied air forces. Most remained operational until either killed, incapacitated or elevated to a staff position. Apart from periods of leave, there were many who served in frontline units throughout the entire war, from the first day of hostilities until the last.

Also, for much of the air war in the east, the *Jagdwaffe* enjoyed undisputed superiority in those three essentials to survival and success – equipment, training and tactics.

The Bf 109 was a far better fighting machine than anything the Soviets possessed during the early years of the air war in the east. In the opinion of some veterans it remained so until the very end – 'unencumbered (i.e. without additional underwing weaponry such as gondolas or rocket tubes), the Bf 109 was superior to the Russian Yak-9'.

The barrel-like shape of an abandoned I-16 sitting alongside this *Friedrich* of II./JG 54 illustrates the yawning chasm in design technology between the Soviet and German fighter arms during the opening phases of *Barbarossa*

Secondly, all *Jagdwaffe* combat leaders had enjoyed the priceless benefit of thorough training. Ironically, some – such as Lützow and Trautloft – had even attended the clandestine fighter training school at Lipezk, north of Voronezh, which the *Reichswehr* had operated in conjunction with the Soviets between the years 1925 to 1933. Many had also flown with the *Condor Legion* in Spain, and more recently a great number of fighter pilots had seen action in Poland, the west and the Balkans. This wealth of expertise and experience in turn gave them the flexibility to devise new and effective tactics to counter any situation they might meet in the air.

Much of the above could equally well apply to all the other campaigns in which the *Jagdwaffe* was involved. What made the eastern front different was the second half of the equation – the nature and make-up of the opposition.

The Stalinist purges of the late 1930s had emasculated the Soviet armed forces, cutting huge swathes through their ranks. Many air force officers, including those with recent combat experience (in Spain, the Far East and Finland), were dismissed, imprisoned or worse. This not only robbed the Red Air Force of an invaluable core of experts, it thoroughly cowed those who remained, stifling any initiative they might otherwise have displayed, and ensuring that they followed every official operational edict to the letter irrespective of the consequences.

In an effort to make good the losses brought about by its own actions, the Kremlin then ordered a rapid expansion of Russia's armed forces. But time was not on the Soviets' side. With the emphasis on numbers rather than quality, pilot training was hurried and perfunctory. Consequently their performance was, in general, of a much lower standard than that of the Luftwaffe during the opening rounds of *Barbarossa*. This inflexibility and inexperience is borne out by the combat reports of German pilots, which are full of accounts of formations of Russian aircraft either 'sticking rigidly to their course and altitude as they were chopped down one by one', or 'milling about in the air like a huge, chaotic swarm of bees'.

Inadequate training does not imply lack of courage on the part of the Soviet pilots. Quite the reverse. Unable to bring down their opponents in any other way, many resorted to ramming. Dubbed 'taran' attacks by the Russians, the first recorded instance of this ultimate act of desperation occurred within minutes of the launch of *Barbarossa*.

Although not a high scorer himself, Hannes Trautloft's wealth of early experience – from the Lipezk training establishment to service with the *Condor Legion* in Spain – made him the archetypal fighter leader. He commanded JG 54, the famous 'Green Hearts', from 1940 to 1943

At 0415 hrs on 22 June Junior Lieutenant D W Kokoryev of the 124th Fighter Regiment knocked the tail off a reconnaissance Do 215 near Sambruv after the guns of his MiG-3 had jammed. Ten minutes later the 46th Regiment's Senior Lieutenant I T Ivanov despatched a He 111 bomber in similar fashion during a dogfight above Rovno. Unlike the former, Ivanov did not survive his encounter. On 2 August he was posthumously awarded the title of Hero of the Soviet Union.

The early battles took a heavy toll of the Red Air Force. Anxious to replace their losses and get pilots to the front as quickly as possible, training programmes did not rise above the barely adequate for many months. It was not until the latter stages of the campaign that a marked improvement came about. But by that time the Luftwaffe's many *Experten* had themselves gained two or three more years of eastern front experience. And although they took no chances with their Soviet opponents – never knowing when they might come up against one of the Red Air Force's 'naturals' – most are convinced that they retained a definite edge over the Russian rank and file throughout.

The same totalitarian obsession with numbers governed the Kremlin's dictates to the Soviet aircraft industry. The portly Polikarpovs which had fought for Republican Spain were obsolete or obsolescent by the summer of 1941. Three 'modern' designs had begun to enter service in 1940. But all suffered severe teething problems and were full of faults.

The Yak-1 was unreliable and had poor firepower. Both the LaGG-3 and MiG-3 lacked manoeuvrability, and were particularly unforgiving to novice pilots. Those selected to fly the LaGG joked grimly (but only amongst themselves) that the aircraft's initials stood for 'Lacquered Coffin Guaranteed'. Even pilots with many hours on Polikarpovs found the new monoplanes sluggish and hard to handle.

Despite this, production figures came before performance. Numbers of aircraft at the front were all that mattered to Moscow. As with the pilot training programmes, the situation gradually improved. Both Lavochkin and Yakovlev subsequently developed excellent fighters out of their original designs. But it all took time. Indeed, the world would have to wait until 1950, and the war in Korea, before discovering what the Mikoyan bureau could really do – and even then the revolutionary

MiG-15 jet fighter relied heavily on captured German research and British engine design.

Much has been made of the Lend-Lease aircraft delivered to the Soviet Union to 'bridge the gap' between the initial shock of *Barbarossa* and Russian industry's gearing up to full production after evacuating its manufacturing plants to safety beyond the Ural mountains. Indeed, between 1941 and 1945 the United States alone despatched close to 10,000 fighters to Russia.

But here, too, quantity ruled over quality, for over 7000 of these machines were mid-engined Bell P-39s and P-63s. The former type was deemed 'specially disappointing' as an interceptor by the USAAF, and rejected by the RAF after just one operational mission. Both Bell fighters were extensively used by the Red Air Force, although mainly for close support and ground-strafing operations. Obsolescent P-40s were also

This LaGG-3 'lacquered coffin', showing signs of combat damage to the starboard wing root, was captured by German troops on a Soviet railway freight wagon before it could be transported to the rear for repair

Not every flyer who was forced to land behind enemy lines was as lucky as the unknown pilot of this II./JG 53 machine. He was picked up by a patrol of the 16. SS Grenadier Division *'Reichsführer SS'* and brought back to safety

supplied in great numbers, although less than 200 P-47s were received by the USSR, and not a single P-51 – the only Mustangs to arrive in Russia were ten Allison-engined Mk Is from RAF stocks.

The British also provided over 4000 Hurricanes and Spitfires, and although both types gave a good account of themselves, the latter, in particular, was not ideally suited to the often primitive conditions to be found on Soviet forward landing grounds.

Lastly, to tactics. Despite the vast distances involved, the air war in the east was essentially a non-strategic conflict. Both air forces concentrated primarily on direct, medium to low-level support of ground operations. For reasons which will become clear, Luftwaffe fighter pilots were loath to venture too far behind the Russian lines.

The Soviet High Command, for its part, was as rigid – and almost as profligate – in the control and use of its pilots and aircrew as it was with its foot soldiers. Just as, on the ground, wave after wave of Red infantrymen would be hurled, regardless of losses, against an entrenched German position in a series of frontal assaults until either none of the attackers was left standing or the defences were overwhelmed, so, in the air, wave after wave of Soviet aircraft were despatched to bomb targets along the German frontline.

The defending Luftwaffe fighter pilots, usually based close to the action, often flew as many as five or six – or even more – sorties per day. Patrolling the front, they would dive on the enemy machines, knock down one or two, break up the formation, and then climb back up to altitude to await the next incoming wave.

Although an oversimplification, such was the essence of air combat on the eastern front. Attempting to swamp the enemy by sheer weight of numbers, the Soviets bore the inevitable attrition with stoicism. The Luftwaffe's *Experten* reaped the rewards.

As to the campaign itself, the eastern front was divided into three main sections, or axes of advance – northern, central, and southern (four, if one includes the somewhat isolated far northern Finnish/Arctic region, which was a more static area of operations).

A crowded airfield towards the close of the campaign in the Balkans. On the original print the markings of the *Emil* seen below the port wing of the Henschel Hs 126 can just be made out. They reveal it to be the machine of the *Gruppen-Adjutant* of II./JG 54, Leutnant Steindl . . .

. . . who is pictured here flying the same E-7 on a *Jabo* mission only a matter of days later at the start of *Barbarossa*. In the interim, however, the narrow yellow band aft of the fuselage cross has been dispensed with, and the unit's distinctive 'crazy paving' camouflage pattern is already beginning to show through the thin coat of yellow wash hastily applied to the engine cowling

Despite the much greater length of the front, the Luftwaffe embarked upon *Barbarossa* in tried and tested fashion – by mounting a series of pre-emptive strikes that were designed to destroy the enemy air force on the ground. In this they proved remarkably successful. But the seeds of Germany's ultimate defeat had already been sown.

Hitler's intention to invade the Soviet Union had first been spelled out in his *Führer* Directive No 21 of 18 December 1940. He originally planned to launch Operation *Barbarossa* in the late spring of 1941. But the difficulties his Axis partner Mussolini was experiencing in Greece, and a revolt by the people of Yugoslavia against joining the Tripartite Pact (of Germany, Italy and Japan) persuaded him instead first to subjugate the Balkans.

This put *Barbarossa* back by a few vital weeks. The Wehrmacht's initial objective was Moscow. By 15 November 1941 a reconnaissance detachment of *Panzerpionierbataillon* 62 was just 12 miles (20 km) short of the Kremlin. But the winter snows brought the German army to a halt. The Russian capital held, and the *Führer* had lost his one chance for a 'speedy conclusion' to the campaign in the east.

The German offensive resumed in the spring of 1942. This time it was aimed not at Moscow, but along the southern sector towards the oilfields of the Caucasus and the city of Stalingrad. The 6. *Armee* reached Stalingrad late in August, only to be encircled and destroyed there during the winter months of 1942-43.

The epic battle of Stalingrad is regarded by many as the turning point of the war in the east. In fact, it was the third annual German offensive, launched on the central sector in the mid-summer of 1943, which really marked the beginning of the end for the Wehrmacht in Russia. Operation *Zitadelle*, better known as the battle of Kursk, was the greatest tank battle in military history. When Hitler ordered his armour to disengage on 13 July, it was more than a tacit admission of a local reversal. It paved the way for the huge Soviet advances of 1944-45, which would end with the Red Army in the centre of Berlin.

This, then, was the broad and sombre canvas against which the most successful fighter pilots the world has ever seen – or is ever likely to see – shone so briefly, and yet so brightly.

BARBAROSSA – THE EARLY ADVANCES

The first kill on the eastern front was claimed by the *Staffelkapitän* of 1./JG 3, Oberleutnant Robert Olejnik, who described the historic action in the following report;

'Everybody knew that I was an early riser and liked to fly the dawn missions. So, shortly before 0330 hrs, I took off with my wingman to reconnoitre the Russian airfields along our stretch of the border.

'Everything seemed quiet in the semi-darkness below. It was not until we were returning to base, and flying back over the first airfield we had visited some 20 minutes earlier, that I spotted signs of activity.

'Two Russian fighters were preparing to scramble. As we circled 700-800 metres (2300-2600 ft) overhead, I saw the Russians start their engines and begin to taxi out. They took off immediately and climbed towards us, obviously looking for a fight.

'They were still some 300-400 metres (980-1300 ft) below us when we dived to the attack. I caught the leader with a short burst on my first pass and he went down in flames. His wingman disappeared.

'Arriving back over our own airfield I waggled my wings to indicate a victory. My comrades, most of whom had only just woken up, peered sleepily from their tent flaps shaking their heads in disbelief.'

But some confusion surrounds the exact time of Olejnik's kill. The unit diary credited him with the destruction of an I-16 at 0340 hrs – just 25 minutes after the opening artillery salvoes of *Barbarossa* had rent the pre-dawn darkness – whereas he himself logged the 'Rata' ('Rat') as going down at 0358 hrs.

Oberleutnant Robert Olejnik who, by his own account, claimed the first aerial kill of *Barbarossa* is greeted by his chief mechanic, Feldwebel Mackert, upon his return from another successful mission some weeks later. The Knight's Cross, awarded for 32 victories, is just visible around Olejnik's neck. Note also I./JG 3's *'Tatzelwurm'* (Dragon) emblem, which would be retained after the *Gruppe's* redesignation as II./JG 1

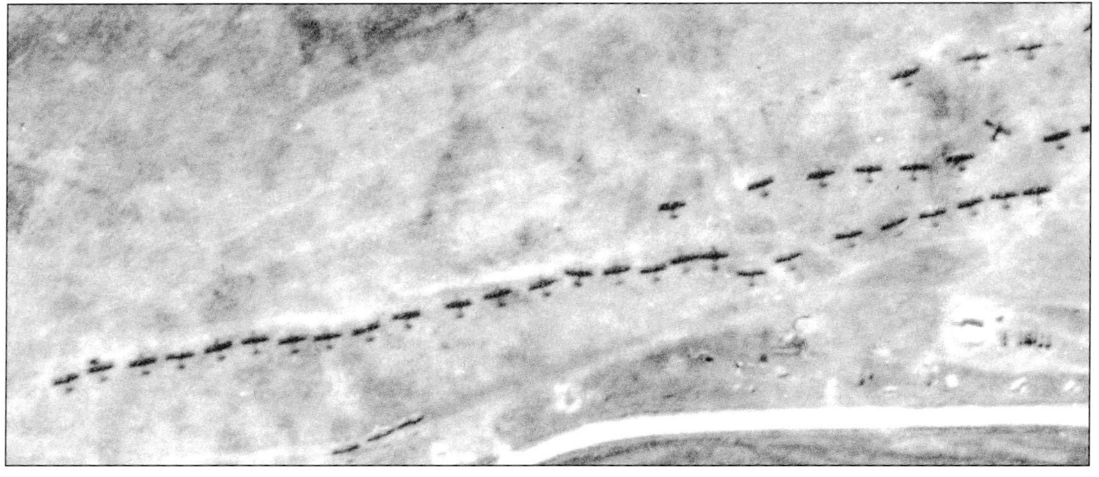

Another strong contender for the distinction of claiming the first aerial kill of the eastern front campaign must therefore be 5./JG 27's Leutnant Hans Witzel, who downed one I-15 at 0354 hrs, followed by another just 60 seconds later.

One fact not in dispute, however, was that the Luftwaffe's pre-emptive strikes had caught the Soviet Air Force completely off guard. All along the front the scene was the same as that described by Robert Olejnik's *Gruppenkommandeur*, veteran Channel front *Experte* Hauptmann Hans von Hahn;

'We could hardly believe our eyes. Every airfield was chock full of reconnaissance aircraft, bombers and fighters, all lined up in long straight rows as if on a parade. The number of landing strips and aircraft the Russians had concentrated along our borders was staggering.'

Staggering, too, was the price the Soviets paid for their unpreparedness. The Luftwaffe fighter pilots had a field day.

In the northern sector Major Hannes Trautloft's JG 54 had claimed 45 Russian aircraft shot down by the close of the first day's fighting, and the attached II./JG 53 had added a dozen more.

A Luftwaffe reconnaissance photo of a Soviet airfield with rows of fighters lined up wingtip to wingtip. The constant chord wings would suggest that the majority of these machines are Polikarpov biplanes. Targets such as this were the first priority of the new *Blitzkrieg* in the east

The result of one early strike. Of the nearly two-dozen aircraft visible here, all but two have been reduced to piles of wreckage. Although seemingly intact, the I-16 at the top of the picture is resting on its starboard wingtip. Below it a biplane is still upright, but no doubt badly damaged by debris from the machine still burning to its right

Hauptmann Wolf-Dietrich Wilcke, *Gruppenkommandeur* of III./JG 53, shot down five Soviet fighters on the opening day of *Barbarossa*

JG 53's other two *Gruppen*, deployed in the central sector – the scene of the invasion's main thrust – accounted for no fewer than 62 Soviet aircraft. Hauptmann Wolf-Dietrich Wilcke, *Gruppenkommandeur* of III./JG 53, was perhaps the eastern front's first ace, for he downed five Soviet fighters in the course of three separate sorties on 22 June. Wilcke's victims comprised a trio of I-15s shortly after 0400 hrs, a single I-16 later in the morning, and an 'I-17' in the afternoon.

Leutnant Jürgen Harder of Wilcke's *Gruppenstab* returned to Sobolevo on the afternoon of 22 June with his first kill under his belt. Like the *Kommandeur's* fifth victory of the day, it was identified as an 'I-17', and has already been recorded by the single bar seen here at the top of the rudder hinge line of Harder's *Friedrich*

The actual identity of Wilcke's fifth and final kill of the day remains conjectural. The shortcomings of Germany's intelligence services, combined with an almost paranoid secrecy on the part of the Soviets, meant that the Luftwaffe embarked upon *Barbarossa* without a proper grasp of the Soviets' – admittedly somewhat complicated – system of aircraft designation. This in turn has meant that there is a great deal of confusion surrounding many of the early claims submitted by German fighter pilots.

The I-17, for example, was a Polikarpov design of the mid-1930s. It was powered by a water-cooled engine in a long streamlined nacelle, but never progressed beyond the prototype stage. Nearly every reference to an 'I-17' (or 'I-18') shot down during the opening months of the war in the east was almost certainly the result of an encounter with one of the 'new'

'If an aircraft looks right, it is right.' But not always. The MiG-3's sleek lines belied its sluggish performance in the air, while on the ground the length of that streamlined cowling meant that forward visibility when taxying was almost nil

generation of Russian in-line engined fighters – almost certainly the MiG-3, which did bear more than a passing resemblance to published photos of the earlier Polikarpov I-17, and which was in service in far greater numbers at the beginning of *Barbarossa* than either of its Lavochkin or Yakovlev contemporaries.

Many Luftwaffe pilots also retained the habit (prevalent in the days of the *Condor Legion*) of referring to Polikarpov biplanes as 'Curtiss' fighters. Likewise, the Soviets' Tupolev SB-2 twin-engined bombers were commonly known as 'Martins' on account of their similarity to the American Martin B-10.

Future Knight's Cross holder Franz Schiess, who flew with the *Geschwaderstab* of JG 53, quickly developed a healthy respect for the agile Polikarpovs;

'We became involved with a group of about 20 Curtiss fighters, whose pilots clearly knew what they were doing. They let us get on their tails and almost into firing position. Then they suddenly pulled a 180-degree turn and we found ourselves shooting at them from head-on. In such a situation a kill becomes a matter of luck.'

Schiess nevertheless managed to claim his first victory – an I-153 – at 0725 hrs on that 22 June.

Also in the central sector, JG 51 was credited with 69 aerial victories. Four of that number had fallen to the guns of the *Geschwaderkommodore*, Oberstleutnant Werner Mölders. This took his personal score to 72, and won him the immediate award of the Swords to his Knight's Cross with Oak Leaves (just one day after the same honour had been conferred upon his arch rival, Oberstleutnant Adolf Galland, *Kommodore* of JG 26 back in France – see Osprey *Aircraft of the Aces 29 - Bf 109F/G/K Aces on the Western Front*).

'Vati' ('Daddy') Mölders, arguably the most famous and revered Luftwaffe fighter pilot of them all, had warned his pilots on the eve of *Barbarossa* that the coming campaign against Russia would not only be hard, but could also last a very long time. He would not live to see his predictions come true.

In just three weeks of action against the Soviets he added another 27 kills to his tally. Then, on 15 July, two more victories brought his total to 101. Mölders, who had not only been the *Condor Legion's* top scorer with 14 kills, but had also been the first Luftwaffe pilot to achieve 20 victories in World War 2, and thus received the *Jagdwaffe's* first Knight's Cross, had now become the first fighter pilot in history to reach the century mark.

This feat earned him the Diamonds to his Swords (in yet another 'first', he was the first of only 27 members of the entire German armed forces – seven of them *Jagdflieger* – to receive this prestigious decoration. But the award of the Diamonds brought

Oberst Werner Mölders, the Luftwaffe's first *General der Jagdflieger*, is seen on a tour of inspection in the early autumn of 1941. He is flanked by Major Günther Lützow, *Kommodore* of JG 3 (right), and Hauptmann Karl-Gottfried Nordmann, *Kommandeur* of IV./JG 51 (left). The latter pair are both already wearing the Oak Leaves to their Knight's Crosses (awarded in July and September for 42 and 59 victories respectively)

with it an immediate ban on all further operational flying. Promoted to the rank of Oberst, Werner Mölders was appointed to the newly-established office of *General der Jagdflieger*.

It was while on a tour of inspection of fighter units on the eastern front in November 1941 that he was informed of the death of World War 1 ace Ernst Udet, and instructed to return forthwith to Berlin to form part of the guard of honour at the late *Generalluftzeugmeister's* (Chief of Aircraft Procurement and Supply's) state funeral.

Mölders took off for the German capital in a Heinkel He 111. The weather was appalling, with the forecasters predicting that even worse was to come. But Mölders overrode the Heinkel pilot's objections and ordered him to continue – he had to get to Berlin on time. After departing Lemberg (Lvov) on the last leg of the flight, however, conditions deteriorated to such an extent that even the *General der Jagdflieger* was forced to admit defeat.

He instructed the pilot to head for the nearest airfield. Now reportedly flying on only one engine, the Heinkel crabbed towards Breslau. During the final approach a factory chimney suddenly loomed out of the murk and driving rain. The experienced NCO pilot managed to avoid the obstacle, but could then no longer hold the wallowing transport. It smashed to earth on Martin Quander's poultry farm at exactly 1130 hrs on 22 November.

The whole nation mourned the passing of one of its greatest heroes. A plaque to mark the spot where Mölders had perished was erected on Quander's premises at No 132 *Flughafenstrasse* (Airfield Road) – they had come that close to making it!

But to return to the opening day of *Barbarossa*.

The third *Jagdgeschwader* deployed on the central sector was JG 27 (more accurately, that unit's II. and III. *Gruppen*, plus the attached II./JG 52, the latter taking the place of the absent I./JG 27, which was currently in North Africa). These *Gruppen* achieved far fewer aerial victories in their first pre-emptive strikes against the Red Air Force. II. and III./JG 27, for example, were credited with just eleven and two kills respectively.

The two southern sector *Jagdgeschwader*, JGs 3 and 77, also submitted far fewer claims than the bulk of the units stationed along the central and northern fronts. JG 3's kills totalled 25, including one (listed as an 'I-18') for *Geschwaderkommodore* Major Günther Lützow.

The majority of the victories, 15 in all, had been achieved by Hauptmann Lothar Keller's II./JG 3. The *Gruppenkommandeur* himself claimed four – a brace each of I-16s and I-153s – which took his overall score to 20. Four of Keller's pilots opened their scoreboards on this day too. Among them was Oberleutnant Walther Dahl – a future Oak Leaves recipient, noted *Sturm* leader, and the Luftwaffe's last *Inspekteur der Tagjäger* (Inspector of Day Fighters) – whose first kill was another 'I-18'.

JG 77's III. *Gruppe* were responsible for all 15 of that *Geschwader's* successes, Oberleutnant Kurt Ubben, *Staffelkapitän* of 8./JG 77, downing two of them – an I-16 and an Ilyushin DB-3 bomber. He too would go on to win the Oak Leaves, but unlike Dahl, he would not survive the war. Risen to the command of JG 2, Major Kurt Ubben was killed in action over France in the spring of 1944 (see *Osprey Aviation Elite 1 - Jagdgeschwader 2 'Richthofen'* for further details).

One of the main reasons for the widely diverging levels of claims for aerial victories submitted by the various *Jagdgruppen* on 22 June 1941 was that many of their number were employed primarily on ground-attack missions throughout the opening phases of *Barbarossa*. Although the Luftwaffe threw some 35 *Kampf-* and *Stukagruppen* into the initial strikes against the Soviet Air Force on the ground, so numerous – and so crowded – were Russia's airfields along her western borders that a substantial proportion of the German fighter force had to fly bombing missions too.

The weapon they were to use was the recently introduced SD-2 *Splitterbombe* (fragmentation bomb, also called the 'Butterfly' bomb). Weighing only 2 kg (4.4 lbs), this devilish little device, which could be fused to explode either on or before impact with the ground, had been developed as an anti-personnel weapon. But, if dropped in sufficient numbers, it could also do a lot of damage to rows of parked aircraft. And each Bf 109 could carry 96 *Splitterbomben*!

The SD-2 *Splitterbombe* in its fully-armed state. After release, the outer casing's two clamshell halves sprang open to form a kind of parachute to retard the bomb's fall. They in turn freed a pair of circular discs which acted as a wind vane as they rotated about, and moved up, the short steel cable. This action fused the bomb's 7.5-oz (212-gr) charge of TNT

Shuttling back and forth between their bases and the target airfields just beyond the frontier, the bomb-laden Bf 109s did indeed wreak considerable havoc. And although of short duration, such missions were not at all popular with the pilots who had to fly them.

Firstly, the four bulky panniers (arranged in two tandem pairs) from which the SD-2 were suspended had a marked effect on the Bf 109's performance and handling characteristics. Secondly, for maximum effect, the bombs had to be salvoed from an altitude of just 40 metres (130 ft), at which height Soviet small-arms fire was at its most vicious.

But, perhaps most alarming of all, the SD-2 had an unfortunate tendency to hang up. At any sort of speed – and, for obvious reasons, pilots did not dawdle when making low-level runs across an enemy airfield – the build-up of air pressure held the SD-2s in place in their racks; particularly the eight bombs of the two front rows.

It was only when the fighter slowed down – on approaching to land back at base, for example – that the last of any remaining bombs fell away. Numerous reports from this time note that incoming Bf 109s could often be distinguished by the trail of small explosions left in their wake. Worst still was the fact that some SD-2s did not release until the fighter was actually taxying in. A number of casualties were incurred.

It soon became standard practice for returning Bf 109s to make a low (but high-speed!) pass across their home fields to allow observers on the ground to confirm that their bomb racks were indeed empty. Only when they got the all-clear from below did the pilots then come in to land.

It is not known how many Soviet aircraft the Bf 109 fighter-bombers accounted for in such raids, but Russian losses on the ground far exceeded the number of machines shot down on 22 June. By the close of the day's operations it was estimated that the Red Air Force had lost 322 aircraft to fighters and flak, but that some 1500 had been destroyed on the ground.

Such was the magnitude of the enemy's losses that Hermann Göring at first refused to believe the reports of his pilots' successes. He ordered an enquiry. Within days the advancing German army had overrun all 31 of the airfields which had been the targets of the Luftwaffe's pre-emptive opening strikes. This allowed examination of the wreckage, and showed that the initial reports submitted to the *Reichsmarschall* had, if anything, erred on the conservative side.

Even the official Soviet history of the Great Patriotic War – not a work noted for its objectivity – conceded that, 'By midday of 22 June our losses totalled approximately 1200 aircraft, including more than 800 machines destroyed on the ground'.

Against this the Luftwaffe recorded the loss of just 35 aircraft of all types. Casualties among the fighter arm were light, but included three unit leaders. Knight's Cross holder Hauptmann Heinz Bretnütz, *Gruppenkommandeur* of II./JG 53, downed a Soviet SB-2 bomber, but was himself wounded. Forced-landing behind enemy lines, Bretnütz was hidden by friendly farmers, who tended his injuries as best they could until the arrival of the first German spearheads on 26 June. Despite an emergency operation to amputate a gangrenous leg, Heinz Bretnütz died in hospital the following day.

Grim as the fate of 'Pietsch' Bretnütz may have been, that of the other two was infinitely worse. Major Wolfgang Schellmann, *Kommodore* of JG 27, and Oberleutnant Willy Stange, *Staffelkapitän* of 8./JG 3, both came down behind Russian lines. The former was forced to take to his parachute when his *Emil* was damaged by debris from the I-16 he had just destroyed, whilst the latter crash-landed his *Friedrich* after being hit by flak. Both fell into the hands of Soviet troops and were killed.

The barbaric treatment meted out to downed flyers, particularly during the early stages of *Barbarossa*, was yet one more facet of the aerial war in the east which set it apart from all other European air campaigns. The threat of capture was never far from the minds of single-engined fighter pilots whenever they were required to fly deep into Soviet-held territory.

Although the Luftwaffe's initial strikes had inflicted enormous damage, the Red Air Force was by no means neutralised. As early as midday on 22 June penny-packet formations of Soviet medium bombers were beginning to hit back at the German invaders. Throughout the last week of June these attacks grew in strength and frequency, but they were ill-planned and lacked both cohesion and adequate fighter cover. Unlike the longer range bombers, much of the western districts' fighter strength had been deployed – and destroyed – on those frontier airfields targeted at the start of the campaign.

As each rigid formation of bombers approached, it was set upon by Luftwaffe fighters. Individual and unit scores began to escalate rapidly as old hands – *'alte Hasen'* ('old hares') in the vernacular of the *Jagdwaffe* – added to their already considerable numbers of western victories and newcomers, their names as yet unfamiliar, achieved their first kills.

On 23 June it was estimated that over 775 Soviet aircraft had been destroyed (again, many of them on the ground). But by the following day most of the action was aloft, with JG 51 being credited with no fewer than 57 'Martin' bombers shot down. Twenty-four hours later II./JG 27 and III./JG 53 each claimed 25 bombers apiece.

5./JG 27's Leutnant Gustav Langanke, whose sole victory to date had been a Hurricane downed in the London area the previous September,

Major Wolfgang Schellmann, *Geschwaderkommodore* of JG 27, was forced to take to his parachute over enemy territory on the opening day of *Barbarossa* and was reportedly shot by the NKVD 48 hours later

was alone responsible for the destruction of seven Tupolevs (but he would add nothing further to his total before being killed in action against South African Marylands over Libya some three months later).

At least three of III./JG 53's pilots claimed triple kills. Among Feldwebel Hermann Neuhoff's trio was an Ilyushin Il-2, one of the earliest examples of the Soviet Air Force's heavily-armoured *Stormovik* ground-attack aircraft to be brought down.

On that same 25 June II./JG 51 produced another 'instant ace' when Oberleutnant Hans Kolbow, the *Kapitän* of 5. *Staffel*, shot down five Russian bombers in a row – Kolbow already had 13 western kills to his credit. To this he would add another 14 in the east, including the five on 25 June, before being brought down by Soviet ground fire on 16 July. He was awarded a posthumous Knight's Cross 11 days later.

The most spectacular success of all came about on 30 June when the Red Air Force hurled hundreds of bombers against the central sector. Everything that could fly was sortied, including antiquated Tupolev TB-3 four-engined heavy bombers.

In reply, JG 51's three *Gruppen* put up 157 individual sorties. Sixty pilots returned to base with one or more victories, resulting in the *Geschwader* being credited with 113 kills in total! Among the total was JG 51's 1000th enemy aircraft destroyed since the outbreak of war. It was the first unit within the *Jagdwaffe* to reach this figure. Three pilots had claimed five kills apiece on this day.

Kommodore Werner Mölders' five took his personal score to 82, thereby surpassing the world record 80 victories set by the immortal 'Red Baron', Rittmeister Manfred Freiherr von Richthofen, in World War 1. The other two claimants were the *Gruppenkommandeur* of I./JG 51, Oak Leaves wearer Hauptmann Hermann-Friedrich Joppien, and a certain Leutnant Heinz 'Pritzl' Bär, who was to become one of the *Jagdwaffe's* true greats.

Several other members of JG 51, including Hauptleute Josef Fözö and Richard Leppla, the *Kommandeure* of II. and III. *Gruppe* respectively, took their scores to 20 or more during the course of the day's fighting. Hitherto the 'magic 20' had automatically brought with it the award of the Knight's Cross. But with the war in the east little more than a week old, a total of just 20 kills no longer guaranteed this coveted honour. So many Soviet aircraft were being shot down that more stringent requirements were already being applied to the winning of the award in order not to devalue it.

The damage being inflicted upon the Red Air Force was undoubtedly enormous. On 29 June the Luftwaffe had reported to the OKW (High Command of the Armed Forces) the destruction of 4017 aircraft on the ground and in the air. No longer the sceptic, *Reichsmarschall* Göring thereupon announced that, 'In the first week of the campaign the Luftwaffe has destroyed 4990 enemy aircraft for the loss of 179 of its own.'

The opening phase of *Barbarossa* was coming to an end. In the air the Luftwaffe had delivered its knockout blow to the Soviet Air Force. Although not mortal, it had succeeded in securing for the Germans mastery of the skies for the months ahead – long enough, it was confidently assumed by most, for the campaign to reach the 'speedy conclusion' demanded by Hitler.

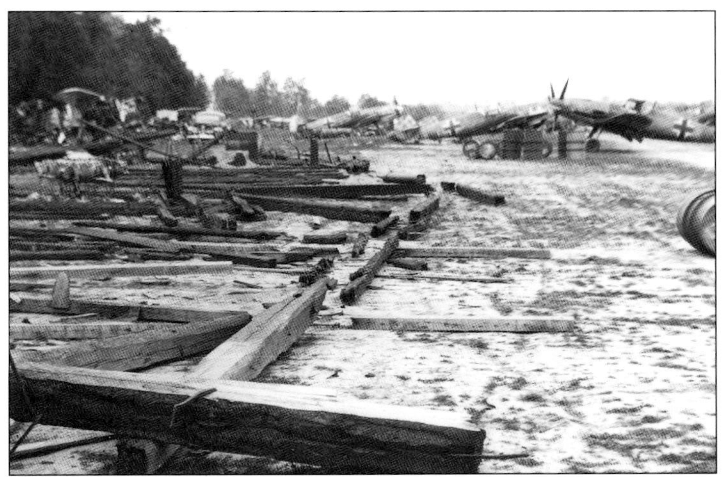

Bf 109s of JG 51 occupy a Russian airfield as the advance into the Soviet Union gets underway. Note the abandoned I-153s among the trees on the left

On the ground, too, the Russian frontier defences had been thoroughly breached. The way now lay open for the advance on Moscow, the key to victory in the east.

At the beginning of July the two armoured groups deployed along the central sector broke out of the Beresina bridgehead and began to push towards the Russian capital. They were supported by the Bf 109s of JG 51. With few Soviet fighters in evidence, the *Geschwader* was rarely called upon for bomber escort duties, instead flying mainly *freie Jagd* sweeps and ground-attack missions. At least one *Staffel* continued to operate in the fighter-bomber role against enemy airfields, but pilots no longer had to contend with the temperamental SD-2 *Splitterbomben*, their aircraft being equipped instead to carry four 50-kg bombs.

On 12 July Hauptmann Leppla claimed JG 51's 500th Soviet victim (which also proved to be the *Geschwader's* 1200th aerial victory of the war). But the pressure of the past three weeks' constant campaigning was beginning to tell. Although only six pilots had been killed or reported missing during that time, the three *Gruppen* had, between them, written off 89 Bf 109s – for which they had received just 49 replacements. The *Geschwader* was operating at less than half its normal establishment. And of those 58 fighters which were serviceable, 22 had engines with more than 50 hours' flying time which needed urgent overhaul.

One of Werner Mölders' earliest duties as *General der Jagdflieger* was to make a welcome return visit to III./JG 53, the *Gruppe* he had formed and first commanded in October 1939. The occasion was the award of the Knight's Cross to Leutnant Erich Schmidt on 23 July for his 30 victories (17 of them in the west). From left to right are Oberst Mölders, *Gruppenkommandeur* Hauptmann Wilcke and Leutnant Schmidt

Just over a month later, on 27 August, and Schmidt (top left) watches the 44th kill bar being applied to the rudder of his *Friedrich*. Four days – and three victories – later still, Erich Schmidt would be reported missing, shot down by Soviet anti-aircraft fire near Dubno, in the Ukraine

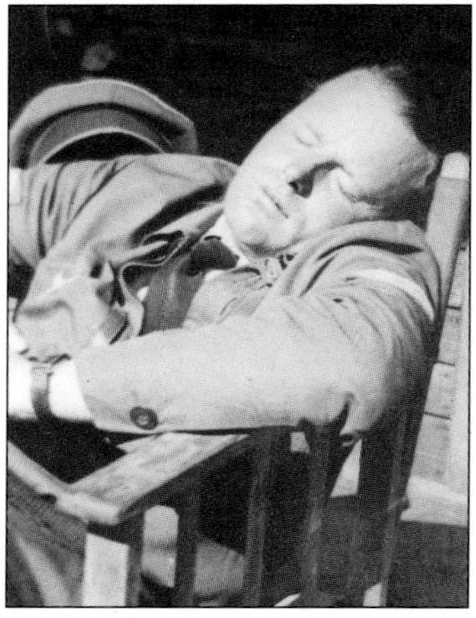

Already a seasoned campaigner – his first kill had been a French Morane claimed on 14 March 1940, the famous 'Day of the Fighters' – Oberleutnant Franz ***'Altvater'*** ('Old Father') Götz of 9./JG 53 knew the value of grabbing 40 winks whenever the chance presented itself. He was another who would remain in frontline service until the very end of the war, by which time he had risen to become ***Kommodore*** of JG 26 in the west

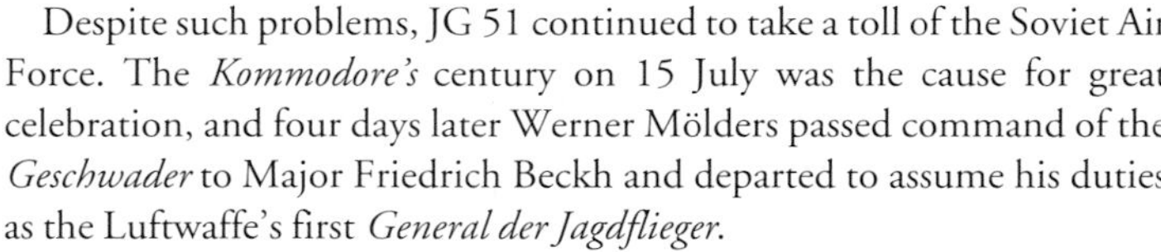

Despite such problems, JG 51 continued to take a toll of the Soviet Air Force. The *Kommodore's* century on 15 July was the cause for great celebration, and four days later Werner Mölders passed command of the *Geschwader* to Major Friedrich Beckh and departed to assume his duties as the Luftwaffe's first *General der Jagdflieger*.

Mölders' new post was no sinecure. It was clear that the *Jagdwaffe* was becoming dangerously overstretched. Already committed in western Europe and the Mediterranean, the German fighter arm was now waging war on three fronts. The very size of the new theatre, the huge distances to be covered and the vast areas to be controlled were simply too much for the number of fighters available.

As a consequence, July was to witness not only the first transfer of units from one part of the eastern front to another (such transfers would become increasingly frequent as the campaign wore on), but also the withdrawal of the first *Jagdgruppe* to meet the more 'pressing' operational demands of another theatre.

The latter was Hauptmann Wolfgang Lippert's II./JG 27. After just four weeks in the east, which had netted a total of 42 victories, II./JG 27 returned to Germany to re-equip with Bf 109Fs, before staging southwards to join I. *Gruppe* in Africa.

To make up for the departed II./JG 27, Hauptmann Wolf-Dietrich Wilcke's III./JG 53 was temporarily subordinated to *Stab* JG 27 (commanded since the disappearance of Wolfgang Schellmann by Major Bernhard Woldenga). Throughout the late summer and early autumn JG 27's three main component *Gruppen* (III./JG 27, II./JG 52 and III./JG 53) also supported the central sector armies' advance on Moscow.

By far the most successful of III./JG 27's pilots at this time was Oberleutnant Erbo Graf von Kageneck, the *Kapitän* of 9. *Staffel*, who added 48 eastern front victories to his previous tally of 17 western kills (and gained the Knight's Cross in the process) before both the *Geschwaderstab* and III./JG 27 withdrew from Russia in mid-October to fight alongside the unit's other two *Gruppen* in North Africa.

During the same period the attached III./JG 53 had claimed some 200 kills. The *Gruppe's* three leading scorers in the east were Oberleutnant Franz Götz, *Staffelkapitän* of 9./JG 53, with 23 victories, 7. *Staffel's* Oberfeldwebel Hermann Neuhoff with 21, and Hauptmann Wilcke with 20. Wilcke was awarded the Knight's Cross on 6 August for achieving 25 kills (the first 13 of them in the west), but both Götz and Neuhoff would have to wait until the following year, and the destruction of 40 enemy aircraft each, before they were similarly honoured.

One member of II./JG 52 also received the Knight's Cross at this juncture. Oberleutnant Johannes Steinhoff, *Kapitän* of 4. *Staffel*, had claimed 35 victories by the time of his award on 30 August. Destined to become one of the *Jagdwaffe's* most

Looking almost as relaxed as ***'Altvater'*** Götz, ***'Fürst'*** ('Prince') Wilcke enjoys a cigarette in the company of two of his ***Gruppe's*** leading ***Experten***, namely Leutnants Herbert Schramm (left) and Erich Schmidt (right). Wilcke and Schramm were both awarded the Knight's Cross on 6 August

A later photograph of Hauptmann Johannes *'Mäcki'* Steinhoff after his promotion to the command of II./JG 52 early in 1942. The lettering on the leading edge of the port wing specifies the largest permissible tyre size for this particular machine's mainwheels

respected unit leaders, 'Mäcki' Steinhoff would amass 148 kills on the eastern front. But there was another pilot within the *Gruppe* who would achieve more than double that total.

Leutnant Gerhard Barkhorn had already served with II./JG 52 for over a year by the time he finally shot down his first enemy aircraft on 2 July – this was his 120th mission! This solitary victory was in itself an unremarkable event, except for the fact that Barkhorn would go on to add exactly 300 more to become the second-highest scoring fighter pilot in history.

While existing scores were being added to, and new reputations being launched on the road to Moscow, other *Jagdgruppen* were achieving similar results on either flank of the German advance into the Soviet Union.

The sole *Jagdgeschwader* deployed on the northern sector was Major Hannes Trautloft's JG 54 (initially with 4. and 5. *Staffeln* of JG 53 attached). Its task was to provide aerial support during *Heeresgruppe Nord's* drive through the Baltic states towards the great Soviet naval base of Leningrad, Russia's second largest city and one-time capital.

The *Geschwader's* first major success came on 29 June when large formations of bombers attacked the Dvina bridges in an attempt to halt the Panzers' advance. By the end of the day JG 54 had downed 65 of their number, and on 18 July the *Geschwader* claimed its 500th Russian victim.

Twenty-four hours later another of the eastern front's true 'greats' opened his scoreboard when 9./JG 54's Leutnant Walter Nowotny destroyed a trio of I-153s over the Baltic island of Ösel. Nowotny's career

JG 54's advance through the Baltic states took them to Schaulen, (Siauliai) in Lithuania, where they found this motley collection of abandoned enemy aircraft. Among the usual assortment of I-16s, MiG-3s and SB-2s, note the ex-Lithuanian Air Force Gloster Gladiator fighters (background left) purchased from Great Britain before the war

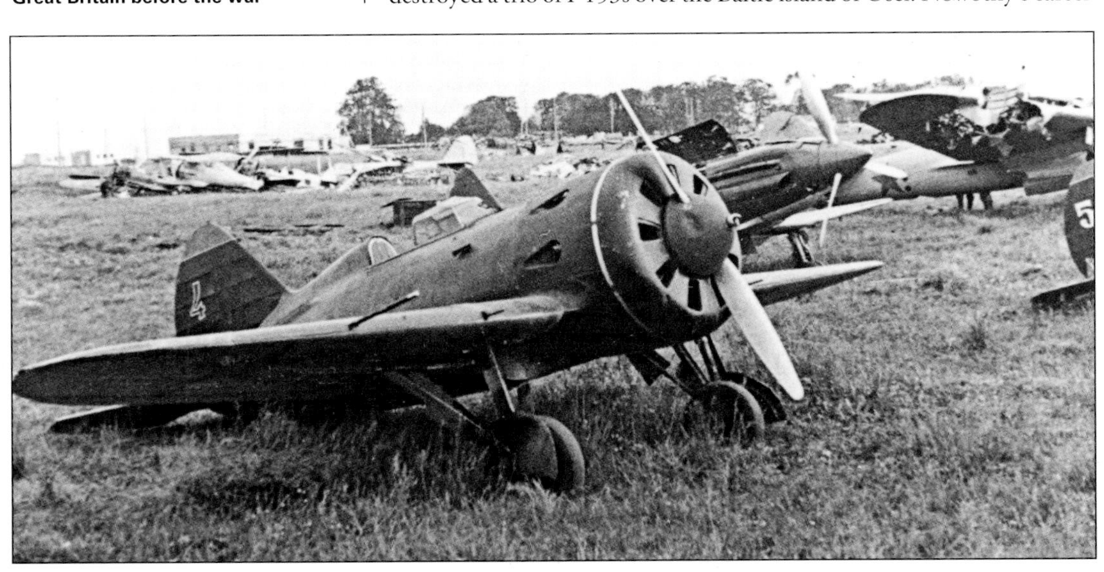

almost ended there and then, however, for he was himself shot down during the engagement and only just survived three days and nights in a rubber dinghy.

Kommodore Hannes Trautloft's Knight's Cross, awarded on 27 July for 20 victories, was but the first of a number conferred upon members of JG 54 during the push on Leningrad. On 1 August JG 54 became the third *Jagdgeschwader* to achieve 1000 aerial victories since the outbreak of war – although widely separated and on different sectors of the front, JG 3's component *Gruppen* had achieved their collective 'thousandth' just the day before.

Already wearing the Knight's Cross, Oberleutnant Hans 'Fips' Philipp, *Staffelkapitän* of 4./JG 54, won the *Geschwader's* first Oak Leaves (for 62 victories) on 24 August. Less than a fortnight later the German army was at the gates of Leningrad. Early in September JG 54 took up residence on the Russian airfields at Siverskaya and Krasnogvardeisk, and these would remain their principal bases for much of the epic 900-day siege of Leningrad that was now about to begin.

Oberleutnant Hans Philipp, who won JG 54's first Oak Leaves, would be killed in action in defence of the Reich late in 1943 when *Kommodore* of JG 1

The city, its naval installations, and the surrounding area were subjected to constant aerial bombardment. One of the first major raids was mounted on 9 September, when JG 54's fighters escorted Ju 87 dive-bombers of StG 2 against units of the Soviet Baltic Fleet. But the day was marred by the loss of Oberleutnant Hubert Mütherich, *Staffelkapitän* of 5./JG 54 and one of the recent Knight's Cross recipients, who was killed when his aircraft somersaulted while attempting a forced-landing. At the time of his death 'Hubs' Mütherich had a total of 43 victories, 33 of them claimed since the beginning of *Barbarossa*.

JG 54 was to lose another Knight's Cross wearer, of longer standing, on 30 September when the *Kommandeur* of III. *Gruppe*, Hauptmann Arnold Lignitz, shed a wing during a dogfight over Leningrad. Before the fighter spun in, Lignitz was able to take to his parachute. He was last seen drifting down over the centre of Leningrad, and reportedly died later in one of the city's gaols. This marked the start of a long war of attrition for JG 54 as the Soviets threw in more and more aerial reinforcements to defend their second city.

In contrast to JG 54's somewhat sedentary existence in the north, the campaign on the southern sector was one of speed and movement as the armoured units of *Panzergruppe* 1 took full advantage of the wide open expanse of the Ukrainian steppe to outmanoeuvre and encircle whole Russian armies. The two main fighter units supporting operations in the south were JGs 3 and 77.

From its jumping-off points south of Warsaw in occupied Poland, JG 3 covered the left-hand flank of the southern front (adjoining the central sector) which was the scene of the main armoured thrust towards the Ukrainian capital Kiev, and thence onwards to the great industrial centre of Kharkov. On their right, JG 77 set out from its fields in Bulgaria and Rumania in support of the ground forces' advances along the shores of the Black Sea towards the Crimea.

The most successful fighter pilot during the early months of the air war over southern Russia was the *Geschwaderkommodore* of JG 3, Major Günther Lützow. He alone was responsible for 83 of the *Stabsschwarm's* 106 victories between June and November 1941, this remarkable string of successes being marked by the award of the Oak Leaves on 20 July (for a total of 42 kills) and the Swords on 11 October (for 92). Exactly a fortnight later a trio of MiG-3s boosted his score to 101.

Günther Lützow thus became the second member of the *Jagdwaffe*, after Mölders, to achieve the century. He too received an immediate ban on all further operational flying, but this did not stop him from adding two more victories to his overall total – during 'involuntary encounters' (!) with Soviet fighters – before he finally relinquished command of JG 3 in August 1942 to join the staff of the *General der Jagdflieger*.

The Russian reaction along the southern front was similar to that on the central sector. After most of its fighter strength had been destroyed on the ground, the Red Air Force sent in waves of unescorted bombers in an effort to prevent a German break-out. They suffered appalling losses. In expressing his appreciation for the support provided by the Luftwaffe, the Chief of the Army High Command spoke of 'entire Russian bomber *Geschwader*, flying without fighter cover' being wiped out.

This is believed to have been a reference to the action of 8 July when JG 3 claimed the destruction of 38 twin-engined bombers. I. *Gruppe* was credited with 20 Ilyushin DB-3s, three of which fell to Oberleutnant Robert Olejnik. This brought the number of Olejnik's Russian victims to 25 since claiming the opening kill of *Barbarossa*. He would achieve half-a-dozen more – and receive the Knight's Cross while so doing – to emerge as I./JG 3's highest scorer before the *Gruppe's* return to the Reich at the end of September 1941, and subsequent redesignation as II./JG 1.

Also pictured wearing the Oak Leaves, awarded on 26 October for 85 victories, II./JG 3's Hauptmann Gordon Gollob subsequently commanded JG 77, before ending the war as the Luftwaffe's third and final *General der Jagdflieger*

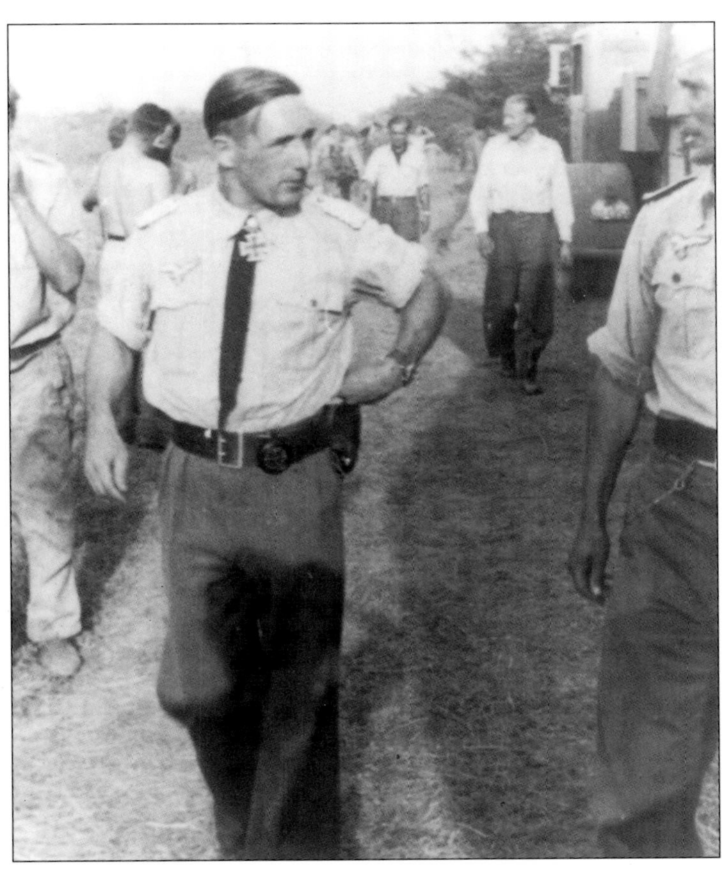

Not too far behind 'Franzl' Lützow in respect of the number of Soviet aircraft destroyed during this period was Hauptmann Gordon Gollob, *Kommandeur* of II./JG 3. He had assumed command of the *Gruppe* on 27 June after the previous incumbent, Hauptmann Lothar Keller, had been killed in a mid-air collision.

An ex-*Zerstörer* pilot, and with six victories already to his credit, Gollob had added 79 Soviet aircraft to his tally by late October. This earned him both the Knight's Cross and the Oak Leaves. In November 1941 II./JG 3 was also withdrawn from the eastern front, but Major Gordon Gollob would reappear in the Soviet Union the following year as *Kommodore* of JG 77. Thereafter, he would serve in various staff positions before replacing the 'disgraced' Adolf Galland on 31 January 1945 as the third, and final, *General der Jagdflieger*.

Yet another high scorer during the opening phase of *Barbarossa* was the *Gruppenkommandeur* of III./JG 3, Hauptmann Walter Oesau. A veteran of the *Condor Legion* who had since claimed 42 World War 2 victories to add to the eight Republican machines he had downed in Spain, he was already wearing the Oak Leaves prior to the invasion of Russia. In just five weeks over southern Russia 'Gulle' Oesau was credited with a further 44 enemy aircraft destroyed, his 80th kill of the war – a DB-3 bomber brought down on 15 July – bringing him the Swords to his Knight's Cross. But less than a fortnight later Walter Oesau relinquished command of II./JG 3 to take over as *Kommodore* of JG 2 in the west.

A number of other pilots were also scoring steadily as the ground forces advanced on Kharkov. At least six members of JG 3 were awarded the Knight's Cross during this period, and several of them went on to take their final totals close to the 100 mark.

In any other theatre, and in any other air force, an achievement of this kind would be considered outstanding. But such is the dominance of the 'select few' of eastern front aces within much post-war aviation literature that the names of numerical lesser lights such as Franz Beyer, Eberhard von Boremski and Walter Ohlrogge are now all but forgotten.

Much the same applies to JG 77, which was operating on JG 3's right flank. By the end of 1941 this *Geschwader* had a collective total of over 1000 Soviet aircraft destroyed, and five Knight's Crosses had been won as several later high-ranking and highly decorated *Experten* took their scores into double figures. The two most successful pilots of JG 77 during this period were Oberleutnants Kurt Ubben and Heinrich Setz, with 54 and 52 kills respectively. Both would subsequently be killed in action on the western front, Ubben as *Kommodore* of JG 2 and Setz as *Kommandeur* of I./JG 27.

Like the *Jagdgeschwader* to the north, JG 77 also inflicted grievous damage on unescorted Soviet bomber formations. Many multiple successes were achieved. On 25 June Oberleutnant Walter Hoeckner, *Staffelkapitän* of 6./JG 77, downed eight SB-2s during a *Freie Jagd* sweep. Eighteen of the following day's 47 kills were claimed by just four pilots, with Oberfeldwebel Reinhold Schmetzer, who was credited with five of the 32 SB-2s shot down on this date, then chalking up another five

This oddly-marked *Emil* was the mount of Oberleutnant Georg Schirmböck, the *Gruppen-TO* of II./JG 77. The symbol behind the chevron, which appears at first glance to be one half of the runic SS insignia, is in fact the emblem of the *'Jungvolk'*, a youth organisation to which *Schirmböck* presumably once belonged. He is reported to have adopted this marking after *Gruppenkommandeur* Hauptmann Anton Mader complained that the *TO's* standard 'Chevron circle' was too similar to his own 'Double chevron'

As well as being the *General der Jagdflieger*, Werner Mölders also temporarily held the post of *Nahkampfführer Krim* (Close-support Leader Crimea). And it was no doubt in the latter role that he toured the Stuka units operating over the Crimea in the autumn of 1941. Here, he appears to be making a forceful point to Hauptmann Helmut Bode, *Gruppenkommandeur* of III./StG 77, while Leutnant Gawlina looks on

victories on 10 July. Half of Oberfeldwebel Eugen Wintergerst's 22 kills were also scored on just two days – four SB-2s on 9 August and seven SB-3s three days later.

These names may be unfamiliar, but there was one very well-known figure who would see brief action with JG 77 early in November, by which time the *Geschwader* was operating over the Crimea. In his dual capacity as *General der Jagdflieger* and temporary *Nahkampfführer Krim* (Close-support Leader Crimea), Oberst Werner Mölders was visiting JG 77 when he heard an NCO pilot complain of a botched attack on an Il-2.

Ilyushin's heavily armoured ground-attack *Stormovik* was undoubtedly the hardest Soviet aircraft to bring down. Mölders took the Oberfeldwebel up the next day to demonstrate his technique;

'He positioned himself off to one side of – and some distance away from – the last Il-2 in a formation of six. He then turned in quickly and opened fire at the enemy's cockpit from an angle of some 30 degrees. The Il-2 immediately burst into flames and crashed. "Do you see how it's done?" Oberst Mölders voice came over the R/T. "Right, now you take the next one".

'I carried out the same manoeuvre and, sure enough, the next Il-2 went down on fire. "And again!" It was like being on a training flight. Another short burst and the third Il-2 was ablaze. The whole lesson had lasted no more than 12 minutes!'

It was a gesture typical of 'Vati' Mölders. Herbert Kaiser never forgot his 23rd and 24th kills. But because the *General der Jagdflieger* was officially banned from operational flying, the first *Stormovik* was never

But it was as a fighter tactician that Mölders excelled. One lesson he passed on was how to bring down the formidable *Stormovik* which, at this early stage of the war, was a single-seater machine with no rear-gunner. The spot to aim at was the unprotected top of the fuel tank immediately behind the cockpit – which is precisely where this early Il-2 has been hit. A fierce fire has already taken hold as the machine starts to go down

This *Friedrich* belongs to III./JG 52, which was the *Gruppe* responsible for guarding the Black Sea coastline during the opening phase of *Barbarossa*. Note the unusual angular '6' and the wavy bar *Gruppe* symbol, both applied in black to denote 8. *Staffel*

added to Mölders' list of victories – there has been much speculation as to how many other such 'demonstrations' went unrecorded!

Oddly, the one *Jagdgeschwader* perhaps associated more than any other with the eastern front, and certainly ultimately the most successful of all in terms of numbers of Soviet aircraft destroyed, made the least impact at the beginning of *Barbarossa*.

This was due entirely to the nature of JG 52's deployment. I. *Gruppe* was not even part of the invading order of battle, but was retained in the west to guard the North Sea coastline. And while Hauptmann Erich Woitke's II. *Gruppe* performed creditably enough on the central sector (claiming no less than 270 victories during its secondment to JG 27), III./JG 52's kill rate was so poor in comparison to all the other *Jagdgruppen* involved in the opening stages of the campaign in the east that Hermann Göring was moved to despatch the following telegram to the *Gruppenkommandeur* on 4 July;

'Your unit continues to distinguish itself by its failure to shoot down the enemy. Just how much longer are the Russians to be allowed into your airspace unhindered?

'Signed - Göring'

This was a perfect example of the *Reichsmarschall's* lack of understanding of the conditions at the front. He now accepted the huge claims of the other *Jagdgruppen* as the norm, and against these III./JG 52's figures were admittedly low. But Major Albert Blumensaat's unit was the southernmost *Gruppe* of the entire front. Its task was to patrol the Black Sea coast. Enemy incursions were few, and such raids as were mounted almost invariably approached undetected from across the sea, struck at some coastal or fringe target, and quickly escaped back over open water again.

Against hit-and-run tactics of this kind, which could be aimed at any point along a stretch of coastline over 200 miles (320 km) long, it is hardly surprising that the *Gruppe's* 35+ serviceable fighters fared badly in the scoring stakes. But when III./JG 52 was re-directed inland, its pilots soon began to make up for their slow start.

III./JG 52's first Knight's Cross was awarded to Feldwebel Gerhard Köppen of 7. *Staffel*. This early 1942 shot shows the 40th kill, which won Köppen the award, marked in black on a rudder now displaying a total of 62 victories – just ten short of the number which would earn him the Oak Leaves on 27 February. Köppen was posted missing after an engagement with Pe-2s over the Sea of Azov on 5 May. His final score stood at 85

During a Stuka-escort mission on 3 August Leutnant Hermann Graf scored the first kill of a career that would transform him into one of the *Jagdwaffe's* truly outstanding combat leaders. At this time Graf was a member of 9./JG 52. The skies above Kharkov were this *Staffel's* favourite hunting ground, and before its capture, the town's three main military airfields ensured that there was no lack of aerial opposition. By 11 October 9./JG 52's collective total had risen to 59, making it the most successful of the *Gruppe's* three *Staffeln*.

The others were not far behind. But on 28 November 8./JG 52 suffered a serious blow when *Staffelkapitän* Oberleutnant Günther Rall was seriously wounded after claiming his 36th kill. Temporarily paralysed, it would be nine months before Rall returned to his *Staffel*. He, too, was destined for great things. Despite being shot down five times, Günther Rall survived the war as the Luftwaffe's third-highest scoring fighter pilot.

A portent of things to come. The *Gruppen-TO* of II./JG 51 (note the *Gruppe* horizontal bar just visible behind the circle – see colour profile 16) casually brushes the first snow of the winter from the wing of his *Friedrich* at Vyazma in October 1941

The winter of 1941-42 quickly tightened its grip. This III. *Gruppe* machine, and the sentry alongside his tripod-mounted MG 34 machine gun, are fortunate to be well-muffled against the sub-zero temperatures

Soon the snow was so deep that hardstands had to be shovelled free. But there was no respite for the groundcrews, and here a pair of 'black men' refuel a winter-camouflaged III./JG 53 aircraft from individual drums

Yet it was a relatively unknown NCO, 7./JG 52's Feldwebel Gerhard Köppen, who was awarded the *Gruppe's* first Knight's Cross, for 40 victories, on 18 December.

By then, however, *Barbarossa* was in serious difficulties. The *Führer's* 'speedy victory' was to be denied him by that one implacable and impartial foe of any invader of Russia's vast open spaces – 'General Winter'. By mid-November autumn's mud had finally given way to snow and ice, and bone-chilling temperatures of -40 degrees descended over the frontlines. Totally unprepared for a winter campaign, and lacking proper clothing and specialised equipment, the Wehrmacht ground to a halt.

Taking full advantage of the Germans' immobility, fresh Soviet divisions that had been hastily brought in from Siberia launched a series of counter-attacks. The leading Panzers were soon pushed back from the approaches to Moscow, and German forces retreated and dug in for the winter. The late Werner Mölders' fears that the campaign in the east could be a long one had become grim reality.

Hangar space was at a premium, and those units lucky enough to be based on ex-Soviet airfields where hangars were still standing made use of every available inch of cover to carry out essential maintenance work

Colour Plates

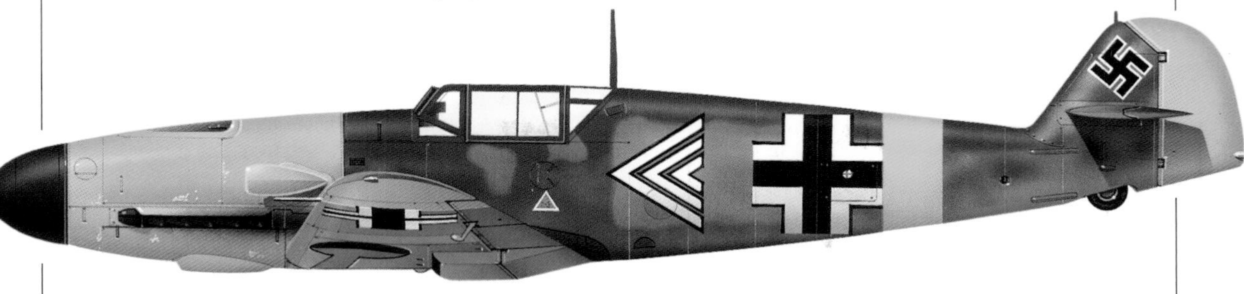

1
Bf 109F-2 'White Triple Chevron' of Major Günther Lützow, *Geschwaderkommodore* JG 3, Hostynne, June 1941

2
Bf 109G-2 'Black Chevron and Bars' of Major Wolf-Dietrich Wilcke, *Geschwaderkommodore* JG 3 'Udet', Morosovskaya, November 1942

3
Bf 109F-2 'Black Chevron and Triangle' of Hauptmann Hans von Hahn, *Gruppenkommandeur* I./JG 3, Luzk, July 1941

4
Bf 109F-2 'Black Chevron and Circle' of Leutnant Detlev Rohwer, *Gruppen-TO* I./JG 3, Byelaya-Zerkov, August 1941

5
Bf 109F-4 'White Double Chevron' of Hauptmann Kurt Brändle, *Gruppenkommandeur* II./JG 3 'Udet', Tusow, August 1942

6
Bf 109F-4 'Yellow 7' of Oberleutnant Viktor Bauer, *Staffelkapitän* 9./JG 3 'Udet', Szolzy, March 1942

7
Bf 109F-4 'Yellow 4' of Oberfeldwebel Eberhard von Boremski, 9./JG 3 'Udet', Zhuguyev, May 1942

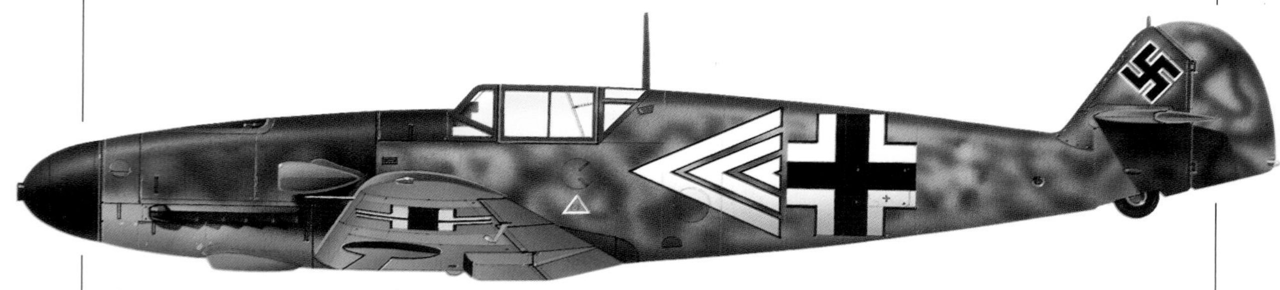

8
Bf 109F-4 'White Triple Chevron' of Hauptmann Franz Hahn, *Gruppenkommandeur* I./JG 4, Mizil/Rumania, January 1943

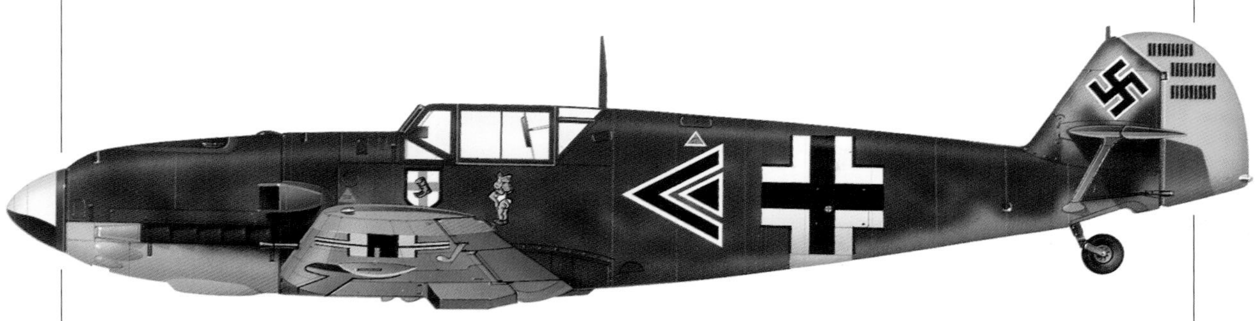

9
Bf 109E-7 'Black Double Chevron' of Hauptmann Günther Scholz, *Gruppenkommandeur* III./JG 5, Petsamo/Finland, September 1942

10
Bf 109G-2 'Yellow 12' of Oberleutnant Heinrich Ehrler, Staffelkapitän 6./JG 5, Petsamo/Finland, March 1943

11
Bf 109G-2 'White 4' of Oberleutnant Theodor Weissenberger, *Staffelkapitän* 7./JG 5, Petsamo/Finland, July 1943

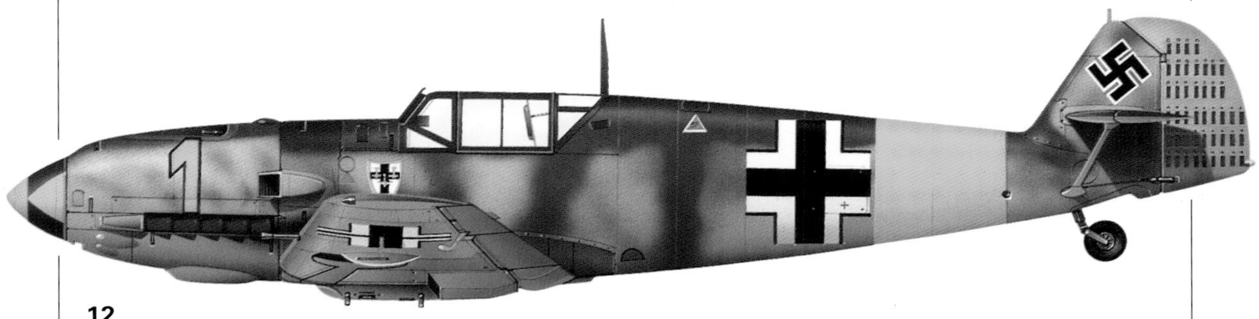

12
Bf 109E-7 'Yellow 1' of Oberleutnant Erbo Graf von Kageneck, *Staffelkapitän* 9./JG 27, Solzy, August 1941

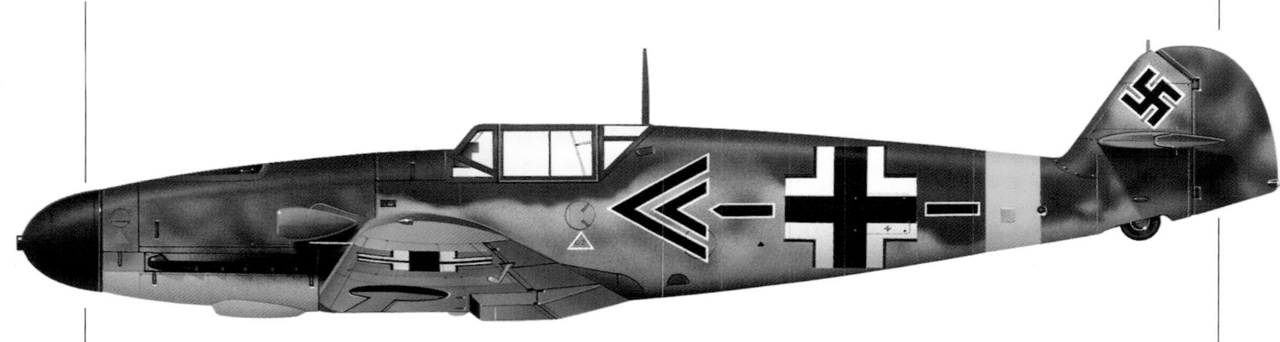

13
Bf 109F-4 'Black Chevron and Bars' of Major Karl-Gottfried Nordmann, *Geschwaderkommodore* JG 51 'Mölders', Shatalovka, Summer 1942

14
Bf 109G-6 'White 9' of Leutnant Günther Josten, 1./JG 51 'Mölders', Bobruisk, Spring 1944

15
Bf 109F 'Yellow 7' of Oberleutnant Heinrich Krafft, *Staffelkapitän* 8./JG 51 'Mölders', Stolzy, March 1942

16
Bf 109F 'Black Double Chevron' of Hauptmann Josef Fözö, *Gruppenkommandeur* of II./JG 51, Stara-Bychov, July 1941

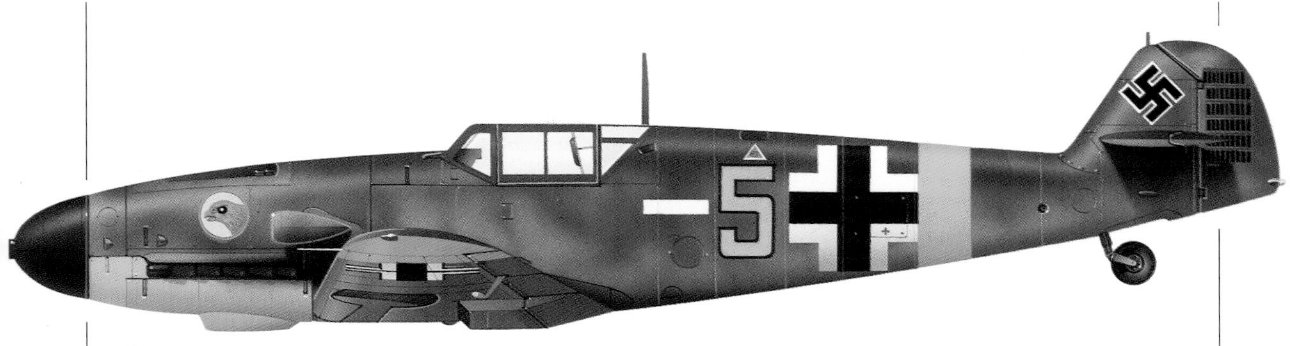

17
Bf 109G-2 'Yellow 5' of Feldwebel Anton Hafner, 6./JG 51 'Mölders', Orel-North, August 1942

18
Bf 109F-4 'Red 12' of Oberfeldwebel Heinz Klöpper, 11./JG 51 'Mölders', Dugino, September 1942

19
Bf 109G-6 'Black Double Chevron' of Hauptmann Gerhard Barkhorn, *Gruppenkommandeur* I./JG 52, Kharkov-South, August 1943

20
Bf 109G-6 'Red 4' of Oberfeldwebel Rudolf Trenkel, 2./JG 52, Poltava, July 1943

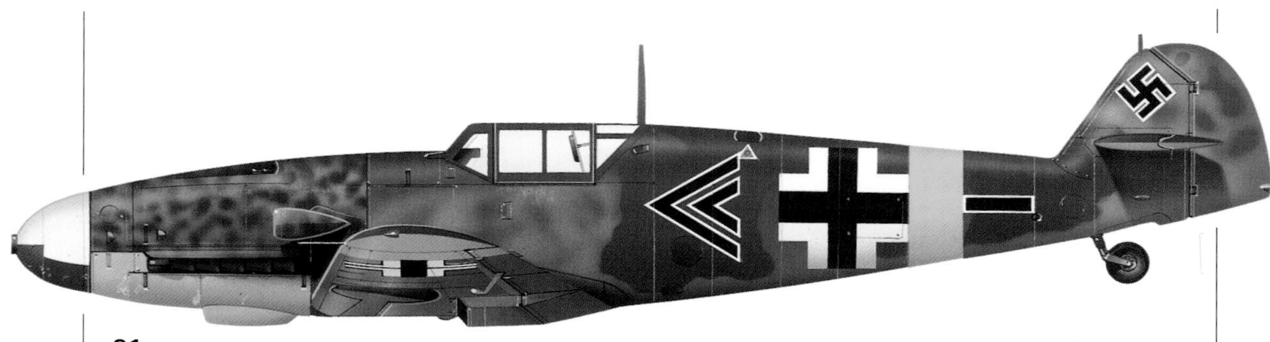

21
Bf 109G-2 'Black Double Chevron' of Hauptmann Johannes Steinhoff, *Gruppenkommandeur* II./JG 52, Rostov, August 1942

22
Bf 109G-6 'White 1' of Hauptmann Erich Hartmann, *Staffelkapitän* 4./JG 52, Budaörs/Hungary, November 1944

23
Bf 109G-4 'Black 12' of Leutnant Peter Düttmann, 5./JG 52, Anapa, May 1943

24
Bf 109G-2 'Yellow 5' of Leutnant Walter Krupinski, 6./JG 52, Armavir, August 1942

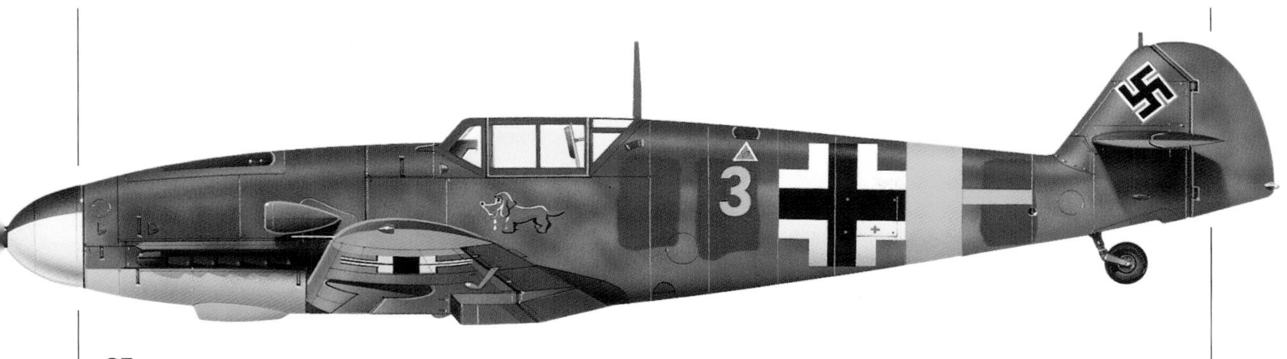

25
Bf 109G-4 'Yellow 3' of Unteroffizier Hans Waldmann, 6./JG 52, Anapa, June 1943

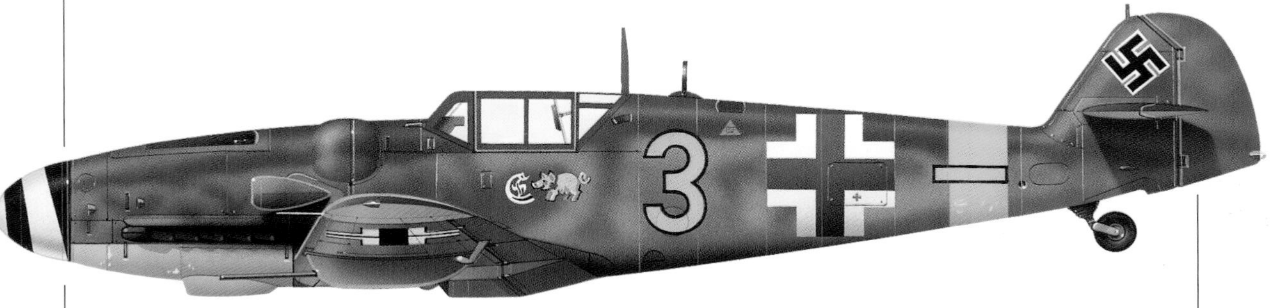

26
Bf 109G-6 'Yellow 3' of Leutnant Heinz Ewald, 6./JG 52, Zilistea/Rumania, June 1944

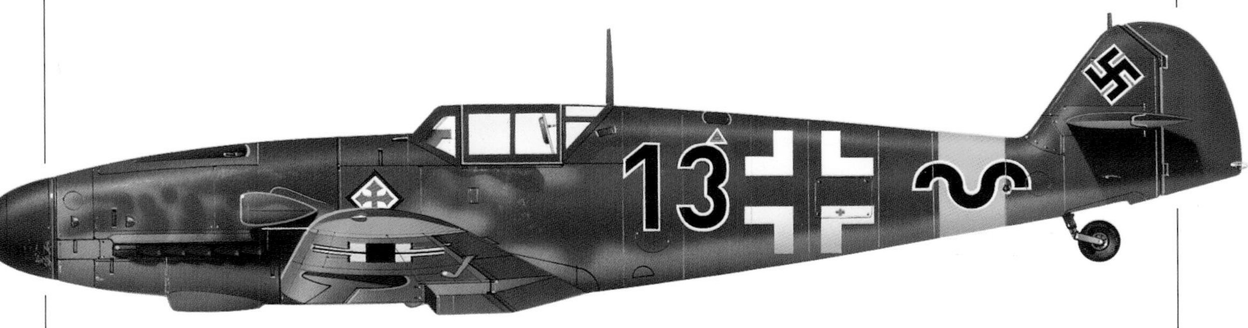

27
Bf 109G-2 'Black 13' of Oberleutnant Günther Rall, *Staffelkapitän* 8./JG 52, Gostanovka, August 1942

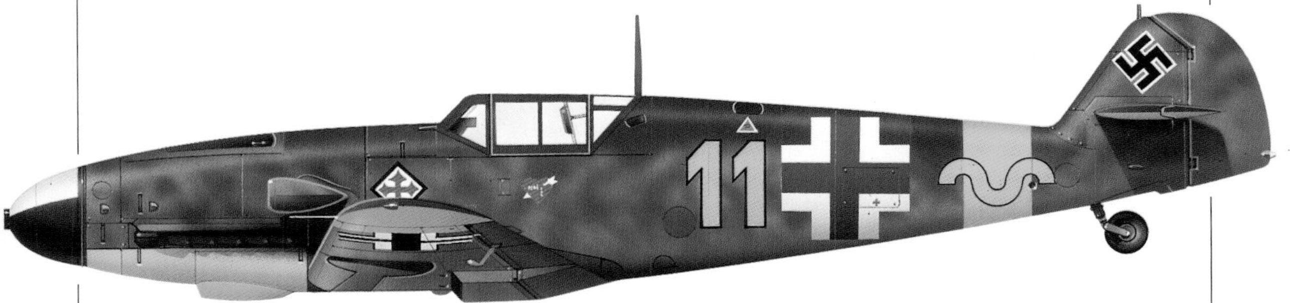

28
Bf 109G-2 'Yellow 11' of Oberleutnant Hermann Graf, *Staffelkapitän* 9./JG 52, Pitomnik, September 1942

29
Bf 109G-6 'Yellow 1' of Leutnant Erich Hartmann, *Staffelkapitän* 9./JG 52, Novo-Zaporozhe, October 1943

30
Bf 109F-2 'Black Chevron and Bars' of Major Günther Freiherr von Maltzahn, *Geschwaderkommodore* JG 53, Byelaya-Zerkov, July 1941

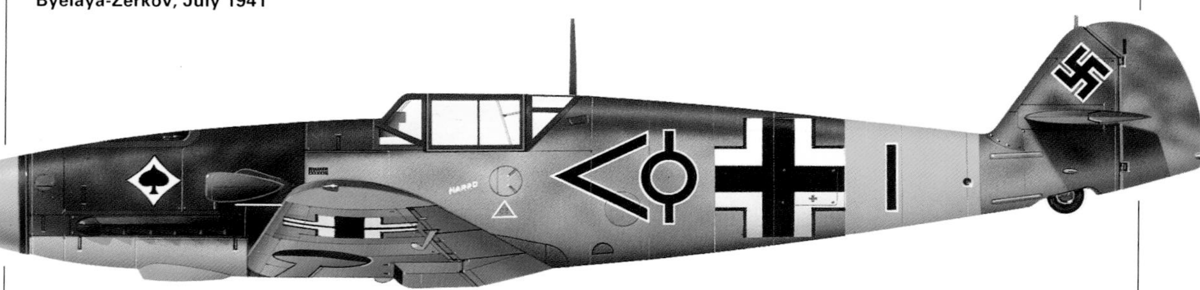

31
Bf 109F-2 'Black Chevron and Circle/Bar' of Leutnant Jürgen Harder, *Gruppenstab* III./JG 53, Sobolevo, June 1941

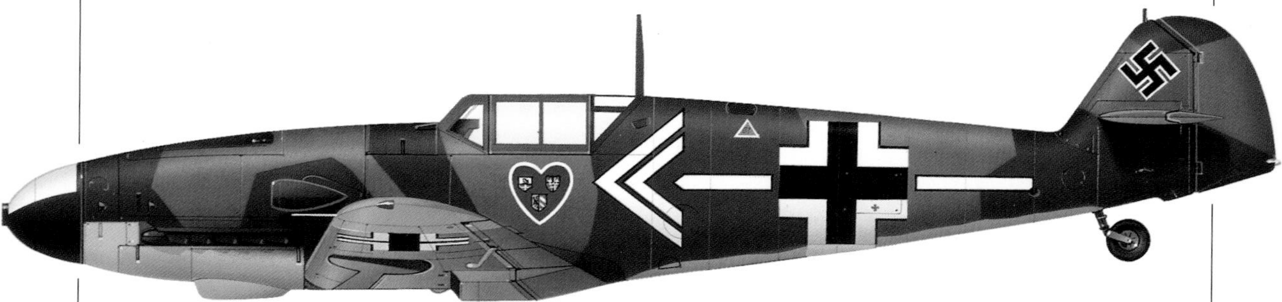

32
Bf 109G-2 'White Chevron and Bars' of Major Hannes Trautloft, *Geschwaderkommodore* JG 54, Siverskaya, Summer 1942

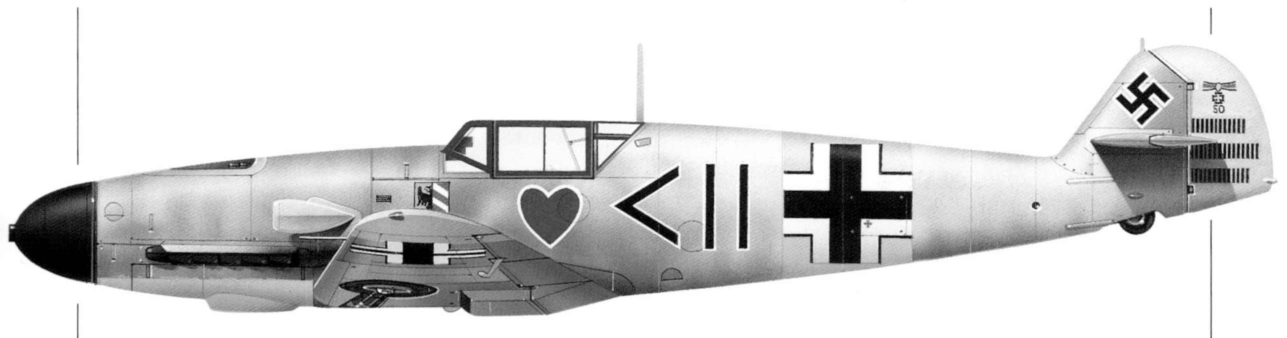

33
Bf 109F-2 'Black Chevron and Bars' of Hauptmann Hans Philipp, *Gruppenkommandeur* I./JG 54, Siverskaya, March 1942

34
Bf 109F 'White 8' of Leutnant Walter Nowotny, 1./JG 54, Ryelbitzi, Summer 1942

35
Bf 109F 'Black 8' of Feldwebel Otto Kittel, 2./JG 54, Krasnogvardeisk, May 1942

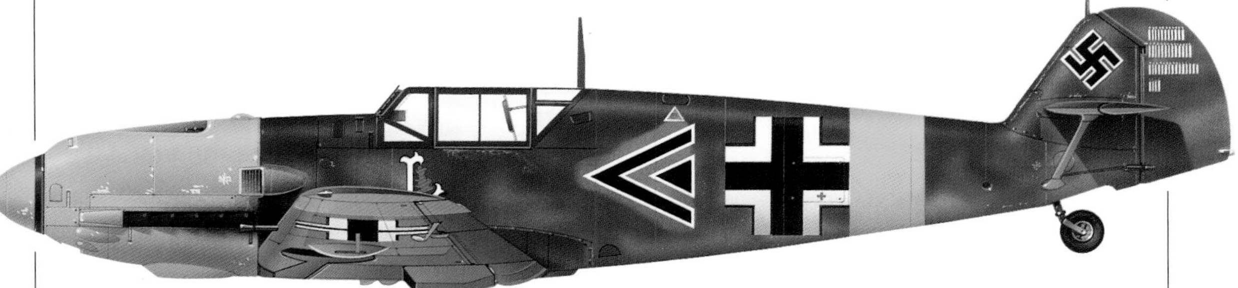

36
Bf 109E 'Black Double Chevron' of Hauptmann Herbert Ihlefeld, *Gruppenkommandeur* I.(J)/LG 2, Jassy/Rumania, July 1941

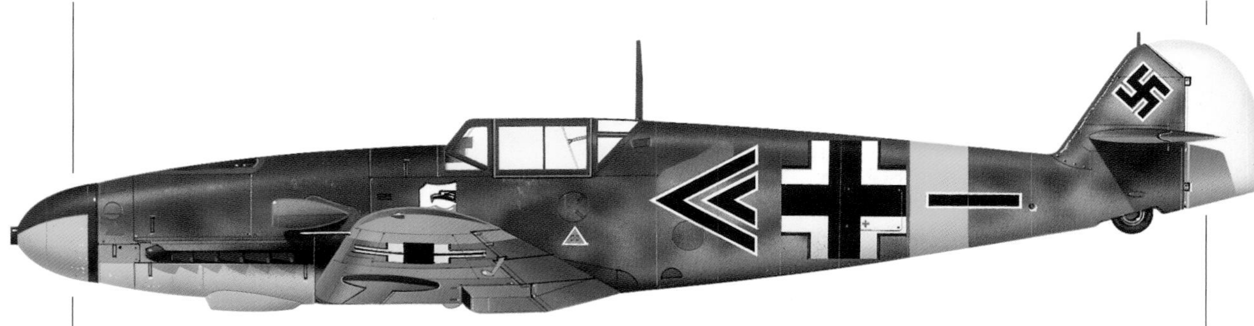

37
Bf 109F-4 'Black Double Chevron' of Hauptmann Anton Mader, *Gruppenkommandeur* II./JG 77, Stary Oskol, September 1942

38
Bf 109F-4 'Black 5' of Oberleutnant Anton Hackl, *Staffelkapitän* 5./JG 77, Kastornoje, September 1942

39
Bf 109G-2 'White Chevron/Yellow 1' of Hauptmann Kurt Ubben, *Gruppenkommandeur* III./JG 77, Lyuban, September 1942

40
Bf 109F 'White 1' of Oberleutnant Wolfdieter Huy, *Staffelkapitän* 7./JG 77, Lunga/Rumania, August 1941

THE ROAD TO DISASTER

The counter-attack on the outskirts of Moscow was not the only surprise the Soviets had in store for the ill-prepared German army. On 9 January 1942 Russian forces launched a second counter-offensive. This thrust was aimed at the boundary between the central and northern sectors. A breach some 60 miles (100 km) wide was soon driven between the two German fronts. This posed a serious threat to the rear of the German units encircling Leningrad to the north, who were now themselves in danger of being surrounded and cut off.

Much of JG 54's activity during 1942 was therefore governed by the twin needs to keep up their own pressure on beleaguered Leningrad while, at the same time, alleviating the Soviet pressure in the Lake Ilmen area at their backs.

In February alone, despite their now being outnumbered, the pilots of JG 54 claimed 201 kills for the loss of 18 of their own. Their successes were recognised by a clutch of awards. On 10 March Oberleutnant Max-Hellmuth Ostermann, *Staffelkapitän* of 7./JG 54, received the Oak Leaves for 62 victories, and two days later Hauptmann Hans Philipp, who had recently assumed command of I. *Gruppe*, became the first member of the *Geschwader* to be awarded the Swords (for 82 victories). On 31 March 'Fips' Philipp scored his century. But it fell to the relatively inexperienced Oberfeldwebel Rudolf Klemm of 8. *Staffel* to claim JG 54's 2000th kill of the war on 4 April.

It would take the *Geschwader* just over five months to add the next 1000 enemy aircraft to its collective scoreboard, although this figure was not achieved without cost. Among the summer's lengthening casualty lists was the *Kapitän* of 7. *Staffel*, Oberleutnant Max-Hellmuth Ostermann. Having been awarded the Swords on 17 May for reaching his century, he would add just two more to that total before falling victim to nine Soviet fighters over the Lake Ilmen front on 9 August.

Twenty-four hours later Hauptmann Karl Sattig, *Staffelkapitän* of 6./JG 54, was also brought down during a dogfight. Sattig was honoured with a posthumous Knight's Cross the following month. He had claimed 53 victories in the east, two of them by night.

The latter were the direct result of an initiative by the *Geschwaderkommodore* back at the beginning of the year. Hannes Trautloft had proposed that selected pilots should take off on bright moonlit nights and circle low over the snowy landscape of the Volkhov front north of Lake Ilmen ready to pounce on unwary Soviet bombers. These first nightfighter sorties of the war in the east soon began to pay dividends.

Between mid-January and the end of July 1942, JG 54 Bf 109s shot down 56 enemy aircraft during the hours of darkness. The most successful of the pilots taking part in Trautloft's 'experiment' was

Hauptmann Reinhard 'Seppl' Seiler, *Kommandeur* of III. *Gruppe*, whose final tally of 96 eastern front victories included 16 night kills during this period. Second came Oberleutnant Günther Fink with nine. But the greatest single achievement was that claimed by Leutnant Erwin Leykauf, for six of his eight nocturnal victories were Russian transports – all downed on the night of 22 June, and all in the space of just one hour!

By day the *Geschwader's* total of victories had continued to rise steadily despite the approach of autumn. Two recent Knight's Cross recipients, Leutnant Hans Beisswenger, *Staffelkapitän* of 6./JG 54, and Oberfeldwebel Max Stotz, had both gone on to double their scores in little more than four months to reach a century apiece. Each was awarded the Oak Leaves, Beisswenger on 30 September and Stotz exactly a month later.

On the other side of the coin there were those who were finding it more difficult to make their mark. Men such as Horst Ademeit, for example, who had joined JG 54 as an Unteroffizier in 1940, and then taken nearly two years to claim his first 20 kills. Another NCO pilot, Feldwebel Otto Kittel, had even fewer with just 15. Yet both these slow starters were also destined to achieve high scores.

In fact Beisswenger, Stotz, Ademeit and Kittel would all share a remarkably similar fate, joining the ranks of the eastern front's top scorers, each with a total of more than 150 Soviet aircraft destroyed, before they themselves were killed or posted missing. These events were to take place after JG 54 had converted to the Fw 190, however (see *Osprey Aircraft of the Aces 6 - Fw 190 Aces of the Russian Front* for further details).

The first *Staffeln* began to re-equip with the radial-engined Focke-Wulfs in February 1943, and almost as if to commemorate the passing of their trusty Bf 109s, Feldwebel Otto Kittel claimed JG 54's 4000th victory of the war on 19 February.

Forty-eight hours later II. *Gruppe* lost their *Kommandeur*. Major Hans Hahn – nicknamed 'Assi', and not to be confused with I./JG 3's Hans von Hahn – had been a long-time member of JG 2, and one of the Channel front's leading *Experten* with 68 western kills to his credit. He had moved east to take command of II./JG 54 on 1 November 1942 after the previous *Kommandeur*, Major Dieter Hrabak, had assumed the leadership of JG 52.

On 26 January 1943 Hans Hahn claimed his 100th victory (the same day, incidentally, that Max Stotz got his 150th). In just under a month he accounted for eight more Soviet aircraft, but then on 21 February engine failure brought him down behind enemy lines south of Lake Ilmen. A popular figure known throughout the *Jagdwaffe* for his natural ebullience, 'Assi' Hahn also possessed great inner strength, as he was to demonstrate during seven long years of Soviet captivity.

On the central sector during the early weeks of 1942 JG 51 had likewise to focus its attentions and energies in two different directions – towards the Soviets pushing westwards from Moscow, and against the counter-offensive simultaneously threatening *Heeresgruppe Mitte's* left flank.

The reappearance in numbers of the Red Air Force afforded JG 51's pilots ample opportunity to add to their growing scores. This in turn led to a number of decorations. Among the first of these was the Swords awarded to Hauptmann Heinz Bär on 16 February for 90 victories. 'Pritzl' Bär was another of the *Jagdwaffe's* true characters. He had been

Wearing his recently-awarded Swords, Heinz *'Pritzl'* Bär (in peaked cap) poses with three of I./JG 51's then leading *Experten*. They are, from left to right, Leutnant Heinrich Höfemeier (96 victories, killed in action on 7 August 1943), Leutnant Erwin Fleig (66 victories, PoW on 29 May 1942), Bär and Oberleutnant Heinrich Krafft (78 victories, missing in action on 14 December 1942)

Staffelkapitän of 12./JG 51 since July 1941. Subsequently serving as *Kommodore* of both JGs 1 and 3, he ended the war flying the Me 262 jet (see *Osprey Aircraft of the Aces 17 - German Jet Aces of World War 2* for further details). His final total of 220 kills included 96 claimed during his time on the eastern front.

On 18 March Oberleutnant Heinrich Krafft and Leutnant Hans Strelow both received the Knight's Cross, for 46 and 52 victories respectively. Six days (and 14 kills) later, Strelow was awarded the Oak Leaves. Just two days short of his 20th birthday, Hans Strelow was then the youngest wearer of the Oak Leaves in the entire *Wehrmacht*, but before the year was out both Krafft and Strelow had forced-landed behind enemy lines. 'Gaudi' Krafft was beaten to death by Russian soldiers, and Hans Strelow reportedly shot himself rather than suffer the same fate.

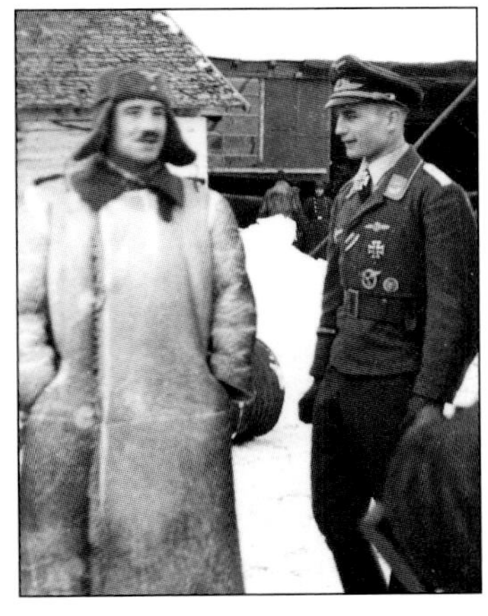

***'Gaudi'* (literally 'Fun and games') Krafft – seen in the photograph at the top of this page – had won his Knight's Cross on 18 March 1942. On the same day 5. *Staffel's* Leutnant Hans Strelow (right) had also been presented with the award during a visit to Bryansk by the new *General der Jagdflieger*, Adolf Galland. The latter appears to be taking no chances with the still bitter Russian winter! Strelow and Krafft shared a similar fate. Both would perish – albeit under very different circumstances – after forced-landing behind Soviet lines**

On 9 April Oberstleutnant Friedrich Beckh, who had succeeded Werner Mölders as *Kommodore* of JG 51, was promoted to a staff position in the RLM. 'Vati' Mölders would have been a difficult act for any commanding officer to follow, but Beckh was a distant and not particularly popular figure. Indeed, a number of pilots apparently did not even know that he had joined the *Geschwaderstab* back in 1940, believing he had been brought in from outside to take over JG 51!

Beckh's successor, the erstwhile *Kommandeur* of IV. *Gruppe*, was an entirely different type. Already sporting the Oak Leaves, Major Karl-Gottfried Nordmann soon stamped his personality on the *Geschwader*. One of the measures he took was to release 2./JG 51 from its predominantly fighter-bomber role – this *Staffel* had been flying mainly *Jabo* sorties since the beginning of *Barbarossa*.

Relieved of this chore, its pilots' scores rose dramatically, and none more so than that of Oberfeldwebel Joachim Brendel. Having been credited with his first kill in the early days of the campaign in the east, Brendel took a further nine months to claim a second. By war's end Hauptmann Joachim Brendel, *Kommandeur* of III./JG 51, and winner of the Knight's Cross and Oak Leaves, had emerged as the *Geschwader's* highest scorer on the eastern front with 189 Soviet aircraft destroyed – including over 90 heavily-armoured Ilyushin *Stormoviks*.

Despite there being something of a lull over JG 51's areas of operations during April and May, the *Geschwader* still suffered a number of

Judging by the guilty smile, Major Karl-Gottfried Nordmann, *Kommodore* of JG 51 'Mölders', is seen here carrying out a well-known pre-op ritual. But has he really been caught on camera in the act of watering the tailwheel – or is that small puddle behind the object in question the last vestige of winter's snow?

Little doubt here that this is the spring thaw proper as a Bf 109, still in winter camouflage, mushes its way across a waterlogged field

Mother Russia is nothing if not resilient and by the summer of 1942 the Luftwaffe's airfields were once again a riot of colour as the wild flowers bloomed. 7./JG 51's 'White 10' enjoys the lull before the coming storm

casualties. On 29 May – exactly a week after the disappearance of Hans Strelow – Leutnant Erwin Fleig, *Staffelkapitän* of 2./JG 51 and 66-victory *Experte*, bailed out over enemy territory and was taken prisoner.

Forty-eight hours later another Knight's Cross holder was lost when the *Kommandeur* of II. *Gruppe*, Hauptmann Josef Fözö, was badly injured in a take-off accident. Ex-Austrian air force and a *Condor Legion* veteran, Fözö would not return to combat flying. Earlier in May Oberleutnant Bernd Gallowitsch, who had since added 22 more kills to the 42 which had earned him the Knight's Cross on 24 February, had also been seriously injured. Unlike Fözö, he would return to operations, flying the He 162 with JG 1 during the final weeks of the war.

Pictured here as an Unteroffizier at the time of the award of his Knight's Cross (for 42 kills) back in October 1941 – hence the fetching fur headgear – Oberfeldwebel Franz-Josef Beerenbrock was the first member of JG 51 to surpass Mölders' century

Hauptmann Richard Leppla, *Kommandeur* of III./JG 51, was severely wounded in combat on 2 August 1942. Despite losing the vision in one eye, he endeavoured to remain operational, only to collide with a landing Ju 52 five days later. After hospitalisation, Leppla commanded various training units before being appointed *Kommodore* of JG 6 in mid-April 1945

In July the skies over the central sector flared into life again as the Soviets prepared for a new offensive. For a brief period the *Geschwader's* scoring rate rose to a level approaching that enjoyed in the opening phases of *Barbarossa*.

On 5 July Hauptmann Hartmann Grasser's II./JG 51 claimed 46 victories, the *Kommandeur* himself being credited with eight of them. Two of his pilots, Oberleutnant Karl-Heinz Schnell and Feldwebel Anton Hafner, accounted for seven each. The latter pilot was awarded the Knight's Cross on 23 August, for 60 kills, and would subsequently become JG 51's highest scorer of all with a total of 204 enemy aircraft destroyed before being killed in action in 1944.

On 2 August Oberfeldwebel Franz-Josef Beerenbrock of IV./JG 51 downed nine Soviet aircraft, taking his score to 102. He thus became the first pilot within the *Geschwader* to surpass Werner Mölders' century, and it earned him the Oak Leaves the following day.

But losses were continuing to rise too. Among August's 16 casualties were Hauptmann Richard Leppla, *Kommandeur* of III. *Gruppe*, who was seriously wounded (but who would return to frontline service for the last three weeks of the war as *Kommodore* of JG 6), and three *Staffelkapitäne*.

A Ju 87D of StG 2 'Immelmann' enjoys a close escort from one of I./JG 51's *Friedrichs* during the late summer of 1942 shortly before the *Gruppe* began to re-equip with the Fw 190

In the far north the new JG 5 was also tasked with Stuka escort duties. A solitary Bf 109 waits in the foreground as a *Staffel* of Ju 87s run up their engines preparatory to a massed take-off

The introduction into service of upgraded versions of the 'new generation' Soviet fighters, and the employment of improved tactics by their pilots, were beginning to erode the *Jagdwaffe's* hitherto undisputed superiority. But JG 51 was also about to receive new aircraft. Early in September I./JG 51 was withdrawn from the front to begin conversion on to the Fw 190. Other *Gruppen* followed in short order.

The Messerschmitt Bf 109 may have been disappearing from the ranks of JGs 51 and 54 on the central and northern sectors, but elsewhere on the eastern front it was still the mainstay of the German fighter force.

Early in 1942 a completely new *Jagdgeschwader* was formed in the far north. Made up of previously autonomous *Gruppen*, JG 5 was somewhat unusual in that it was deployed to combat both western and eastern opponents. While two of its *Gruppen* were stationed in central and southern Norway to guard against RAF incursions from across the North Sea, II. and III./JG 5 were based in northern Norway and Finland facing the Soviet Air Force.

Operating astride and above the Arctic Circle, the pilots of the two latter *Gruppen* fought an isolated, almost self-contained war. Their tasks included bomber- and Stuka-escort missions against the Russian port of Murmansk and the strategically vital railway line linking it to the south, as well as the defence of the Wehrmacht's own northernmost bases and lines of supply.

Heavily outnumbered from the outset, JG 5 nevertheless produced some of the highest scorers of the eastern front. Foremost amongst them was Leutnant, later Major, Heinrich Ehrler.

JG 5 had their own ideas about suitable camouflage for the Arctic theatre. This *Friedrich* of IV. *Gruppe* (note the small solid circle behind the fuselage cross) displays a favourite scheme consisting of a light wave-mirror 'scribble' over all upper surfaces

Arctic *Experte* Oberleutnant Walter Schuck of 7./JG 5 returns to Petsamo, zooming in low, wings waggling, to indicate to those watching below that he has just claimed another victory to add to his lengthening list of kills

Third in JG 5's trio of top scorers was ex-*Zerstörer* pilot Oberleutnant Theodor Weissenberger, *Kapitän* of 7. *Staffel*, who is pictured here wearing the Oak Leaves awarded on 2 August 1943 for 112 enemy aircraft destroyed . . .

Initially a member of the flak arm, Ehrler retrained as a fighter pilot in 1940. Rising through the ranks of JG 5, he commanded both the highly successful 6. *Staffel*, and then III. *Gruppe*, before being appointed *Geschwaderkommodore* in May 1944. References quoting his final tally of kills vary between 200 and 220. Despite having been awarded the Oak Leaves – on 2 August 1943 for 112 victories – and being nominated for the Swords, Major Ehrler left JG 5 under something of a cloud after being held officially responsible for the Luftwaffe's failure to protect the battleship *Tirpitz* from the RAF bombing raid which sank her in Norway's Tromsö Fjord on 12 November 1944.

Although sentenced by court-martial to three years' imprisonment (to commence after the 'final victory'), Heinrich Ehrler retrained yet again, this time on to the Me 262 jet fighter. Serving with JG 7, he was killed in action on 6 April 1945 – by deliberately ramming a B-17, according to some reports.

Two other Oak Leaves winners from JG 5 went on to fly the Me 262 with JG 7. Oberleutnant Walter Schuck's eastern front total fell just two short of 200, while Hauptmann Theodor Weissenberger claimed 175

. . . and a close-up of the rudder of Weissenberger's *Gustav* when his score had risen to 131 (a minor mystery here – a record of Weissenberger's victories lists kill no 131 as the second of a trio of Yak-9s all downed within the space of three minutes south of Luga on the afternoon of 16 February 1944, so why not 132 kill bars?). Compare this machine's camouflage scheme and elaborate rudder decoration with his earlier G-2 depicted in colour profile 11

Although not a high scorer himself (his final tally was 56), Oberleutnant – later Major – Horst Carganico was another of the *Jagdwaffe's* natural leaders. He commanded, in turn, the original *Jagdstaffel* Kirkenes (ex-1./JG 77, later 1./JGrzbV), 6./JG 5 and then II. and I./JG 5. Revealing a closer affinity to the art of Walt Disney, rather than the designs of ancient heraldry, his cowling is here embellished with a miniature Mickey Mouse . . .

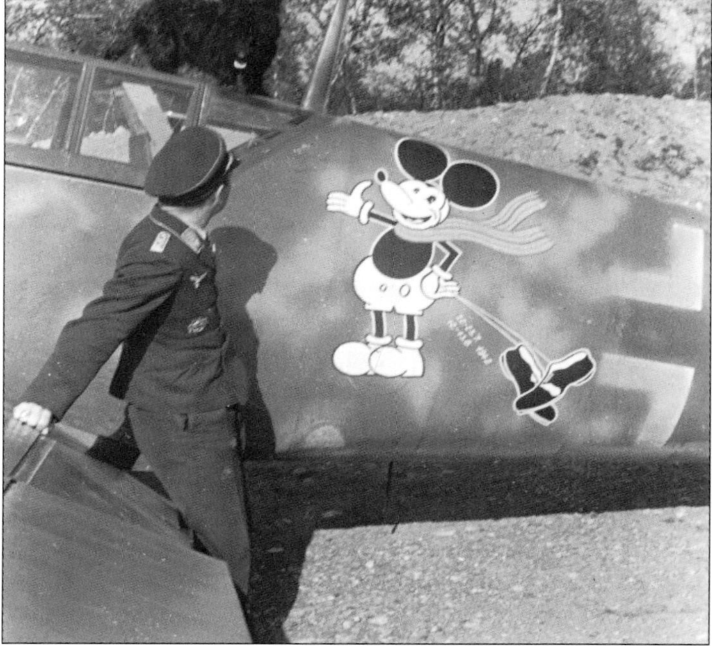

. . . which was later to grow somewhat in size! The extra pair of shoes, and the dates close alongside (22-23 July and 12-13 August 1942), refer to occasions when Carganico forced-landed and had to return to base on foot. His pet scottie, perched on the cockpit roof, had provided the inspiration for an earlier personal emblem when he was *Kapitän* of 1./JG 77. Major Carganico was killed in France on D-Day +10

Soviet aircraft, latterly as *Kommandeur* of II./JG 5, before assuming command of I. *Gruppe* in the west immediately prior to D-Day. Unlike Ehrler, both Schuck and Weissenberger survived the war. Coincidentally, each was credited with eight jet victories while serving with JG 7.

More than a dozen members of JG 5 received the Knight's Cross. Although not the first to be so honoured, Feldwebel Rudolf 'Rudi' Müller emerged as one of the *Geschwader's* first true *'Experten'*, downing five Red Air Force Hurricanes over the Kola Inlet on 23 April 1942. Twelve months later, almost to the day, he was himself shot down in the same area – by then his score stood at 94. Forced-landing on a frozen lake close to Murmansk, Rudolf Müller died in post-war Soviet captivity.

Like Müller, Oberfeldwebel Jakob Norz was another high-scoring NCO belonging to 6. *Staffel*. His final total of 117 included 12 Soviet aircraft downed in a single day. Later commissioned, Leutnant 'Jockel' Norz lost his life when he crashed in northern Norway following engine failure.

Spectacular as some of these individual Arctic successes undoubtedly were, the main focus of attention in 1942 was fixed on the southern sector of the front. This was to be the scene of the Wehrmacht's major summer offensive. *Fall Blau* (*Case Blue*) was launched on 28 June along a front stretching some 500 miles (800 km) from Kursk down to the Sea of Azov. Its initial objectives were quickly reached, and within days Hitler had expanded *Blau* into *Braunschweig* (*Brunswick*).

This new, more ambitious operation had twin aims – the seizure of both Stalingrad, an important industrial and communications centre on the River Volga, and the rich oilfields of the Caucasus. This meant, however, that the two armies involved had to proceed along dangerously diverging lines of advance until, finally, a yawning 185-mile (300-km) gap had opened up between 6. *Armee* in Stalingrad and 17. *Armee* on the Caucasus front. Furthermore, for the first time since the campaign in Poland, the German ground forces were lacking the one essential ingredient to a successful *Blitzkrieg* – overwhelming air support.

Back to the spring of 1942 and the southern sector for these four shots, illustrating the aftermath of a spectacular synchronised somersault. Coming in to land side-by-side at Otozeni, near Kharkov, on 5 May 1942, these two pilots of III./JG 77 failed to spot that part of the field was waterlogged. The result was a simultaneous nose-over, with both machines ending up on their backs

A closer look at one of the hapless *Friedrichs* ('Yellow 5'), wheels in the air and cockpit partially open

It is estimated that the Luftwaffe units deployed on the southern sector at this time amounted to only a quarter of the strength required to properly cover *Braunschweig's* two-pronged offensive. Combined with the growing numbers of Soviet aircraft appearing in the area, it was a recipe for disaster.

Having remained responsible for the southernmost part of the front, including the Black Sea coast and the Crimea, throughout the winter and spring of 1942, JG 77's component *Gruppen* began to be dispersed within days of the launch of the summer offensive. This seemingly inexplicable move, weakening yet further the *Jagdwaffe's* already inadequate presence in southern Russia, serves to illustrate just how overstretched Germany's fighter forces were becoming.

Early in July I./JG 77 was transferred to the Mediterranean. At the same time Hauptmann Anton Mader's II. *Gruppe* moved to the region north of Kharkov to support the left flank of the 6. *Armee* as it set out on its fateful drive on Stalingrad. Having completed its re-equipment with Bf 109G-2s in August, III./JG 77 deployed even

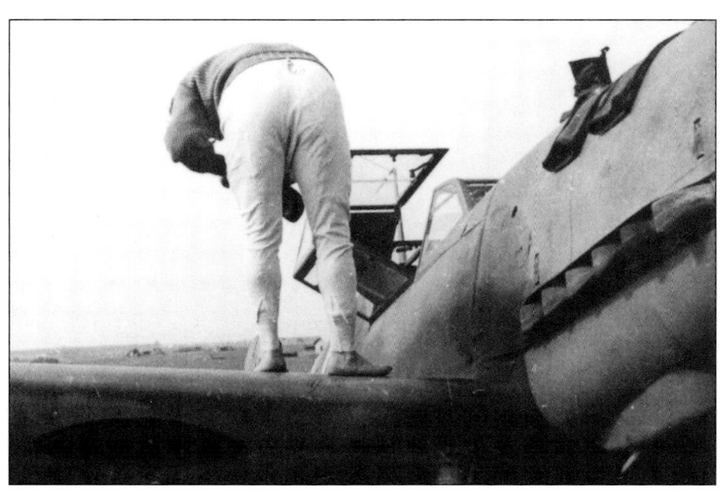

Fortunately both pilots were able to escape unharmed, suffering nothing worse than a ducking

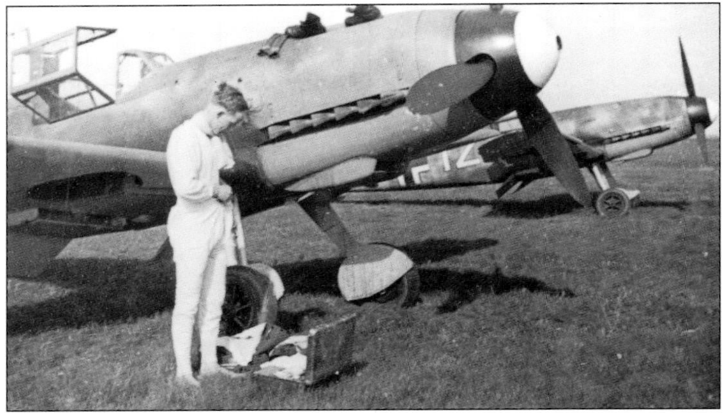

With his boots and socks laid out to dry in the gun troughs of a neighbouring machine, at least one of the pair was able to retrieve his *Jabuko* (fighter pilot's overnight case) from his own overturned aircraft and change into dry underclothes!

further northwards in September adding its weight to the continuing pressure on Leningrad. The following month II. and III. *Gruppen* were withdrawn from Russia altogether to join I./JG 77 in North Africa.

During their final four months on the eastern front II. and III./JG 77 had been credited with some 775 Soviet aircraft destroyed between them. Over a quarter of this total had been claimed by just four pilots, all of whom were members of II. *Gruppe*, and included the three *Staffelkapitäne*.

Hauptmann Heinrich Setz, *Kapitän* of 4./JG 77, was the only one of the four to have been awarded the Knight's Cross prior to the launch of *Braunschweig*. Yet all would be sporting the Oak Leaves before leaving for North Africa, for

In August 1942 III./JG 77 exchanged its Bf 109Fs for early model *Gustavs*. The pilot to the right in front of this G-2 *'Kanonenboot'* (Gunboat), pictured on the Leningrad front in September, is future *Experte* and Knight's Cross winner Oberfeldwebel Johann Pichler. Note III. *Gruppe's* 'Wolf's head' badge

Hauptmann Heinrich Setz, *Staffelkapitän* of 4./JG 77, was already wearing the Oak Leaves when he downed a brace of Yak-1s on 24 July 1942 to take his total to exactly 100. The newly fledged 'centurion' clambers from the cockpit of his *Friedrich*. This time the badge on prominent display is the 'Sea eagle's head' of II. *Gruppe*

each had added 50 or more kills to his individual score to take it above the century mark.

Setz's 54 victories in these closing weeks had raised his eastern front total to 132. Oberleutnant Erwin Clausen, 6./JG 77's *Staffelkapitän*, scored 63 between July and September, which took his tally of Soviet victories to 114. Both Setz and Clausen would be killed in action in the west the following year while serving as *Gruppenkommandeure* of I./JG 27 and I./JG 11 respectively.

The *Staffelkapitän* of 5./JG 77, Oberleutnant Anton 'Toni' Hackl, claimed 56 victories during this period and left Russia with 105 eastern front kills. Feldwebel Ernst-Wilhelm Reinert, a member of Setz's 4. *Staffel*, achieved similar results, his 50 victories raising his Soviet total to 103. Subsequently adding a considerable number of western kills to their scoreboards, and winning the Swords in the process, Hackl and Reinert both managed to survive the war – the former as *Kommodore* of JG 11 with a final total of 192, and the latter as *Kommandeur* of IV./JG 27 with 174.

The transfer of JG 77 meant that yet another *Jagdgeschwader* had departed the Russian scene. But one *Jagdgruppe* which had left earlier for the Mediterranean was brought back in the later spring of 1942 to help bolster the *Jagdwaffe's* support of the coming summer offensive.

Between the end of May and the beginning of October I./JG 53 claimed an amazing 900+ victories as it, too, accompanied 6. *Armee's* advance on Stalingrad. And although many pilots added significantly to their individual totals during the *Gruppe's* temporary recall to the eastern front, once again there were four outstanding performances, which this time accounted for more than a third of all claims made.

Oberleutnant (later Hauptmann) Friedrich-Karl Müller, the *Staffelkapitän* of 1./JG 53, had already been awarded the Knight's Cross (for 22 victories) in September 1941, and had since added a trio of Hurricanes over Malta. On the road to Stalingrad he amassed 76 more kills, culminating in a brace of Soviet aircraft downed on 19 September, which took his score to 101, and earned him the Oak Leaves.

Hard on Müller's heels came two others – 3./JG 53's *Staffelkapitän*, Oberleutnant Wolfgang Tonne, and his erstwhile wingman, Feldwebel Wilhelm Crinius, both of whom had claimed their 96th victim on that same 19 September. Each got another kill 24 hours later. Although no longer flying together as a *Rotte* (two-aircraft formation), officer and NCO agreed to try for simultaneous centuries the next day. But luck was not with them. Tonne managed just one victory, while Crinius claimed a double. Success came on 22 September, however, with Crinius getting one more for his hundred and Tonne's three taking his score to 101.

Tonne had originally arrived back in Russia in May with a mere 13 kills to his credit. He had added 41 more to win his Knight's Cross on 6 September, and now, just 18 days later, he received the Oak Leaves. Crinius' feat was all the more remarkable in that his century had been achieved entirely in the Soviet Union over the past 16 weeks (he had opened his scoreboard on 9 June with a pair of *Stormoviks*). On 22 September his 100 victories won him the Knight's Cross and the Oak Leaves both on the same day! The two pilots' careers continued to run on parallel lines until each came to an end over Tunisia early in 1943 (see

Every century achieved gave rise to celebrations involving congratulatory placards and/or garlands and suitable liquid refreshment. Oberleutnant Friedrich-Karl *'Tutti'* Müller, *Kapitän* of 1./JG 53, appears to be coping admirably with two out of the three at Tusow, on the Stalingrad front, on 19 September. Like Setz (featured at the bottom of the previous page), Müller would later be killed in action on the western front

Another of I./JG 53's high scorers on the road to Stalingrad was Oberleutnant Wolfgang Tonne, *Kapitän* of 3. *Staffel*. He is pictured here (along with his canine friend) earlier in the campaign while still a leutnant, and with a victory tally only just into double figures

Osprey Aircraft of the Aces 2 - Bf 109 Aces of the Mediterranean and North Africa for further details).

The fourth most successful pilot during the *Gruppe's* brief sojourn in Russia would not survive to make the return trip to the Mediterranean in October. 1. *Staffel's* Leutnant Walter Zellot scored his 70th kill of the present offensive on 9 September. It took his overall total to 85, but would also be his last. The following day the tail of his *Gustav* was shot off – reportedly by 'friendly' flak – over Stalingrad. Having been caught at low-level, there was insufficient height for his parachute to open.

As the above suggests, the Battle of Stalingrad had now been joined. In fact, 6. *Armee* had reached the outskirts of the city late in August. To the south, German mountain troops had raised their flag on Mount Elbrus, the highest peak in the Caucasus. But this was a gesture more for home newsreel consumption than of strategic significance, for neither of *Braunschweig's* stated objectives had been secured. The defenders of Stalingrad were holding on grimly, and the coveted oilfields remained tantalisingly out of reach on the far side of the Caucasus range.

Following the departure of JG 77 and I./JG 53, there were just two *Jagdgeschwader* left to cover the huge southern sector area as the second winter of the war in the east closed in – JG 3, which had accompanied von

Wearing the Oak Leaves with Swords, awarded on 19 May 1942 for 106 victories, Oberleutnant Hermann Graf (second from right) relaxes in the company of three of his 9./JG 52 Knight's Cross NCO *Experten*. They are, from left to right, Oberfeldwebel Ernst Süss (approximately 60 kills, killed in action on 20 December 1943), Feldwebel Hans Dammers (113 kills, died of wounds on 13 March 1944) and Oberfeldwebel Josef 'Jupp' Zwernemann (approximately 106 kills, killed in action on 8 April 1944)

Hermann Graf's 150th kill was reportedly claimed while flying this 'Yellow 11' . . .

. . . although the achievement was 'officially' recorded on the rudder of his regular mount, 'Yellow 1'

Paulus' 6. *Armee* across the steppe to Stalingrad, and JG 52, which had taken over JG 77's responsibilities for the Black Sea and Caucasus fronts.

1942 was to witness the start of JG 52's steady rise to prominence as the most successful, and highest-scoring, of all eastern front Bf 109 *Jagdgeschwader* – not least because, for much of the time thereafter, it was the only eastern front Bf 109 *Jagdgeschwader*! But it was also fortunate in having a considerable number of truly exceptional pilots within its ranks.

Most of 1942 was dominated by the outstanding success of Leutnant Hermann Graf, who was awarded all four of Germany's highest decorations in the space of just eight months. On 24 January he won the Knight's Cross for 42 eastern front kills. Exactly two months later he became *Staffelkapitän* of 9./JG 52. Seven victories on 14 May elevated his score to 104, for which he received the Oak Leaves three days later. And just two days and two kills after that, he was honoured with the Swords.

On 4 September Graf became the second pilot to reach 150 (behind Major Gordon Gollob, who had achieved this total on 29 August while serving as caretaker *Kommodore* of JG 52). Now promoted to Oberleutnant, Graf's score continued to mount. 172 victories earned him the highest award of all, the Diamonds, on 16 September. And on 2 October he became the first member of the *Jagdwaffe* to attain the double century.

Although overshadowed by Graf's achievements, many other pilots were also putting in sterling performances. It is a measure of JG 52's growing success that over 20 Knight's Crosses and seven sets of Oak Leaves were awarded to the *Geschwader* during the course of 1942.

A typical *Feldflugplatz* (forward landing ground) as occupied by I./JG 52 in the late summer of 1942. The air of apparent tranquillity is deceptive, however, for each camouflaged pup tent is topped by its owner's steel helmet. A necessary precaution . . .

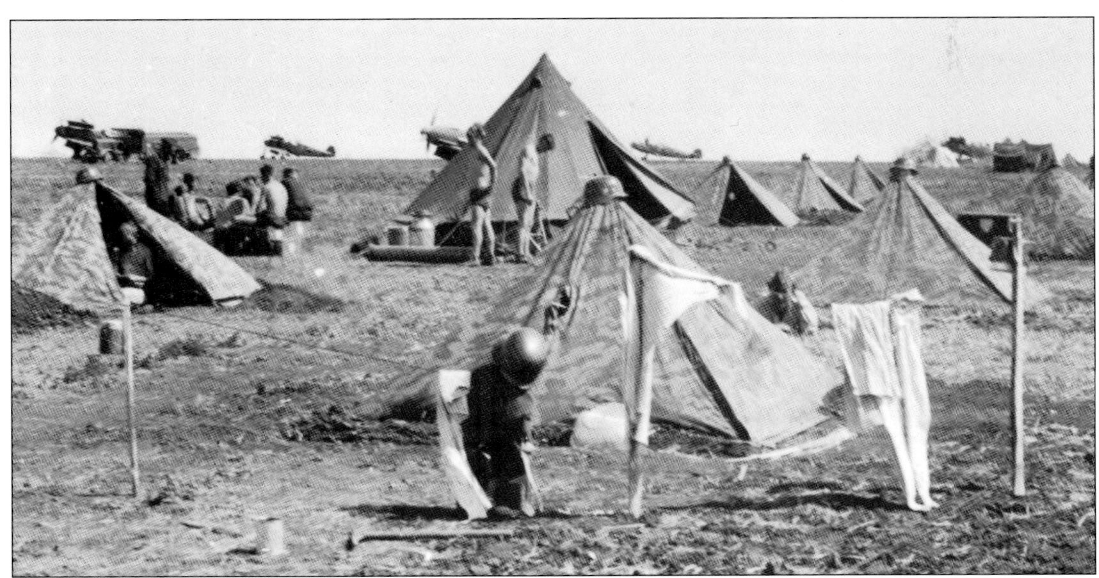

... for Soviet air raids were becoming increasingly frequent. The result of one such strike by Russian ground-attack aircraft – a Bf 109 totally wrecked by cannon fire (note the dead mechanic by the starboard wing root), with another blazing furiously in the background

But the groundcrews had to carry on with their essential duties despite the danger. Ever resourceful, the 'black men' of II./JG 52 have rolled the main wheels of these F-4s into shallow trenches, and jacked up their tails, to make it easier to work on the engines and adjust the armament

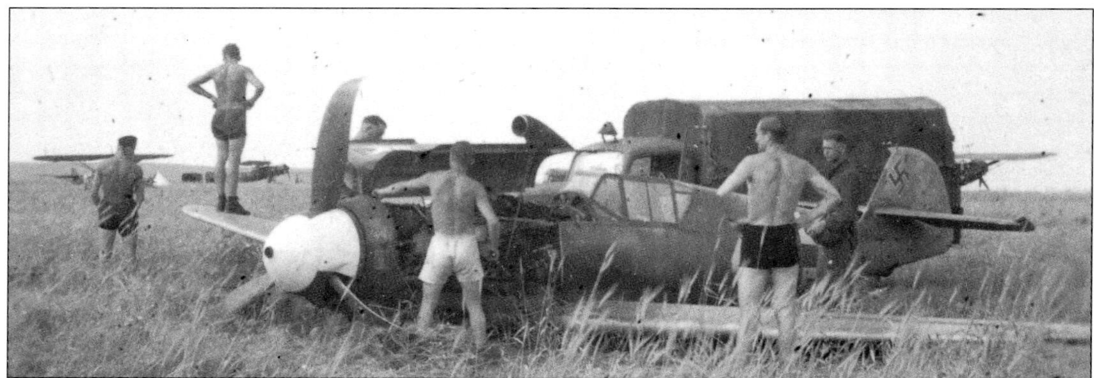

Soviet resistance in the air was also on the increase. This damaged *Friedrich* of II./JG 52 has made it back to friendly territory – a decidedly lush meadow housing the Hs 126s of a tactical reconnaissance *Staffel* . . .

. . . but the pilot of this III. *Gruppe* machine has not been so fortunate. A Red Army infantryman peers suspiciously into the radio compartment

A line-up of II./JG 52's new *Gustavs* in the early autumn of 1942. Although none display any unit badges, the two nearest machines have the densely mottled engine cowlings associated with this *Gruppe*

The majority of the recipients – the likes of Karl Hammerl, Ernst Süss, Heinz-Wilhelm Ahnert and Karl Steffen, all with scores in the high 50s and 60s – are now little remembered, but some deserve fuller mention. One such pilot is Feldwebel Leopold Steinbatz, who received JG 52's second Knight's Cross of the year on 14 February for 42 kills.

'Bazi' Steinbatz regularly flew as wingman to Hermann Graf. During May he scored 35 kills, and on 2 June won the Oak Leaves when his total reached 83. Less than a fortnight later, on 15 June, three victories took him to one short of his century, but he failed to return from this last mission, having himself fallen victim to AA fire while still over enemy territory. On 23 June Oberfeldwebel Leopold Steinbatz became the first NCO of the entire *Wehrmacht* to be honoured with the Swords, albeit posthumously.

On 3 June a Petlyakov Pe-2 twin-engined bomber despatched by Oberleutnant Helmut Bennenmann, *Staffelkapitän* of 3./JG 52, had provided the *Geschwader* with its 2000th victory of the war. But the rapidly lengthening scoreboard was not being achieved without cost. Only the day before, on 2 June, JG 52 had lost its first *Kommodore* to enemy action when Major Wilhelm Lessmann was also downed by Soviet flak.

His successor lasted less than three weeks. Returning to frontline service after his short stint at the RLM, the aloof Oberstleutnant

Featuring a similar cowling, 'Chevron 2' was often flown by Unteroffizier Hans Waldmann as wingman to II./JG 52's *Gruppenkommandeur* Johannes Steinhoff. The future *Experte* had a narrow escape in September 1942 when a Soviet anti-aircraft shell shredded his rudder (for a later aircraft of Waldmann's see colour profile 25)

Major Helmut Bennemann who, as a Hauptmann and *Kommandeur* of I./JG 52, claimed his *Gruppe's* 600th and 800th kills of the war. A month prior to the latter event Bennemann had received the Knight's Cross for a personal score of 50

Friedrich Beckh, who had made such little impression at the head of JG 51, was given scant time to leave his mark on JG 52. He was posted missing after a ground-attack mission east of Kharkov on 21 June. It was following Beckh's unexpectedly quick loss that JG 77's Major Gordon Gollob was brought in as acting *Kommodore* for eight weeks (during which time he claimed 43 kills, culminating in his 150th).

In mid-July I. and III. *Gruppen* began re-equipping with *Gustavs*. By this stage *Braunschweig's* southern spearheads were biting deep into the Caucasus. But while II. and III./JG 52 dutifully followed the ground advance, I. *Gruppe*, commanded now by Hauptmann Helmut Bennemann, was employed as a 'fire brigade' formation – Luftwaffe parlance for a unit sent at short notice to any area where sudden danger threatened (another telling indication of the paucity of fighter forces on the eastern front).

One of Bennemann's then *Staffelkapitäne*, and his successor at the head of I./JG 52, was Hauptmann Johannes Wiese. His Knight's Cross was awarded on 5 January 1943 for 51 victories

Shuttling between the southern and central sectors – ranging from the Kerch Peninsula on the Black Sea to the Moscow region and beyond – I./JG 52 was in near constant action. On 23 August another Pe-2 brought down by Bennemann was the *Gruppe's* 600th victory since hostilities began. Just over a month later, on 29 September, a LaGG-3 claimed by Hauptmann Johannes Wiese, *Staffelkapitän* of 2./JG 52, took their collective total to 700. The *Kommandeur's* 62nd, a MiG-3 downed on 2 November, raised the figure to 800. Such pressure could not be sustained indefinitely, however, and 48 hours later I./JG 52 handed over its remaining *Gustavs* to JG 3 and retired to Rostov to re-equip yet again.

Nor had there been any lack of aerial opposition over the Caucasus front in the interim, as the growing scores and associated awards among

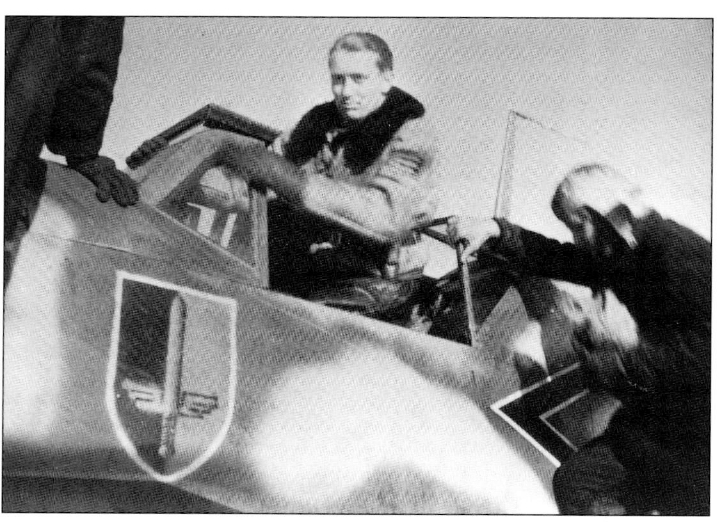

Hauptmann Johannes Steinhoff, *Kommandeur* of II./JG 52, is seen easing himself into the cockpit of his *Gustav* – complete with the *Geschwader's* 'Winged sword' badge – in the Crimea in the late autumn of 1942

II. and III. *Gruppen* amply demonstrated.

Two of the Knight's Crosses won on 23 August had gone to members of Hauptmann Johannes Steinhoff's II./JG 52. Oberleutnant Gerhard Barkhorn, *Kapitän* of 4. *Staffel*, received his for 59 victories. Leutnant Heinz Schmidt had eight fewer kills, yet it was the latter who first reached the century, which earned him the Oak Leaves on 16 September. 'Johnny' Schmidt, who later became *Staffelkapitän* of 6./JG 52, might well have emerged as one of the true 'greats' of the eastern front had he not been shot down – in error, it is believed, by a Hungarian fighter – in September 1943 when his score was standing at 173.

II./JG 52's Leutnant Heinz 'Johnny' Schmidt. The combination of Bf 109F and the state of undress of the mechanic would seem to indicate that this photograph was taken a little earlier than the one featuring his *Kommandeur*, 'Macki' Steinhoff – the floral tribute suggests that this event was perhaps Schmidt's 50th kill, or the announcement of his Knight's Cross shortly thereafter on 23 August

In III. *Gruppe* Hermann Graf continued to reign supreme. But one of his fellow *Staffelkapitäne*, Oberleutnant Günther Rall of 8./JG 52, was just resuming the climb which would ultimately take him into the *Jagdwaffe's* top three. Rall had been seriously wounded back in November 1941. Now, on 3 September 1942, and less than a week after returning to operations, he was awarded the Knight's Cross for 65 kills. The following month, on 26 October, Rall's century would bring with it the Oak Leaves.

During that same October – by which time eastern front scores in triple figures, if not exactly commonplace, were no longer altogether rare – four young leutnants, 'freshly-baked' from fighter training school, arrived at JG 52's *Stab* HQ at Maikop in the Caucasus.

Geschwaderkommodore Major Dietrich Hrabak's welcoming pep talk was cut short by the crash-landing of a flak-damaged Bf 109 on the field outside. Somewhat chastened by this introduction to the realities of frontline service, the four were flown on 48 hours later to Soldatskaya, the home of Major Hubertus von Bonin's III. *Gruppe*. Here, they were paired off between 7. and 9. *Staffeln*, and each was assigned to an experienced NCO pilot whose job it was to show them the ropes.

Oberfeldwebel Edmund Rossmann's charge was eager – perhaps too eager. On their first contact with the enemy he overtook his leader, sprayed bullets in the general direction of 'two dark green aircraft', got lost, and forced-landed out of fuel 32 km (20 miles) away from base. It was not an auspicious beginning.

Three weeks later, on 5 November, he got a second chance. One of a *Schwarm* (formation of four aircraft) attacking a force of 18 Il-2s, escorted by ten LaGG-3 fighters, he succeeded in downing one of the heavily-armoured *Stormoviks*. Although debris from his victim damaged his own machine, and resulted in another forced-landing, Leutnant Erich Hartmann – destined to become the most successful fighter pilot in aviation history – had scored his first kill.

It would take him three months to claim a second – three months which were to seal the fate of the 6. *Armee* at Stalingrad.

Severely wounded the previous year, and following a long convalescence, Oberleutnant Günther Rall returned to his 8./JG 52 on 28 August. Within two months he was awarded the Knight's Cross and the Oak Leaves, and would end the war as the world's third-highest scoring fighter pilot

STALINGRAD AND ZITADELLE

The main fighter unit tasked with supporting the ground troops' advance on Stalingrad was Oberstleutnant Günther Lützow's JG 3. This *Geschwader* had been re-assembled on the southern sector in the late spring of 1942, with *Stab* and II. *Gruppe* returning from the Mediterranean, and III./JG 3 being brought back from a brief stint in the Lake Ilmen area in the north. A new I. *Gruppe* had been activated to make good the original I./JG 3's transfer to the west and re-designation as II./JG 1.

As von Paulus' army forged eastwards across the dry, dusty steppe towards the Volga, JG 3 faced increasing opposition in the skies overhead. The determination of the enemy to blunt the German offensive and to defend Stalingrad is indicated by the severity of their losses. By year's end JG 3's pilots would have claimed over 2200 aerial victories.

Wearing JG 3's distinctive 1942 'Mediterranean mix' camouflage scheme (see colour profile 7), an F-4/trop of the new I. *Gruppe* displays the recently introduced 'Winged U' (for 'Udet') *Geschwader* badge on the cowling, and I./JG 3's own 'crossed cutlasses' below the windshield

Groundcrew swarm over the F-4/trop (note mounting holes for the absent dust filter immediately below the gun trough) of Hauptmann Wolfgang Ewald. This photograph was reportedly taken in July 1942, although the reason for the obvious excitement remains unknown – unless perhaps it is the announcement of Ewald's appointment as *Kommandeur* of III./JG 3 (he replaced Major Karl-Heinz Greisert, who was killed in action against I-16s on 22 July)

The markings on this *Friedrich* identify it as the mount of III./JG 3's *TO*, Leutnant Heinrich Graf von Einsiedel, and the five kill bars on the rudder (two surmounted by roundels and three by red stars) definitely date it as July 1942 – von Einsiedel's fifth was a Pe-2 downed on the 4th of that month. Both von Einsiedel and Ewald, seen in the photograph at the base of the previous page, would come down behind enemy lines, near Stalingrad and Kursk respectively, and spend many years in Soviet hands

The *Geschwader's* success was broad-based. During this period no fewer than 19 pilots, all with totals ranging between the high 40s and 60s, were awarded the Knight's Cross, but only one actually claimed 100 kills on the road to Stalingrad.

Ever since *Kommodore* Günther Lützow's century the previous October – and its attendant ban on his further combat flying – the *Stabsschwarm* had been without a regular leader in the air. In May 1942 Hauptmann Wolf-Dietrich Wilcke, ex-*Kommandeur* of III./JG 53, was brought in to fulfil this function. Already wearing the Knight's Cross, and with 38 victories to his credit, 'Fürst' Wilcke quickly proved his worth, accounting for 118 of the *Geschwaderstab's* final 191 kills on the eastern front (34 of the remainder went to Adjutant Hauptmann Walther Dahl of later Fw 190 *Sturm* fame).

On 12 August Wolf-Dietrich Wilcke officially assumed command of JG 3. Less than a month later, on 9 September, he was awarded the Oak Leaves for 100 victories. A further 55 kills by the end of December earned him the Swords, and then it was Major Wilcke's turn to face a ban on all further operational flying.

Two of the earlier Knight's Cross winners had also received the Oak Leaves for attaining an overall total of 100 victories by the late summer of 1942. The three victories (a solitary Hurricane and a pair of *Stormoviks*) claimed by Oberleutnant Viktor Bauer, *Staffelkapitän* of 9./JG 3, on 25 July took his score to 102, and resulted in the Oak Leaves the following day.

Almost exactly a month later II. *Gruppe's Kommandeur*, Hauptmann Kurt Brändle, was also credited with three victories – including a brace of LaGG-3s – which raised his total to 102. He was presented with the Oak Leaves on 27 August. Unlike Bauer, who was transferred to a training unit shortly after receiving his award, and survived the war, Major

Wearing the Oak Leaves (awarded on 27 August for achieving his century four days earlier) Hauptmann Kurt Brändle, *Kommandeur* of II./JG 3, displays more than a passing interest in an engine change being carried out on one of his *Gruppe's* fighters

Kurt Brändle was killed in action in the west late in 1943 with a final score standing at 172.

By late August 6. *Armee* was fighting its way into Stalingrad. During the second week of September JG 3 began moving up to Pitomnik, a small airstrip some 12 miles (20 km) to the west of the city. Suitably enlarged and fortified, it would serve as the *Geschwader's* main base for the next two months. It also briefly housed elements of JG 52 and I./JG 53.

But the storm was about to break . . .

Despite a long and bloody struggle, von Paulus' men were unable to prise Stalingrad's defenders from their last desperate toeholds among the ruined buildings lining the west bank of the Volga. Then, on 19 November, as the street-fighting in the city was approaching its climax, the Soviets suddenly counter-attacked.

In a huge pincer movement, strong forces crossed the Volga to the north and south of Stalingrad. Smashing through the Axis flanks, they joined up 43 miles (70 km) to the west of the city three days later. The

Come the Russian autumn, come the Russian mud. A pilot of II./JG 3 wades towards his G-2 *'Kanonenboot'* as groundcrew struggle to remove its protective tarpaulin . . .

. . . having clambered up on to the wing, the pilot tries to lend a hand . . .

. . . before lowering himself down on to the port mainwheel and letting the experts finish the job. Now all he has to do is get 'White 6' out of that flooded dispersal!

As the second winter of the campaign closed in on the eastern front the *Jagdwaffe* put into practice the lessons hard-learned from the previous year's unpreparedness. Dispersal pens were strengthened against both the elements and enemy bombing raids . . .

. . . and its fighters had their wheel and undercarriage leg covers removed to prevent compacted snow building up between them and causing take-off and landing accidents . . .

besiegers had become the besieged. Over 20 German and satellite divisions were encircled and cut off, and among the 250,000 men trapped within the Stalingrad perimeter were more than 200 JG 3 groundcrew, mainly from I. *Gruppe*, who had been unable to escape from Pitomnik.

Meanwhile, the bulk of the *Geschwader* had retreated to Tazinskaya and Morozovskaya, about 185 miles (300 km) to the south-west of Stalingrad. These two airfields, universally referred to as Tazi and Moro, were the

. . . and suitably attired groundcrew used rubber hammers and wooden mallets to keep flying surfaces free from snow and ice

There was also an efficient aircraft recovery and repair organisation. But the speed of the surprise Soviet counter-offensive at Stalingrad overran the Chir railhead collecting point before these damaged machines could be transported to the rear. The black triangle on the Bf 109E in the foreground identifies it as a ground-attack aircraft of II./SchlG 1. But note JG 53's 'Ace-of-Spades' and JG 3's 'Winged U' on the noses of the Bf 109s to the left . . .

. . . while this shot of another area of the Chir facility (including the wing of a Rumanian Air Force Bf 109) shows at right, below the gantry, 3./JG 3's 'Yellow 7' still wearing the modified Mediterranean camouflage of the previous spring

major bases from which was mounted the ill-fated attempt to supply 6. *Armee* by air. And to offer the gallant but near defenceless Ju 52 transports some protection while inside the perimeter, and during turnaround on the ground at Pitomnik, Major Wilcke called for volunteers to form the so-called *Platzschutzstaffel* (Airfield defence squadron) Pitomnik.

Some 22 pilots responded to the appeal. Led by Hauptmann Rudolf Germeroth, *Staffelkapitän* of 3./JG 3, they would remain in Pitomnik – under conditions and amidst scenes which quickly degenerated from the merely appalling to the truly horrific – until mid-January 1943.

During these two months of unimaginable hardship, they nonetheless managed to claim 130 Soviet aircraft destroyed. The *Platzschutzstaffel's*

This anonymous *Gustav*, following another's tracks across a snow-covered field in the gloom of a mid-winter's day, typifies the conditions under which the *Platzschutzstaffel* Pitomnik operated. However, it cannot convey the horror that was unfolding around them as 6. *Armee* fought, suffered and died

most successful pilot was Feldwebel Kurt Ebener of II. *Gruppe*, whose 35 kills took his total to 52, and won him the Knight's Cross. But, inevitably, there were casualties too. Among those lost was an earlier Knight's Cross recipient, I. *Gruppe's* Oberleutnant Georg Schentke, who was forced to bail out over Soviet-held territory beyond the perimeter after downing a bomber – his 90th kill of the war – on Christmas Day.

By 15 January 1943 Pitomnik was in imminent danger of being overrun as the Red Army tightened its noose around Stalingrad. And 48 hours later the remaining *Gustavs* of the *Platzschutzstaffel* were ordered to fly out.

The epic Battle of Stalingrad is rightly regarded as the turning point of the war in the east. But it was the third and final great German summer offensive of the eastern front campaign – code-named *Zitadelle* – which finally dashed any remaining hopes Hitler may have had of defeating his arch enemy Stalin.

Although JG 52 was not directly involved in the closing stages of the fight for Stalingrad, Hauptmann Johannes Steinhoff's II. *Gruppe* had been brought up from the Caucasus front in mid-December 1942 to support the abortive attempt by 4. *Panzer-Armee* to break through to the besieged city from the south-west. It was at the height of this action, on 19 December, that Oberleutnant Gerhard Barkhorn, *Staffelkapitän* of 4./JG 52, was able to attain his century.

Both JGs 3 and 52 would, however, be committed to *Zitadelle*. But first a new danger threatened. 17. *Armee*, the southern arm of the now defunct *Braunschweig* operation, was still deep in the Caucasus, and at grave risk of being cut off by Red Army advances to its north. To avoid another Stalingrad, these troops would have to be evacuated from the Kuban, across the Kerch Straits, to the Crimea. Throughout the first half of 1943 much of the two *Geschwaders'* activities were consequently centred on these areas of the Black Sea coast.

Knight's Cross wearer Georg 'Peterle' Schentke of the Pitomnik volunteer *Staffel*, who was posted missing after bailing out over enemy territory on Christmas Day 1942. He is pictured here as an Oberfeldwebel serving with 9./JG 3 earlier in the year. Note the Bf 109F-4's segmented 'Mediterranean' camouflage, III. *Gruppe's* 'Double-headed axe' badge, and Schentke's nickname (which he shared with his pet cat!) below the cockpit

I./JG 3 had already been withdrawn back to the Reich late in January, before the final surrender at Stalingrad. But two pilots of Major Kurt Brändle's II. *Gruppe* would reach their centuries over the Kuban bridgehead on consecutive days in the spring. On 27 April one of a pair of lend-lease Bostons gave Oberleutnant Joachim Kirschner his 100th victory. Kirschner, the *Kapitän* of 5. *Staffel*, was already wearing the Knight's Cross (awarded on 23 December for 51 victories), and he would duly

Although the featureless expanse of the southern steppe gives nothing away as to the exact location, the two German rifles leaning against the trailing edge of 'White 2's' port wing, and the cavalry patrol just visible in the right background, would seem to suggest that this unknown 4./JG 3 pilot just managed to reach friendly lines before making a successful belly-landing in the spring of 1943

Studying a map with a group of his pilots, 5./JG 3's Oberleutnant Joachim Kirschner (centre, wearing a lifejacket and fur collar) wears the Knight's Cross, awarded at the height of the battle of Stalingrad (for 51 kills), and the Oak Leaves, won in the aftermath of *Zitadelle* (for 170 kills)

become JG 3's top scorer – with 175 kills – before being posted to the command of IV./JG 27 in October.

Twenty-four hours after Kirschner's century, a trio of LaGG-3s took the score of 4. *Staffel's* Leutnant Wolf Ettel to exactly 100. But Ettel would have to wait until 1 June for his Knight's Cross – by which time his total was standing at 120!

Based to the north of the Crimea, only one member of III. *Gruppe* reached treble figures in the months leading up to *Zitadelle*. Another of 1942's Knight's Cross winners, Leutnant Wilhelm Lemke, *Staffelkapitän* of 9./JG 3, had achieved his 100 with the destruction of a La-5 on 16 March.

Meanwhile, JG 52 was evacuating its forward bases down in the Caucasus. These fields, along the line of the River Terek, which flows into the Caspian Sea, were the easternmost airstrips occupied by the Luftwaffe during the war against the Soviet Union. By mid-March II. and III. *Gruppen* were back guarding the all-important Kerch Straits, which was the most vulnerable bottleneck along 17. *Armee's* main line of retreat.

Although displaying the insignia of Major Wolfgang Ewald, *Kommandeur* of III./JG 3, the *Gustav* in the foreground was being flown by Leutnant Adolf von Gordon of the *Gruppenstab* when it was lost in action against Il-2s on 24 April 1943. Note the Stukas taking off overhead

The original Soviet caption claims this to be 'a Nazi plane shot down by pilots of the air squadron named after Chkalov in action over the Kuban area in May 1943'. Although it is unlikely that the Russian pilots had deliberately targeted this machine, the 15 kill bars on its rudder reveal it to be the regular mount of one Erich Hartmann, wingman to 'Graf Punski' Krupinski of 7./JG 52 (Hartmann's 15th victory was a U-2 biplane downed on 15 May). But 'White 2' was being piloted by Unteroffizier Herbert Meissler when it was forced to land behind enemy lines. It is not known whether the smoke has been caused by combat damage, or by Meissler's deliberately setting fire to the aircraft after landing. Incidentally, the confusion of markings on the rear fuselage was caused by III. *Gruppe's* white wavy bar being painted across the yellow theatre band, which had itself been applied directly over the last two letters of the fighter's original delivery KJ+GU *Stammkennzeichen*

On 2 March 1943 66-victory *Experte* Oberleutnant Walter Krupinski had assumed command of 7. *Staffel.* It was Krupinski's spectacular crash-landing which had greeted Erich Hartmann's arrival at JG 52 back in October, and now 'Graf Punski' ('Count Punski'), as Krupinski was popularly known, selected the same promising young Leutnant – whose score by this time had risen to four – as his wingman.

In contrast, 4. *Staffel's* Oberfeldwebel Willi Nemitz was one of the oldest frontline pilots serving in the Luftwaffe. Nicknamed 'Altvater' ('Old Father') on account of his advanced years, the 32(!)-year-old Nemitz was awarded the Knight's Cross, for 54 kills, on 11 March. But exactly one month – and 27 victories – later Oberfeldwebel Nemitz would be killed in action against Soviet fighters above II. *Gruppe's* Anapa base.

On 20 April Hauptmann Günther Rall, *Staffelkapitän* of 8./JG 52, claimed the *Geschwader's* 5000th enemy aircraft destroyed. Another 11 weeks would see that total climb to 6000, but success on this scale could not be achieved without loss. Among the many casualties was Hauptmann Rudolf Miethig, long-serving *Kapitän* of 3. *Staffel.* Miethig was one of the *Geschwader's* 20+ Knight's Cross winners of the previous year, having received the award (for 50 kills) on 29 October – the same day as Walter Krupinski (for 53).

By 10 June 1943 Rudolf Miethig's score had reached the century. But he was himself killed on that date over the Kuban bridgehead when he brought down his 101st victim by ramming.

In the first days of July *Stab*, I. and III./JG 52 moved up from the Black Sea coast into the Ukraine in preparation for Operation *Zitadelle.* This third summer offensive was aimed at eradicating the Soviet salient at

Kursk, which projected westwards into the German front like a huge fist, and threatened to split the central and southern sectors wide open.

Zitadelle was very much a ground battle. In fact, it developed into the largest armoured confrontation in military history, although air power played an important part, too. Fighter cover was to be provided by eight *Jagdgruppen*, divided between the northern and southern flanks of the 'bulge' around Kursk. To the north were four *Gruppen* of Fw 190s, and to the south, four of Bf 109Gs – II. and III./JG 3 and I. and III./JG 52.

Operation *Zitadelle* was launched early on the morning of 5 July. And for a few brief hours those fighter pilots who had participated in *Barbarossa* experienced again the kind of success that had marked the opening rounds of the air war in the east. By the end of the first day of *Zitadelle* it is estimated that the Soviets had lost 432 machines – mainly bombers and ground-attack aircraft attempting to halt the advancing Panzers.

Major Kurt Brändle's II./JG 3 accounted for 77 of them, with a couple of Il-2s downed seven hours apart providing the 150th victories for two members of the *Gruppe*. The first had been claimed by Oberleutnant Joachim Kirschner, *Staffelkapitän* of 5./JG 3, and was one of nine kills credited to him that day. The second was among the *Kommandeur's* own bag of five (four Il-2s and a single Yak-1). Another pilot to bring down five was Oberleutnant Werner Lucas, *Kapitän* of 4. *Staffel*, who thereby took his total to 92.

III. *Gruppe's* top scorer of the day was Oberleutnant Emil Bitsch, *Staffelkapitän* of 8./JG 3, with six – his 75th to 80th victories. Fellow *Kapitän* Oberleutnant Wilhelm Lemke of 9. *Staffel* also claimed six, but three of these were unconfirmed.

The most successful of all were two *Staffelkapitäne* of JG 52. Hauptmann Johannes Wiese of 2./JG 52 shot down no fewer than 12 Soviet machines, which left him five short of his century – a situation he remedied exactly five days later. And 7. *Staffel's* Walter Krupinski was just one behind with 11 aircraft destroyed. But 'Graf Punski' was severely wounded claiming the last of these, and for the next six weeks 7./JG 52 would be led by acting *Staffelkapitän* Leutnant Erich Hartmann, whose own four victories on this day had elevated his score to 21.

Hauptmann Walter Krupinski, *Staffelkapitän* of 7./JG 52 from March 1943 to March 1944, is seen here wearing the Oak Leaves awarded to him on 2 March 1944 (for 177 eastern front victories). He was transferred to the west shortly after this photograph was taken, where he in turn served with JGs 5, 11 and 26, before finally joining Me 262-equipped JV 44

***Gustavs* of I./JG 52 enjoy the sun on a forward landing strip near Bessonovka, east of Byelgorod, at the time of Operation *Zitadelle* in July 1943**

After all the pictures of snow and ice, a blazing sun is not something immediately associated with the war in the east – but this unteroffizier of 4./JG 3 is no doubt grateful for the improvised sunshade as he sits at readiness at Kharkov-Rogan during a break in the *Zitadelle* operations

Forty-eight hours later a kill by one of Wiese's 2. *Staffel* pilots, Oberleutnant Paul-Heinrich Dähne, provided I./JG 52 with its 800th kill of the war – and the *Geschwader* with its 6000th.

Despite these undoubted successes in the air, on the ground *Zitadelle* was already in deep trouble. The Red Army had also been planning a major offensive in the same area, and the two forces were soon locked in a titanic struggle. Although deploying the mighty 55-ton Tiger tank for the first time in any significant numbers, Germany's Panzer divisions were unable to achieve a breakthrough.

After only eight days Hitler conceded that Operation *Zitadelle* had failed in its purpose. Citing the imminent loss of Sicily and the growing threat to southern Europe as the more important of his priorities, he ordered much of the armour to be withdrawn.

On 21 July two of JG 3's recent multiple scorers, Emil Bitsch and Walter Lucas, both attained their century. Before the month was out Brändle and Kirschner, each having reached 150 on the opening day of *Zitadelle*, had raised their totals to 170 a piece. This brought Joachim Kirschner the Oak Leaves on 2 August – Kurt Brändle had received this award exactly one year earlier for just 100 victories!

The *Staffelkapitän* of 5./JG 3, Oberleutnant Joachim Kirschner (in the dark flight blouse), is congratulated by Oberleutnant Förster of the *Geschwaderstab* on his 150th kill (an Il-2 downed in the opening minutes of *Zitadelle* on 5 July 1943). This claim also reportedly represented 5. *Staffel's* 500th collective victory, and the 2000th of the war for II. *Gruppe*!

Among JG 3's rank and file at this period was a young NCO pilot with just 32 kills. But Unteroffizier Gerhard Thyben's time was yet to come. After transferring to JG 54 and converting on to the Fw 190, he too would ultimately join the top two dozen eastern front *Experten*. First, however, he would have to see some months' service in the west, for at the beginning of August 1943 II. and III./JG 53 were pulled out of Russia to join the *Geschwaderstab* and I. *Gruppe* in defence of the Reich.

This left JG 52 alone in the east.

FIGHTING RETREAT

The *Führer's* abrupt abandonment of *Zitadelle* set the scene for the closing chapter in the story of the Bf 109 on the eastern front. In the months that followed, the component *Gruppen* of JG 52 would be constantly on the move. As the Red Army grew in strength and gathered momentum in its drive towards Germany, they found themselves being shuttled from one point of danger to the next with increasing frequency and desperation.

Under such conditions – often operating from makeshift landing strips, threatened with being overrun by Soviet tanks on the ground, and facing ever-mounting odds in the air – it is a wonder that they survived. That they produced the most successful fighter pilots the world has ever seen is little short of incredible.

JG 52's nomadic existence commenced within days of the Kursk offensive's being called off, with I. *Gruppe* transferring from Polatava to Kharkov-South, and III. *Gruppe* moving to Orel on the northern flank of the 'bulge'. But after just five days at Orel III./JG 52 returned southwards. It was now that Leutnant Erich Hartmann's extraordinary abilities began to reveal themselves.

The last of four Soviet fighters claimed on 3 August gave Hartmann his half-century. By the middle of the month a succession of multiple daily kills in the Kharkov area had raised that total to more than 80. And when the *Staffelkapitän* of 9./JG 52, 113-victory *Experte* Leutnant Berthold Korts, was reported missing in action on 29 August (the same day, incidentally, that the award of his Knight's Cross was announced), it was Hartmann who was chosen by *Gruppenkommandeur* Major Günther Rall to replace him.

With 90 kills already to his credit, Erich Hartmann's year-long leadership of 9./JG 52 would see his personal score rise to an incredible 301. His distinctively-marked aircraft, latterly each with its black

In the month following his promotion to *Staffelkapitän* of 9./JG 52 on 2 September 1943, Leutnant Erich Hartmann regularly flew this Bf 109G-6 (see colour profile 29) in combat

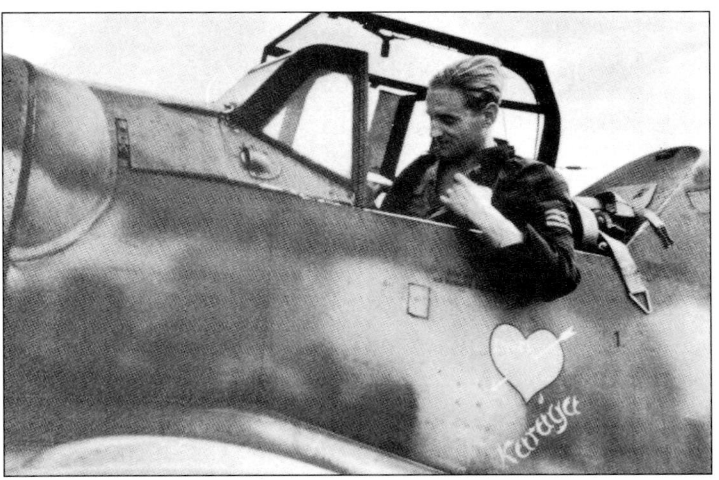

Erich Hartmann, as an oberleutnant, is seen in the cockpit of a later G-6 (note the clear-vision Erla canopy). 9. *Staffel's* famous 'Pierced heart' emblem and 'Karaya' call-sign are also clearly evident – less so is the name *'Ursel'*, in white, in the top left segment of the heart. It appears that Hartmann used two familiar names for his girlfriend/fiancée/wife Ursula – 'Ursel' and 'Usch'

'tulip'-patterned nose, reportedly earned him the nickname of 'The Black Devil' among his opponents.

His own pilots, inspired by their *Kapitän's* simple but effective four-part formula for success in the air – 'locate, decide, attack, break away' – keenly followed his example. Many achieved high scores. Soon the entire 'Karaya' *Staffel* (so named after 9./JG 52's radio call-sign) was as famous as its youthful leader. Dismissive of his own achievements, however, Erich Hartmann took far greater pride in the fact that he never lost a wingman in combat.

Meanwhile II./JG 52, which had remained in the Kuban during the abortive *Zitadelle* offensive, was also transferred up into the Kharkov-Poltava region. Hauptmann Gerhard Barkhorn had assumed command of the *Gruppe* on 1 September. And six days later fledgling *Experte* Leutnant Helmut Lipfert took over at the head of 6. *Staffel* after the previous *Kapitän*, 173-victory Oak Leaves wearer Hauptmann Heinz Schmidt, had been shot down – purportedly in error by that Hungarian fighter.

Back at III. *Gruppe*, September had also seen both the award of the Swords to *Kommandeur* Hauptmann Günther Rall (on the 12th for his double century), and Erich Hartmann reaching his 100th – an Airacobra brought down, along with a trio of La-5s, over the River Dnieper on the 20th.

Just over a month later another Airacobra claimed by Hartmann, on 29 October, raised his total to 148, and resulted in a long overdue Knight's Cross. He was now just behind his good friend, and mentor, Oberleutnant Walter Krupinski, *Staffelkapitän* of 7./JG 52 (whose Knight's Cross had

Celebrating his 200th kill, Hauptmann Günther Rall (left), *Kommandeur* of III./JG 52, poses at Makeyevka on 29 August 1943 with Walter Krupinski (centre) and an unknown pilot

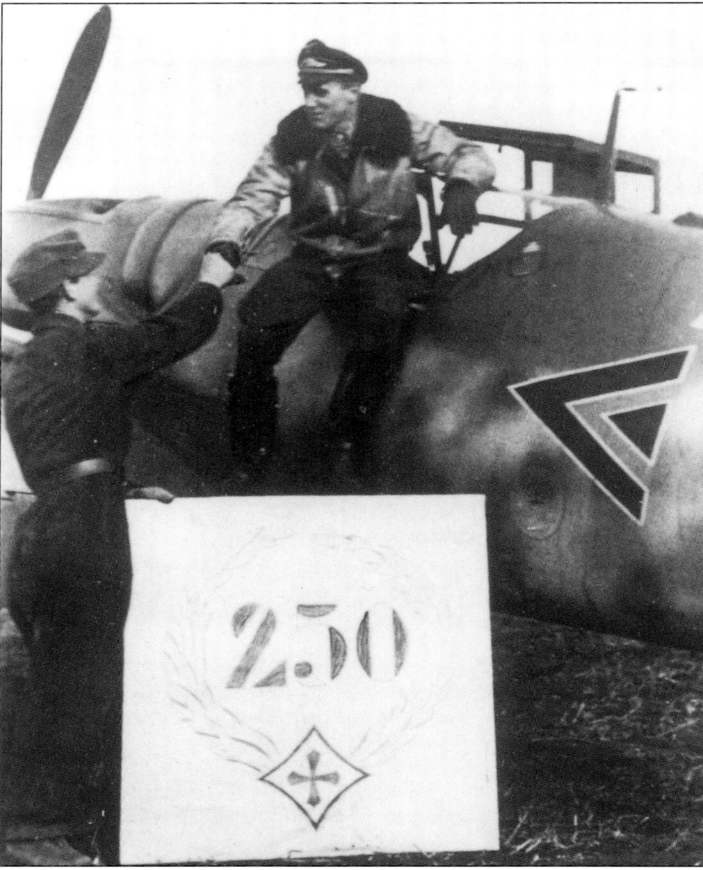

Over the next three months Rall claimed 50 more Soviet victims, and is here being congratulated by his mechanic for having just despatched the 250th on 28 November

been awarded exactly one year earlier – for 53 victories), who had reached 150 on 1 October.

A welcome spell of home leave meant that Hartmann's own 150th would not be achieved until the last day of the year. JG 52's two high-scoring *Gruppenkommandeure* were still well in the lead, however. Günther Rall's 250th had gone down on 28 November, and Gerhard Barkhorn's 200th just 48 hours later.

But, as so often in the past, such individual successes in the air could do little to influence events unfolding on the ground. On 6 November the Soviets had recaptured Kiev. The whole southern sector was in danger of collapse. I./JG 52, commanded now by Hauptmann Johannes Wiese, was brought up from its Crimean bases to the exotically named Malaja-Wiska (inevitably 'Malaya-Whisky' to the troops) south of the Ukrainian capital. Here they were joined by elements of both II. and III./JG 52.

In the early hours of 14 January 1944 Russian armour attacked the packed airfield. Before the enemy could be repulsed a number of casualties had been suffered by the groundcrews, and eight aircraft had been damaged when their tails were apparently crushed by Soviet tanks driving over them. The remaining *Gustavs* escaped shortly after first light and dispersed on neighbouring strips.

Although the third winter of the war on the southern sector was by no means as severe as the previous two, the all-pervading mud posed huge

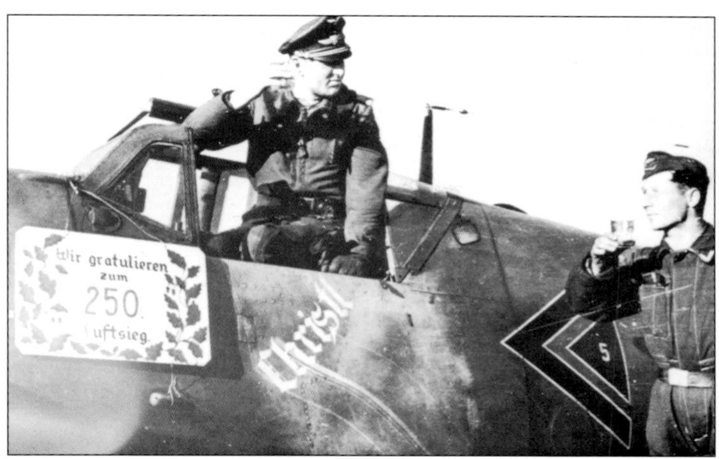

Fellow *Gruppenkommandeur* Hauptmann Gerhard Barkhorn of II./JG 52 reached the 250 mark on 13 February 1944. Once again, the chief mechanic is on hand to toast 'his' pilot's success

problems. At least half-a-dozen pilots were lost in take-off and landing accidents, and sorties had to be broken off prematurely as engines overheated, their radiator intakes clogged with mud thrown up while taxying. Aviation fuel had to be distributed in 200-litre (45-gal) drums by horse and cart, which was the only wheeled transport that could cope with the boggy conditions on many airfields.

Nevertheless, missions continued to be flown. Operating over the Uman region, III. *Gruppe* claimed 50 victories in 60 days. On 2 March Erich Hartmann's ten kills took his total to 202, this achievement winning him the Oak Leaves. Walter Krupinski and Johannes Wiese were similarly honoured on the same day (for 177 and 125 victories respectively), and all three men were summoned to Hitler's Alpine retreat to receive their awards.

On the penultimate leg of their journey, by rail to Salzburg, they were joined by Gerhard Barkhorn, also en route to Berchtesgaden to be pre-

Here is another of Barkhorn's numerous Bf 109s – probably an earlier G-6 (note the length of the aerial mast and the absence of direction-finding loop mounting) photographed shortly after his appointment as *Kommandeur* of II. *Gruppe*. The photograph reveals obvious differences in the application of both his wife's name below the cockpit and his 'lucky 5' incorporated in the command chevrons. Both were Barkhorn's personal markings throughout the war

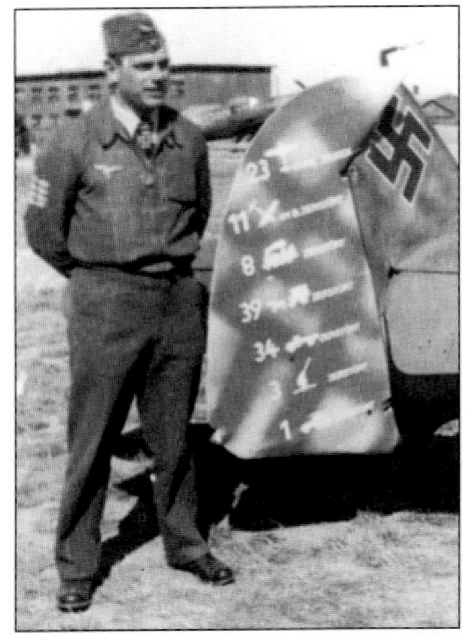

A long-serving member of the famed 'Karaya' *Staffel*, Oberfeldwebel (later Leutnant) Hans Dammers was most meticulous in recording his achievements. He is seen here wearing his Knight's Cross, which was awarded to him back in August 1942 for 51 kills. These, and his many more aerial victories since, are presumably depicted on the port side of that rudder. On the starboard surface are listed, from top to bottom, 23 unconfirmed kills, 11 aircraft destroyed on the ground, as well as 8 locomotives, 39 horse-drawn wagons, 34 trucks, 3 anti-aircraft guns and 1 command half-track!

sented with the Swords for his 250th. Liquid refreshment flowed a little too freely – courtesy of a friendly train conductor – and, despite the drive in sub-zero temperatures up to the *Führer's* eyrie in an open-topped car (a desperate ploy by a worried aide), they were still far from sober on arrival.

While in an ante-room waiting to be ushered in to the Presence, Erich Hartmann took a fancy to a smart peaked cap which he had spotted hanging on a hat-stand. It was four sizes too large, and came down over his ears. Fortunately, while the other three were convulsed with laughter, the same harassed, but quick-thinking aide snatched the hat off Hartmann's head, thus sparing the *Führer* the ludicrous sight of his own uniform cap half-hiding the face of the young Luftwaffe officer he was about to decorate.

Such moments of light-hearted relaxation were few and far between, and it was soon back to the harsh realities of the front. On 13 March another of JG 52's little-known 'centurions', Leutnant Hans Dammers, was rammed by a crashing Soviet aircraft. A Knight's Cross wearer and 113-victory *Experte*, Dammers, who was a member of Hartmann's own 9. *Staffel*, died of his injuries four days later.

On 18 March Erich Hartmann was promoted to oberleutnant. By now III./JG 52 was the most successful *Gruppe* of the *Geschwader*, scoring its 3500th collective kill of the war on 21 March. But such figures accounted for little in the present crisis. A new Soviet spring offensive was underway, and at the end of the month III. *Gruppe* departed Russian soil, withdrawing to Lemberg (Lvov), in Poland.

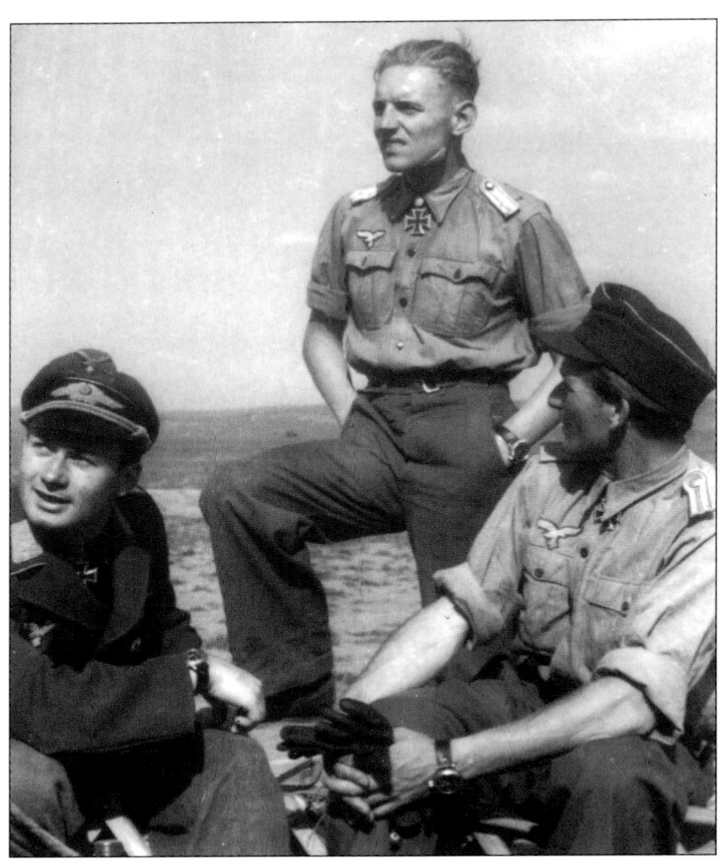

Among the decorations awarded to III./JG 52 in March 1944 were the Oak Leaves on the 2nd to Leutnant Erich Hartmann (centre), *Kapitän* of 9. *Staffel*, for 200 victories, and the Knight's Cross on the 23rd to Leutnant Friedrich Obleser (left), *Kapitän* of 8. *Staffel*, for 80. Leutnant Karl 'Charlie' Gratz, on the right, had received his Knight's Cross in July 1942 for 54 victories. All three would add substantially to their respective scores before war's end

Meanwhile, I. and II./JG 52 had been involved in the final days' fighting in the Crimea. II. *Gruppe's Staffelkapitäne* were particularly prominent at this period. Relative newcomer Feldwebel Hans Waldmann, whose 84th kill on 5 February had earned him the Knight's Cross and promotion to leutnant, took over 4. *Staffel* from fellow Knight's Cross holder and 80+ *Experte* Leutnant Heinrich Sturm on 17 April. After claiming 121 victories in the east, 'Dackel' Waldmann would be transferred to Defence of the Reich duties and lose his life in a mid-air collision between two Me 262s on 18 March 1945.

Another trio of JG 52's leading *Experten*, who achieved a staggering 669 eastern front kills between them. Pictured in the summer of 1944, they are, from left to right, Hauptleute Gerhard Barkhorn and Wilhelm Batz, *Kommandeure* of II. and III. *Gruppen* respectively, and Leutnant Otto Fönnekold, *Kapitän* of 5. *Staffel*

Longer-serving *Experte* Oberleutnant Wilhelm Batz, who had commanded 5. *Staffel* since May 1943, received the Knight's Cross for 75 kills on 26 March. On 19 April he would take over III. *Gruppe* from Major Günther Rall when the latter – his eastern front total having reached 271 – was appointed *Kommandeur* of II./JG 11 in the west. Batz's position at the head of 5. *Staffel* was in turn filled by another Knight's Cross holder, 100+ *Experte* Leutnant Otto Fönnekold.

Lastly, 6. *Staffel's* Leutnant Helmut Lipfert was also scoring steadily. His 90th on 5 April had won him the Knight's Cross. Six days later an 'all-white *Stormovik*' provided him with his century.

But, here too, individual achievements in the air were having little effect on events on the ground. The last German troops were evacuated from the Crimea on 13 May, and II./JG 52 had been withdrawn a week earlier. Retiring to Kherson, it was joined by III. *Gruppe*, brought back down from Poland in a forlorn attempt to help stem the Red Army's inexorable advance westwards along the Black Sea coast.

At Kherson the two *Gruppen* were subjected to near-constant Soviet bombing raids, and Lipfert's 6./JG 52, in particular, lost a number of aircraft. By 9 May the field was under Russian artillery bombardment, although III. *Gruppe* had prepared for this contingency. Having removed the armour-plating and radio equipment, there was room in each *Gustav's* rear fuselage for two extra bodies. Every pilot took off for Zarnesti, in Rumania, with two mechanics aboard.

One of the last to taxi out, Lipfert's machine was damaged by Soviet shell-fire, and the *Staffelkapitän* of 6./JG 52 was forced to complete his journey as a rather cramped passenger in the *Gruppen*-Adjutant's fighter.

On 10 May JG 52 claimed its 9000th enemy aircraft of the war. But it was a war now entering its final year, already irretrievably lost. The *Geschwader's* withdrawal into Rumania did not bring any easing of pressure. Quite the reverse in fact, for now also assigned the additional task of helping to defend the vital Rumanian oilfields, all three *Gruppen* found themselves facing a new enemy – the Americans.

This 2nd Bomb Group B-17G was a typical *'Starflight'* victim. It is not known with certainty which *Gruppe* was responsible for downing the US 'heavy' near Mährisch-Ostrau in mid-August 1944. The feather-hatted gentlemen guarding the scene appear to be members of the local *Feldgendarmerie*

Code-named *Sternflüge* (*Starflights*), the missions undertaken against the US heavy bombers, and their fighter escorts, flying in across the Adriatic from Italy proved both unrewarding and costly. Surviving records indicate that JG 52's six-week defence of Rumania's oil netted just 15 American aircraft, of which only three were four-engined 'heavies'. Two of the latter – both B-24s – were claimed by Oberleutnant Helmut Lipfert and his wingman Unteroffizier Tamen during the *Starflight* mission of 24 June. II. *Gruppe* had despatched its entire strength – nine *Gustavs* – against the incoming Americans. By the day's end it had two left!

Bad as things were in the east, they were apparently even worse in the Homeland, where much of the Reich's defensive fighter strength had been rushed to the Normandy invasion front. Already stretched to the limit, JG 52's position was further weakened when it was ordered to give up three *Staffeln* (one per *Gruppe*) for service in the west. Although

In the spring of 1944 pilots within JG 51 began reverting from Fw 190s back on to the Bf 109. Focke-Wulf *Experte* Leutnant Günther Josten of 1. *Staffel* – soon to be appointed *Kapitän* of 3./JG 51 – gets to grips with the cockpit layout of his new *Gustav* at Bobruisk in April

The pilots of JG 51 were soon demonstrating their mastery of their new mounts. One of the unit's G-6s carries out a low-level pass for the benefit of the photographer

completely new 2., 4. and 7. *Staffeln* would be activated later in the year, it would by then be far too late to reverse the *Geschwader's* fortunes.

For in June 1944 the Red Army had unleashed its last great summer offensive, which was aimed at smashing open the central sector and paving the way for the drive on Berlin. From now on JG 52 would regularly be facing aerial odds of 40-to-1 or more against.

Late in June III. *Gruppe* was transferred northwards to the Minsk area of the central front, where it was to operate under the control of JG 51. This *Geschwader* had converted back on to Bf 109s a few weeks earlier (reportedly because of the demands for the Fw 190 from other fronts), and would remain almost entirely equipped with Messerschmitts until war's end.

Despite the enemy's overwhelming superiority, JG 51 would produce some half-dozen 100+ *Experten* during these final months, although most, if not all, of them had already claimed the majority of their victims while flying the Focke-Wulf. One such was the *Geschwader's* highest scorer, Oberleutnant Anton Hafner, *Staffelkapitän* of 8./JG 51, who had received the Oak Leaves on 11 April for 134 kills. He had added another 70 to that total by the time of his death in action during a low-level dogfight with a Yak-9 on 17 June.

Three more of the *Geschwader's* current *Staffelkapitäne* were also very successful in battling the odds, and all would survive the war with the Oak

But nothing could now halt the advance of the victorious Red Army. This winter-camouflaged *Gustav*, captured by the Soviets towards the close of 1944, is believed to be a machine abandoned by JG 51

Leaves. 1./JG 51's Oberleutnant Joachim Brendel amassed 189 kills in the east, more than 90 of which were *Stormoviks* – universally regarded as the most difficult enemy aircraft to bring down. Leutnant Günther Josten of 3./JG 51 also included more than 60 Il-2s in his overall total of 178. The third, Leutnant Günther Schack of 9./JG 51, who had been awarded the Oak Leaves (for 133 victories) just nine days after Anton Hafner, took his final score to 174.

But none could compete with JG 52's leading *Experten*. On 4 July Erich Hartmann won the Swords for 239 kills. It took him another fortnight to reach his 250th – one of a trio of *Stormoviks* downed on 18 July. He was the fourth *Jagdwaffe* pilot (three of them from JG 52) to attain this figure.

By this time III./JG 52 was back with the rest of the *Geschwader* again operating in the Lemberg (Lvov) region of Poland. On 2 July *Gruppenkommandeur* Hauptmann Wilhelm Batz received the Oak Leaves for 175 victories. It was a period of intense activity for JG 52 as the *Gruppen* were rushed back and forth along the front from Poland up into Lithuania, back to Poland, then south to Rumania.

Nothing could stop Erich Hartmann, however. Another string of successes culminated in eight kills on 23 August, and no fewer than eleven the day thereafter. The last five of these latter, all claimed in the space of twenty minutes, took his total to an amazing 301! He was the first fighter pilot in the world to score a triple century. A telegram from Adolf Hitler arrived 24 hours later, awarding him the Diamonds, and summoning

On 26 August 1944 in a cramped wooden hut in his East Prussian HQ, Adolf Hitler awards the now Oberleutnant Erich Hartmann with the Diamonds for his 301 aerial victories – the first fighter-pilot in the world to top the triple century!

Returning to 9./JG 52's base south of Warsaw the following day, Erich Hartmann poses with his devoted friend and indispensable other half of the successful team – his chief mechanic Heinz 'Bimmel' Mertens

136-victory *Experte* Leutnant Otto Fönnekold of 5./JG 52 was killed by a ground-strafing P-51 while landing at Budak, in Hungary, on 31 August 1944

him to the *Führer's* 'Wolf's Lair' forest HQ in East Prussia for the presentation ceremony the following day.

Afterwards over coffee and tea, Hitler, with unusual candour, admitted to his highest-scoring fighter pilot that, 'militarily, the war is lost, Hartmann'. Nevertheless, the young Oberleutnant returned to his *Staffel* and, like the rest of JG 52, continued to fight on as the eastern front collapsed about them.

The end of August brought with it a change of government, and a change of sides, for Rumania. The one-time Axis ally now declared war on Germany, so II./JG 52, which had been operating in Rumania, retired to Budak, in Hungary, on 31 August. The move was taking them dangerously close to the western Allies at their backs, as was demonstrated

Oberstleutnant Dietrich Hrabak commanded JG 52 from 1 November 1942 through to 30 September 1944. He is seen here in the cockpit of his G-6 with Erich Hartmann, *Kapitän* of 9. *Staffel*, who is helping him with his harness straps. 8./JG 52's Friedrich Obleser and Karl Gratz appear amused by Hartmann's solicitude. The presence of the latter pair, and the sticking plaster on Hartmann's cheek, would seem to suggest that this photograph was taken at about the same time as that on page 74

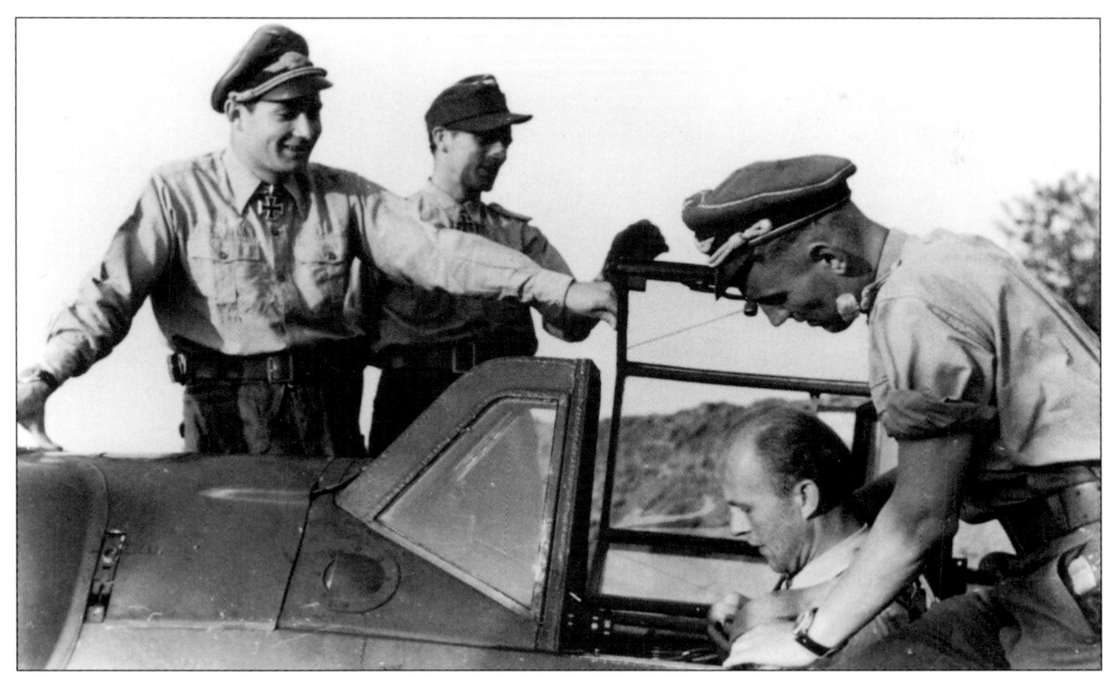

Hrabak's successor at the head of JG 52 was no stranger to the *Geschwader*. Having recovered from wounds suffered during his spell undertaking Defence of the Reich missions, the erstwhile *Kapitän* of 9. *Staffel*, Oberstleutnant Hermann Graf, returned to the eastern front to lead JG 52 for the remaining seven months of the war

on that very same day. 136-victory *Experte* Leutnant Otto Fönnekold, *Staffelkapitän* of 5./JG 52, had just landed at Budak and was taxying in when he was strafed and fatally injured by a solitary Mustang.

Also involved in the retreat from Rumania was I./JG 53. This *Gruppe* had been transferred up from the Mediterranean to help protect the Ploesti oilfields back in May. Its pilots had seen action mainly against the USAAF in the interim, and they had scored only a handful of successes against the Soviet air force – including a quartet of Yak-9s and a single Il-2 for *Gruppenkommandeur* Major Jürgen Harder – before they too withdrew into Hungary.

I./JG 53 would remain in the east until the end of the war, vacating Hungary for Austria towards its close. During these final six months the *Gruppe* claimed some 90 kills. The vast majority of these were Russian, but the tally did include a couple of American aircraft – and one Rumanian-flown Bf 109.

Hauptmann Erich Hartmann is seen here shortly before leaving the famed 'Karaya' *Staffel* to set up the new 4./JG 52. His replacement as *Kapitän* of 9./JG 52 was . . .

The most successful of the *Gruppe's* pilots was Hauptmann Helmut Lipfert, erstwhile *Staffelkapitän* of 6./JG 52, who assumed command of I./JG 53 on 15 February 1945. Lipfert's first kills as *Kommandeur* – two Soviet fighters exactly one week after his arrival – raised his score to 181. His last claim, for a Yak-9 downed on 16 April, took his final tally to 203. It also won him the *Jagdwaffe's* last Oak Leaves of the war 24 hours later.

Meanwhile, JG 52 had been continuing the unequal struggle, responding as best it could to each fresh new danger, scoring victories, suffering casualties.

On 1 September 1944 Erich Hartmann was promoted to hauptmann. The following day Hauptmann Adolf Borchers, who had succeeded Johannes Wiese as *Kommandeur* of I./JG 52, claimed his 118th kill – and the *Geschwader's* 10,000th since the beginning of the war! This unique accomplishment provided a propaganda highlight in those days of otherwise almost unrelieved gloom for the German people. A special *Geschwader* march was even composed and broadcast on the national radio.

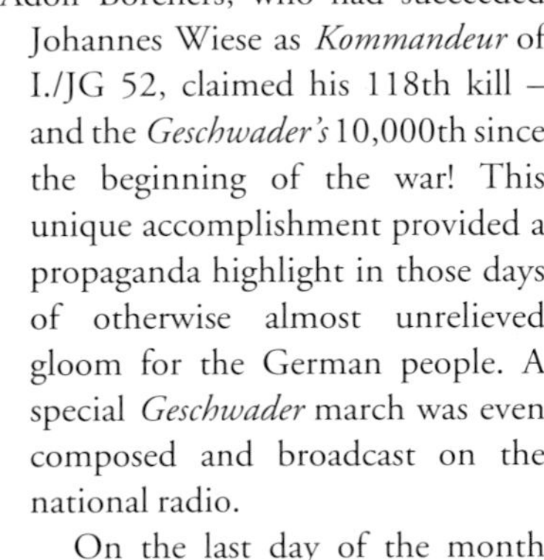

On the last day of the month JG 52 lost its longest-serving *Kommodore* when Oberstleutnant Dietrich Hrabak left to take over JG 54. His successor proved no stranger to JG 52 – Oberstleutnant Hermann

. . . Leutnant Hans-Joachim Birkner, who claimed 117 kills during his brief 14-month combat career

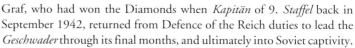

Graf, who had won the Diamonds when *Kapitän* of 9. *Staffel* back in September 1942, returned from Defence of the Reich duties to lead the *Geschwader* through its final months, and ultimately into Soviet captivity.

On that same 30 September Hauptmann Erich Hartmann relinquished command of the famous 9. 'Karaya' *Staffel* to activate the newly formed 4./JG 52. His replacement as leader of 9./JG 52 was Leutnant Hans-Joachim Birkner, who had often flown as Hartmann's wingman. A relative newcomer, Birkner had claimed his first kill exactly a year earlier. On 14 October he would achieve his century.

By then III. *Gruppe* had been rushed up into East Prussia, the area where the Red Army had just set foot for the first time on German soil. III./JG 52 were later joined there by I. *Gruppe*. In the meantime, II. *Gruppe* was operating over Hungary where, its pilots reported, the *Stormoviks'* rear-gunners had taken to lobbing hand grenades at them if they got too close to their tails!

Bad weather during the closing weeks of the year restricted operational activity. In December two Knight's Cross *Staffelkapitäne* were killed in take-off accidents – 9./JG 52's Hans-Joachim Birkner suffered engine failure at Cracow, in Poland, on 14th, and Hauptmann Heinrich Sturm of 5./JG 52 somersaulted when his wheels clipped a truck at Csor in Hungary eight days later.

Hauptmann Hartmann climbs from the cockpit of the all-white G-6 depicted in Iain Wyllie's cover painting, reportedly after just claiming his only non-JG 52 victory of the war – a Yak-9 destroyed on 4 February 1945 while serving as temporary acting *Kommandeur* of I./JG 53

Sturm was succeeded by another Knight's Cross wearer, Leutnant Peter Düttmann, whose exploits during his two-year operational career with II. *Gruppe* resulted in his crashing or forced-landing no fewer than 19 times – mostly as a result of anti-aircraft fire. Düttmann nevertheless survived the war at the head of 5. *Staffel*. His final number of confirmed victories totalled exactly 150 – plus a brace of Soviet tanks which, in 1945, were being equated with aerial kills!

On 4 January 1945 Major Gerhard Barkhorn became the second, and only other, *Jagdwaffe* pilot to achieve 300 victories. Less than a fortnight later he left II./JG 52 to take command of JG 6 in Defence of the Reich. II. *Gruppe's* new commander was to be Hauptmann Wilhelm Batz, who moved across from III./JG 52 on 1 February.

Batz's position was in turn filled by Hauptmann Adolf Borchers, *Kommandeur* of I./JG 52. This left vacant the leadership of I. *Gruppe*, which was assumed by 331-victory Hauptmann Erich Hartmann.

This frenetic round of command re-shuffling paled into insignificance against movements on the ground. By now the rapidly advancing Soviet Army was chasing I. and III./JG 52 out of one Silesian airfield after the other on an almost daily basis. In mid-March it retired down into Czechoslovakia. II. *Gruppe*, meanwhile, crossed the Hungarian border into Austria.

At the beginning of March 1945 Hauptmann Erich Hartmann was taken off operational flying and ordered to report to Lechfeld for conversion training on the Me 262 jet. Just what the world's most successful fighter pilot – now with 346 kills – could have achieved in one of these revolutionary machines must remain conjectural. For Hartmann turned down Adolf Galland's subsequent invitation to join his elite JV 44, opting instead to return to I./JG 52 in the east as requested in a telegram from Oberstleutnant Hermann Graf.

There, on 17 April, he claimed his 350th enemy aircraft destroyed. Four days later fellow *Gruppenkommandeur* Hauptmann Wilhelm Batz became the last member of the *Jagdwaffe* to receive the Swords. By now, however, such individual successes, and such decorations – increasingly irrelevant of late – were totally meaningless. The centre of Berlin was already coming under Soviet artillery fire. On 30 April Adolf Hitler would commit suicide.

Hauptmann Erich Hartmann's 352nd and final kill, an unidentified Yak fighter, went down over Brünn (Brno), in Czechoslovakia, on 8 May 1945 – the last day of the war in Europe.

The fate of I./JG 53 was closely bound up with that of JG 52 during the final weeks' hostilities. Located in Czechoslovakia at the time of the capitulation, members of I. and III./JG 52 suffered long years of post-war Soviet captivity. Only Austrian-based II./JG 52 succeeded in surrendering to the Western Allies. Pictured at Neubiberg in May 1945, the late-model *Gustav* in the foreground is a machine of II./JG 52. But the diamond-shaped patch of overpainting on the cowling, obliterating the famous 'Ace-of-Spades' insignia, suggests it has been taken over from I./JG 53

Lastly, and dedicated to every pilot – *Experte* or otherwise – who suffered the rigours of the eastern front, one final reminder of the two greatest of them all – Gerhard Barkhorn (20 March 1919 to 8 January 1983) . . .

. . . and Erich Hartmann (19 April 1922 to 20 September 1993)

APPENDICES

Pilots with 100+ Eastern Front Victories

	Eastern Front Victories (1)	*Others (2)*	*Knight's Cross (3)*	*Oak Leaves*	*Swords*	*Diamonds*	*Eastern Front JG(s)*
Hptm Erich Hartmann	352	-	148	200	239	301	52
Maj Gerhard Barkhorn	301	-	59	120	250		52
Maj Günther Rall	271	4	65	100	200		52
Oblt Otto Kittel (+)	267	-	123	152	230		54*
Maj Walter Nowotny (+)	255	3	56	189	218	250	54*
Maj Wilhelm Batz	232	5	75	175	?		52
Hptm Helmut Lipfert	203	-	90	203			52, 53
Oberst Hermann Graf	202	10	42	104	106	172	52
Maj Heinrich Ehrler (+)	200+	-	41	112			5
Oblt Walter Schuck	198	8	84	171			5
Hptm Joachim Brendel	189	-	95	156			51*
Oblt Anton Hafner (+)	184	20	60	134			51*
Oblt Gunther Josten	178	-	84	161			51*
Obstlt Hans Philipp (+)	177	29	(20)	62	82		54
Maj Walter Krupinski	177	20	53	177			52
Maj Theodor Weissenberger	175	33	38	112			77, 5
Hptm Günther Schack	174	-	116	133			51*
Hptm Heinz Schmidt (+)	173	-	51	102			52
Hptm Max Stotz (+)	173	16	53	100			54*
Hptm Joachim Kirschner (+)	167	21	51	170			3
Maj Horst Ademeit (+)	165	1	53	c120			54*
Maj Kurt Brändle (+)	160	20	49	100			53, 3
Hptm Heinrich Sturm (+)	c157	-	82				52
Oblt Gerhard Thyben	152	5	116	?			3, 54*
Oblt Hans Beisswenger (+)	151	1	47	100			54*
Lt Peter Düttmann	150	-	91				52
Oberst Johannes Steinhoff	148	28	35	101	(167)		52
Hptm Emil Lang (+)	148	25	119	144			54*
Lt Fritz Tegtmeier	146	-	99				54*
Oberst Gordon Gollob	144	6	42	85	107	150	3, 77
Oblt Albin Wolf (+)	144	-	117	144			54*
Hptm Rudolf Trenkel	138	-	75				77, 52
Oberst Wolf-Dietrich Wilcke (+)	137	25	25	100	155		53, 3
Oblt Walter Wolfrum	137	-	126				52
Maj Erich Rudorffer	136	86	(19)	130	210		54*
Hptm Karl-Heinz Weber (+)	136	-	100	136			51*
Oblt Otto Fönnekold (+)	136	-	100+				52
Maj Johannes Wiese	133	-	51	125			52
Maj Heinrich Setz (+)	132	6	c50	76			77
Maj Anton Hackl	c130	c62	48	104	(150)		77
Maj Franz Eisenach	129	-	107				54*
Maj Adolf Borchers	127	5	78				51, 52*

	Eastern Front Victories (1)	Others (2)	Knight's Cross (3)	Oak Leaves	Swords	Diamonds	Eastern Front JG(s)
Oblt Heinrich Sterr (+)	127	3	86				54*
Lt Kurt Tanzer	126	17	35				51*
Lt Gerhard Hoffmann (+)	125+	-	125				52
Oblt Hans Waldmann (+)	125	9	84	(?)			52
Hptm Wilhelm Lemke (+)	125	6	50	(c125)			3
Hptm Franz Schall (+)	c123	c14	117				52
Hptm Franz Dörr	122	6	95				5
Lt Karl Gratz	121	17	54				52
Oblt Wolf Ettel (+)	120	4	120	(124)			3
Ofw Heinz Marquardt	120	1	89				51*
Oblt Friedrich Obleser	120	-	80				52
Lt Franz-Josef Beerenbrock	117	-	42	102			51
Lt Hans-Joachim Birkner (+)	117	-	98				52
Lt Jakob Norz (+)	117	-	70				5
Lt Heinz Wernicke (+)	117	-	112				54*
Oberst Adolf Dickfeld	115	21	47	101			52
Maj Erwin Clausen (+)	114	18	52	101			77
Lt Hans Dammers (+)	113	-	51				52
Lt Berthold Korts (+)	113	-	113				52
Hptm Alfred Grislawski	109	24	40	(114)			52
Oberst Dietrich Hrabak	109	16	(16)	118			54, 52*
Oblt Bernhard Vechtel	108	-	93				51*
Oblt Franz Woidich	108	2	80				52
Oblt Josef Zwernemann (+)	c106	c20	57	101			52
Hptm Werner Lucas (+)	105	1	52				3
Hptm Emil Bitsch (+)	104	4	105				3
Oblt Ernst-Wilhelm Reinert	103	71	53	103	(?)		77
Lt Heinz Sachsenberg	103	1	101				52
Oberst Viktor Bauer	102	4	34	102			3
Hptm Rudolf Miethig (+)	101	-	50				52
Lt Ulrich Wernitz	101	-	82				54*
Obstlt Friedrich-Karl Müller (+)	100	40	c30	100			53, 3
Lt Wilhelm Crinius	100	14	100	100			53

Key

(1) = includes US aircraft claimed over Rumania and Hungary
(2) = kills claimed in West, Mediterranean, Balkans and Reich
(3) = figures in awards columns indicate number of victories at the time of award
(figures in brackets for award won in another theatre)
(*) = after JG indicates pilot's score includes kills on Fw 190
(+) = after name indicates killed or missing
(c) = *circa*

Bf 109s on the Eastern Front – Representative Orders of Battle

21 June 1941 – Operation *Barbarossa*

	Unit	Commander	Base	**Variant**	**Est/Serv**
Luftflotte 1 (Northern Sector)					
	Stab JG 54	Maj Hannes Trautloft	Lindental	F	4-3
	I./JG 54	Hptm Hubertus von Bonin	Rautenberg	F	40-34
	II./JG 54	Hptm Dieter Hrabak	Trakehnen	E/F	40-33
	III./JG 54	Hptm Arnold Lignitz	Blumenfeld	F	40-35
	II./JG 53	Hptm Heinz Bretnütz	Neusiedel	F	35-33
Luftflotte 2 (Central Sector)					
	Stab JG 27	Maj Wolfgang Schellmann	Sobolevo	E	4-4
	II./JG 27	Hptm Wolfgang Lippert	Berzniki	E	40-31
	III./JG 27	Hptm Max Dobislav	Sobolevo	E	40-14
	II./JG 52	Hptm Erich Woitke	Sobolevo	F	39-37
	Stab JG 51	Obstlt Werner Mölders	Siedlce	F	4-4
	I./JG 51	Hptm H-F Joppien	Staravis	F	40-38
	II./JG 51	Hptm Josef Fözö	Siedlce	F	40-23
	III./JG 51	Hptm Richard Leppla	Halaszi	F	38-30
	IV./JG 51	Maj Friedrich Beckh	Crzevica	F	38-26
	Stab JG 53	Maj Frh G von Maltzahn	Crzevica	F	6-6
	I./JG 53	Oblt Wilfried Balfanz	Crzevica	F	35-29
	III./JG 53	Hptm Wolf-Dietrich Wilcke	Sobolevo	F	38-36
Luftflotte 4 (Southern Sector)					
	Stab JG 3	Maj Günther Lützow	Hostynne	F	4-4
	I./JG 3	Hptm Hans von Hahn	Dub	F	35-28
	II./JG 3	Hptm Lothar Keller	Hostynne	F	35-32
	III./JG 3	Hptm Walter Oesau	Modorovka	F	35-34
	Stab JG 52	Maj Hans Trübenbach	Bucharest/Mizil	F	4-3
	III./JG 2	Maj Gotthard Handrick	Mizil/Pipera	F	43-41
	Stab JG 77	Maj Bernhard Woldenga	Bacau	E	2-2
	II./JG 77	Hptm Anton Mader	Roman	E	39-19
	III./JG 77	Hptm Alexander von Winterfeld	Bacau	E/F	35-20
	I.(J)/LG 2	Hptm Herbert Ihlefeld	Janca	E	40-20

Totals: 793-619

July 1942 – *circa* Operation *Braunschweig*

Luftflotte 1 (Northern Sector)				
Stab JG 54	Obstlt Hannes Trautloft	Siverskaya	F	2-1
I./JG 54	Hptm Hans Philipp	Krasnogvardeisk	F/G	40-25
II./JG 54	Maj Dietrich Hrabak	Ryelbitzi	F	40-28
III./JG 54	Hptm Reinhard Seiler	Siverskaya	F	22-18
Lw.Kdo Ost (Central Sector)				
Stab JG 51	Obstlt Karl-Gottfried Nordmann	Orel	F	2-1
I./JG 51	Hptm Heinrich Krafft	Vyasma	F	31-15
II./JG 51	Hptm Hartmann Grasser	Orel	F	34-30
III./JG 51	Hptm Richard Lappla	Vyasma	F	37-22
IV./JG 51	Hptm Hans Knauth	Sechinskaya	F	36-29
Luftflotte 4 (Southern Sector)				
Stab JG 3	Obstlt Günther Lützow	Millerovo-North	F	3-2
I./JG 3	Hptm Georg Michalek	Morosovskaya	F	24-9
II./JG 3	Maj Kurt Brändle	Millerovo	F	22-10
III./JG 3	Maj Karl-Heinz Greisert	Millerovo	F	25-12
Stab JG 52	Maj Herbert Ihlefeld	Taganrog	F	4-4
II./JG 52	Hptm Johannes Steinhoff	Taganrog	F	40-24
III./JG 52	Maj Hubertus von Bonin	Kharkov	F/G	35-20
I./JG 53	Maj Herbert Kaminski	Kharkov	F/G	40-8
Stab JG 77	Maj Gordon Gollob	Kastornoye	F	4-4
II./JG 77	Hptm Anton Mader	Kastornoye	F	23-16
III./JG 77	Hptm Kurt Ubben	Kerch-IV	F	27-21
Luftflotte 5 (Arctic)				
II./JG 5	Hptm Horst Carganico	Petsamo	E/F	35-25
III./JG 5	Hptm Günther Scholz	Petsamo	E/F	23-17

Totals: 549-341

July 1943 – *circa* Operation *Zitadelle*

Luftflotte 4 (Southern Sector)				
II./JG 3	Maj Kurt Brändle	Kharkov-Rogan	G	46-30
III./JG 3	Maj Walther Dahl	Bessonovka	G	36-25
Stab JG 52	Obstlt Dietrich Hrabak	Krivotorovka	G	4-2
I./JG 52	Hptm Helmut Bennemann	Poltava	G	36-27
II./JG 52	Hptm Helmut Kühle	Anapa	G	42-27
III./JG 52	Maj Günther Rall	Orel	G	31-14
Luftflotte 5 (Finland/Arctic)				
II./JG 5	Obstlt Kurt Kettner	Alarkurtti	E/F/G	23-18
III./JG 5	Maj Heinrich Ehrler	Petsamo	E/F/G	26-24

Totals: 244-167

26 June 1944 – Soviet Summer Offensive

Luftflotte 6 (Central Sector)				
I./JG 51	Maj Erich Leie	Orscha	G	35-20
III./JG 51	Hptm D von Eichel-Streiber	Bobruisk	G	31-14
Luftflotte 4 (Southern Sector)				
Stab JG 52	Obstlt Dietrich Hrabak	Manzar	G	1-1
I./JG 52	Hptm Adolf Borchers	Leipzig (Rum)	G	23-20
II./JG 52	Hptm Gerhard Barkhorn	Manzar	G	11-7
III./JG 52	Hptm Wilhelm Batz	Roman	G	19-15
I./JG 53	Maj Jürgen Harder	Targsorul-Nou	G	28-24
Luftflotte 5 (Arctic)				
III./JG 5	Hptm Franz Dörr	Petsamo	G	24-21
				Totals: 172-122

April 1945

Lw.Kdo. Ostpreussen (Northern Sector)				
I./JG 51	Hptm Günther Schack	Littausdorf	G	10-8
III./JG 51	Hptm Joachim Brendel	Junkertroylhof	G/K	23-7
Luftflotte 6 (Central Sector)				
Stab JG 52	Obstlt Hermann Graf	Deutsch-Brod	G	8-7
I./JG 52	Hptm Erich Hartmann	Chrudim	G	37-34
III./JG 52	Maj Adolf Borchers	Deutsch-Brod	G/K	40-33
Luftflotte 4 (Southern Sector)				
II./JG 51	Oblt Otto Schulz	Fels am Wagram	G	7-5
II./JG 52	Hptm Wilhelm Batz	Hörsching	G/K	55-36
I./JG 53	Hptm Helmut Lipfert	Hörsching	G	27-25
				Totals: 207-155

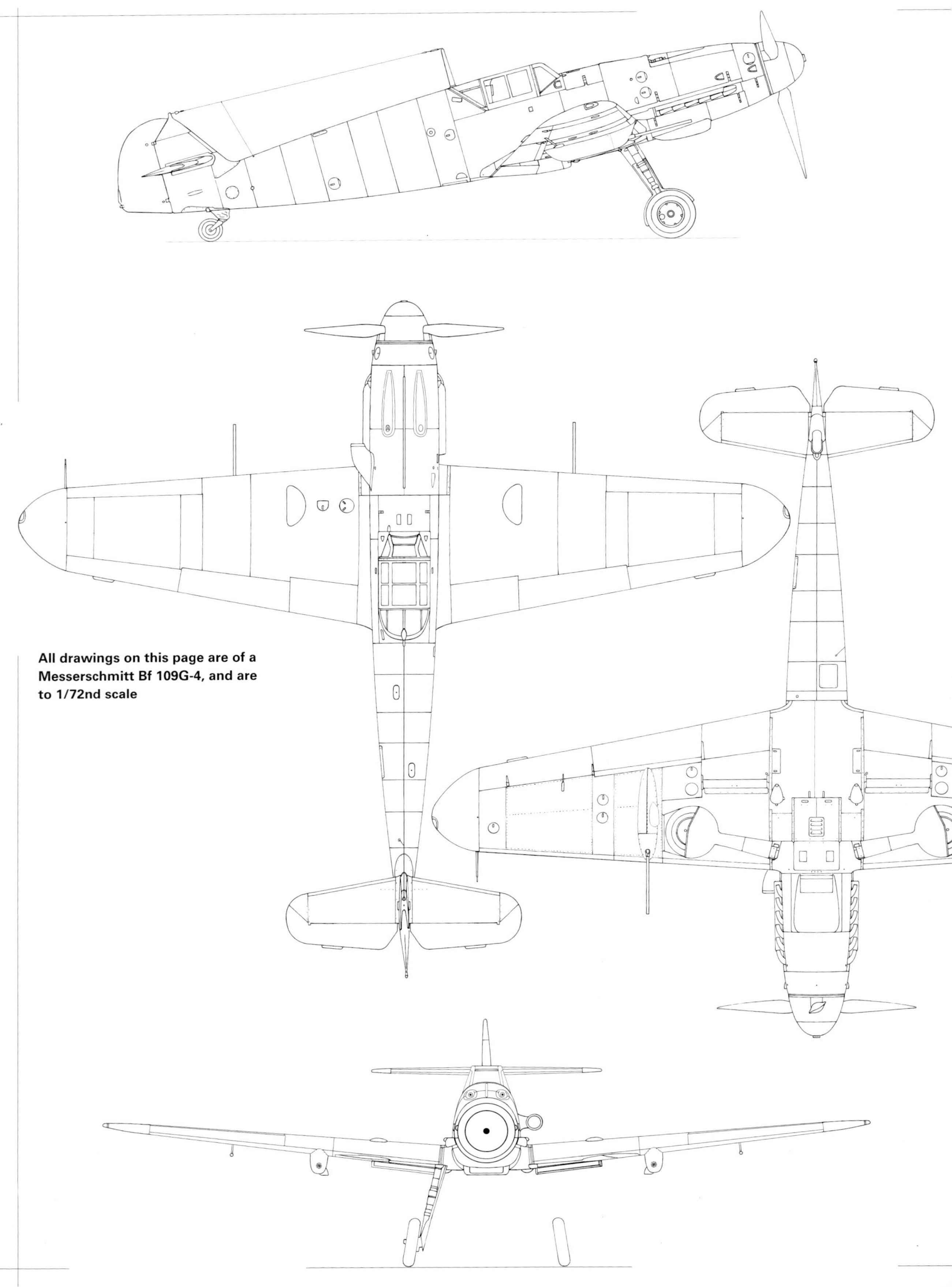

All drawings on this page are of a Messerschmitt Bf 109G-4, and are to 1/72nd scale

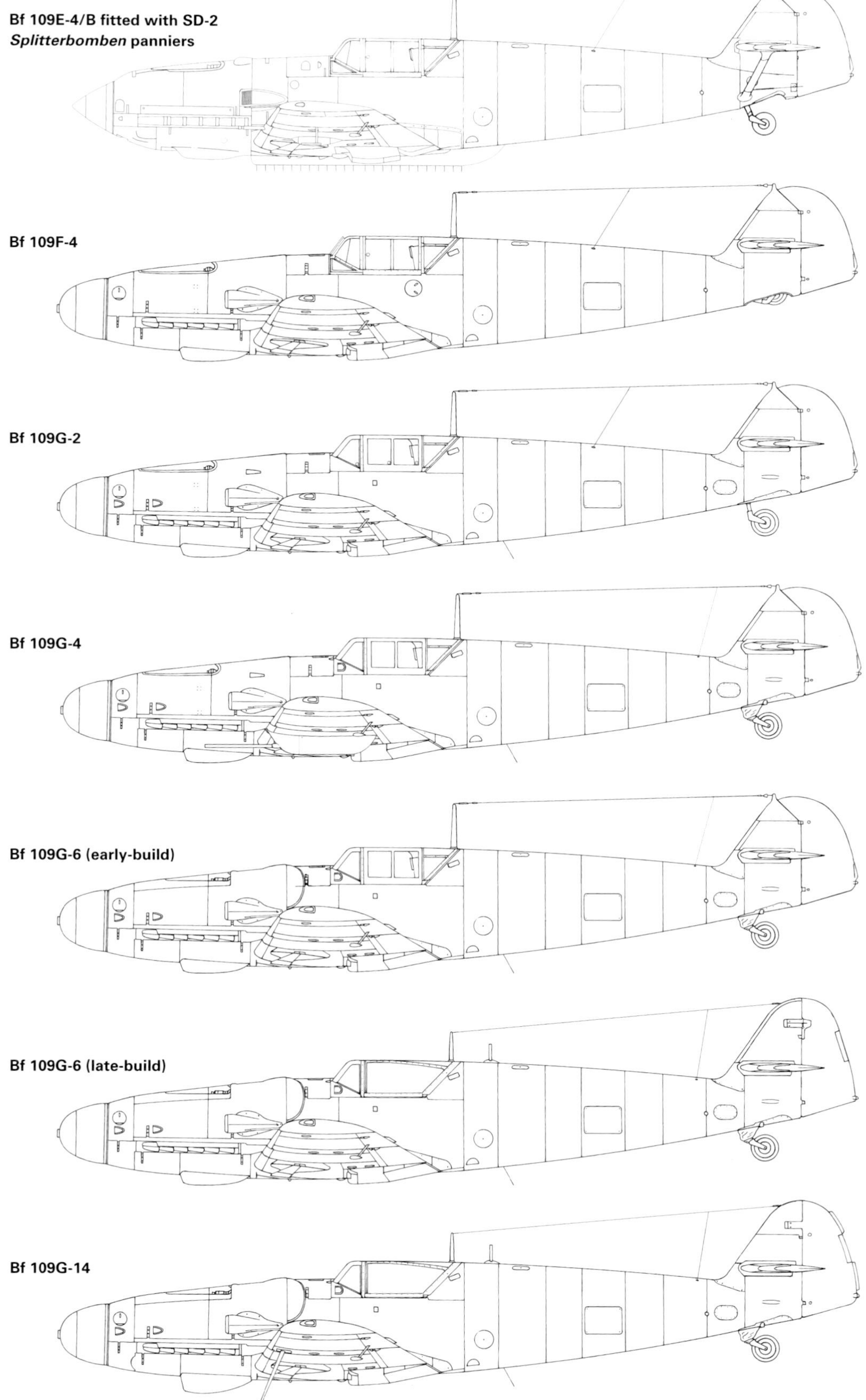

Bf 109E-4/B fitted with SD-2
Splitterbomben panniers
Bf 109F-4
Bf 109G-2
Bf 109G-4
Bf 109G-6 (early-build)
Bf 109G-6 (late-build)
Bf 109G-14

COLOUR PLATES

1

Bf 109F-2 'White Triple Chevron' of Major Günther Lützow, *Geschwaderkommodore* JG 3, Hostynne, June 1941

One of three *Friedrichs* available to Günther Lützow at the start of *Barbarossa*, this machine carries prominent early eastern front yellow theatre markings. It also wears Lützow's preferred style of *Kommodore* insignia – a triple chevron. Although superficially similar to the aircraft he had flown in France immediately prior to JG 3's transfer eastwards (see *Aircraft of the Aces 29*, colour profile 11), this is not the same machine, as it displays several minor differences.

2

Bf 109G-2 'Black Chevron and Bars' of Major Wolf-Dietrich Wilcke, *Geschwaderkommodore* JG 3 'Udet', Morosovskaya, November 1942

Lützow's successor at the head of JG 3 also enjoyed a *Kommodore*'s perks, for this is one of at least two *Gustavs* kept at Major Wilcke's disposal during the winter of 1942-43. They wore the more usual style of markings for a *Geschwaderkommodore*, and featured a much broader aft fuselage yellow theatre band. Note, too, the winged red 'U' unit badge, which was introduced when JG 3 was formally named the *Jagdgeschwader* 'Udet' on 1 December 1941 following the death of Ernst Udet, the Luftwaffe's Chief of Aircraft Procurement and Supply.

3

Bf 109F-2 'Black Chevron and Triangle' of Hauptmann Hans von Hahn, *Gruppenkommandeur* I./JG 3, Luzk, July 1941

A somewhat unusual camouflage scheme and set of *Kommandeur's* insignia adorned Hans von Hahn's F-2 during the opening weeks of *Barbarossa*. In addition to the *Gruppe's 'Tatzelwurm'* emblem on the nose, the machine sported von Hahn's personal badge under the windscreen. Like his namesake, Hans *'Assi'* Hahn of western front fame, von Hahn chose a rooster's head ('Hahn' meaning cockerel in German). Below the cockpit sill on the starboard side was the coat-of-arms of von Hahn's home town, Frankfurt-am-Main. At this stage the rudder scoreboard displays fifteen western kills (plus three balloons) and the first nine of his Soviet victories. He would add ten more to the latter before I./JG 3 left the eastern front to become II./JG 1.

4

Bf 109F-2 'Black Chevron and Circle' of Leutnant Detlev Rohwer, *Gruppen-TO* I./JG 3, Byelaya-Zerkov, August 1941

The *Friedrich* of von Hahn's Technical Officer sported an even more distinctive camouflage pattern. Rohwer's machine also retained the yellow nose (with rectangular cut-out for the *Gruppe* emblem) more associated with the Battle of Britain period. His personal badge was a cartoon rendition of Germany's medieval knight-adventurer Götz von Berlichingen in a decidedly bawdy pose (depicting Götz's invitation to his enemies to 'kiss my a..e'!). Four western victories and all but one of Rohwer's final tally of 24 Russian kills are carried on the rudder. The half-length bars (also seen on von Hahn's machine above) indicate aircraft destroyed on the ground.

5

Bf 109F-4 'White Double Chevron' of Hauptmann Kurt Brändle, *Gruppenkommandeur* II./JG 3 'Udet', Tusow, August 1942

Kurt Brändle was one of JG 3's highest scorers, with a final overall total of 180 enemy aircraft destroyed (160 in the east). The 95 kill bars on the rudder of his *Friedrich* show that he is already over halfway to achieving that tally, and also offer a clue as to time and place – mid-August 1942 on the road to Stalingrad. Note that in addition to the *Geschwader's* 'Winged U', Brändle's machine is wearing II. *Gruppe's* heraldic gyronny shield below the windscreen.

6

Bf 109F-4 'Yellow 7' of Oberleutnant Viktor Bauer, *Staffelkapitän* 9./JG 3 'Udet', Szolzy, March 1942

With its pilot yet to reach the halfway mark of his final score of 106 (as witness the 42 victory bars on the rudder), Bauer's F-4 displays a somewhat worn overall white finish as the first winter of the war in the east nears its end. Note that the slushy conditions have necessitated the removal of the mainwheel leg covers. As was common with III./JG 3, this machine does not carry the *Geschwader* badge, but wears in its place the *Gruppe's* own 'Double-headed axe'.

7

Bf 109F-4 'Yellow 4' of Oberfeldwebel Eberhard von Boremski, 9./JG 3 'Udet', Zhuguyev, May 1942

In early spring 1942 III./JG 3 retired briefly to Germany for re-equipment. Its new aircraft had been destined for the Mediterranean – some even retained tropical filters – and wore that theatre's standard tan and light blue camouflage scheme (see *Aircraft of the Aces 2*). This was toned down by large segments of dark green and light grey before the *Gruppe* returned to the east. In addition, every 9. *Staffel* machine apparently sported the name of its pilot's wife or girl friend below the cockpit. Von Boremski's 'Maxi' (for Maxine?) also displays 43 kills on the rudder. His final eastern front total would reach 84.

8

Bf 109F-4 'White Triple Chevron' of Hauptmann Franz Hahn, *Gruppenkommandeur* I./JG 4, Mizil/Rumania, January 1943

Arguably one of the least known fighter units to see service in the east was JG 4. Its I. *Gruppe* was initially deployed in defence of the Rumanian oilfields, where the opposition was predominantly American. Although the *Geschwader* produced no outstanding aces, this profile is included not only for the sake of completeness, but also on the strength of its pilot – yet another Hahn! – Franz *'Gockel'* ('Rooster') Hahn having already scored some 17+ kills as *Staffelkapitän* of 11./JG 51 (the ex-2./JG 77), prior to assuming command of I./JG 4 in the autumn of 1942. Hahn's choice of command insignia (the triple chevron more usually associated with a *Geschwaderkommodore* – see profile 1 for example), may perhaps be explained by the fact that I. *Gruppe* was still the only component of JG 4 in existence at this time.

9

Bf 109E-7 'Black Double Chevron' of Hauptmann Günther Scholz, *Gruppenkommandeur* III./JG 5, Petsamo/Finland, September 1942

Spending much of its time astride and above the Arctic Circle, and thus somewhat isolated from the major ground battles along the main fronts, JG 5 nonetheless produced five 100+ *Experten*. Although Günther Scholz was not one of them – his score climbing little higher than the 30 depicted here – he did end the war as *Kommodore* of the *Geschwader* (while at the same time serving as *Jafü Norwegen*). Note III. *Gruppe's* badge (a Lapland fur boat on a Finnish cross) and Scholz's personal emblem – a cute young lady baring the same part of her anatomy as Götz von Berlichingen!

10

Bf 109G-2 'Yellow 12' of Oberleutnant Heinrich Ehrler, Staffelkapitän 6./JG 5, Petsamo/Finland, March 1943

Most successful of the Arctic's 'Big Five' was Heinrich Ehrler. References to his final score vary between 201 and 220. To provide a camouflage scheme more suited to the terrain over which it was operating, Ehrler's early *Gustav* has been given a coat of washable white paint (including the fuselage cross), to which large irregular patches of dark green have been added. Note the 77 Soviet kills that have been carefully recorded on the rudder.

11

Bf 109G-2 'White 4' of Oberleutnant Theodor Weissenberger, *Staffelkapitän* 7./JG 5, Petsamo/Finland, July 1943

Like Ehrler, Weissenberger also scored over 200 victories, but 'only' 175 of these were claimed in the east. His G-2 is seen here in the same standard grey finish which is hidden by the temporary winter camouflage of 'Yellow 12' (above). His rudder, too, displays a meticulous scoreboard – a Knight's Cross garlanded with oak leaves and surmounted by an eagle to denote his century, plus 12 individual kill bars below. The last five of these were a brace or Airacobras and a trio of Pe-2s all claimed on 25 July 1943. They would bring him the Oak Leaves proper eight days later.

12

Bf 109E-7 'Yellow 1' of Oberleutnant Erbo Graf von Kageneck, *Staffelkapitän* 9./JG 27, Solzy, August 1941

Although JG 27 did not remain in the east long enough for its pilots to rack up huge scores, several of its members enjoyed considerable success in the opening phases of *Barbarossa*. One such was Erbo Graf von Kageneck, who claimed 48 Soviet kills between June and October 1941 – 27 of them are recorded here, along with 18 earlier western victories. Note the lack of a III. *Gruppe* vertical bar, III./JG 27's unique practice of displaying its aircraft's individual numbers on the engine cowling (a custom introduced during its time as the original I./JG 1) presumably being deemed sufficient for purposes of in-*Geschwader* identification.

13

Bf 109F-4 'Black Chevron and Bars' of Major Karl-Gottfried Nordmann, *Geschwaderkommodore* JG 51 'Mölders', Shatalovka, Summer 1942

Bearing standard finish plus a textbook set of eastern front markings and *Kommodore's* insignia, this *Friedrich* is otherwise devoid of any form of unit or personal badge. It is, in fact, the mount of Major Karl-Gottfried Nordmann, who commanded JG 51 from April 1942 to March 1944. Nordmann had added 69 Soviet kills to his earlier tally of nine western victories by the time his involvement in a mid-air collision on 17 January 1943 ended his frontline career.

14

Bf 109G-6 'White 9' of Leutnant Günther Josten, 1./JG 51 'Mölders', Bobruisk, Spring 1944

After having re-equipped with Fw 190s towards the end of 1942, JG 51 converted back on to the Bf 109 early in 1944. Despite being seen here with a ventral bomb-rack, this anonymous *Gustav* was flown by one of the *Geschwader's* foremost *Experten*. For as well as carrying out some 80 fighter-bomber sorties, Günther Josten claimed 178 aerial victories in the east. This total included more than 60 *Stormoviks*, plus one Eighth Air Force B-17 (downed on a supply-dropping mission to Warsaw on 18 September 1944).

15

Bf 109F 'Yellow 7' of Oberleutnant Heinrich Krafft, *Staffelkapitän* 8./JG 51 'Mölders', Stolzy, March 1942

This winter-camouflaged *Friedrich* displays on its rudder the 46 victories (all but four scored in the east) which won the Knight's Cross for its pilot on 18 March 1942. *'Gaudi'* Krafft would be promoted to *Kommandeur* of I. *Gruppe* on 1 June, and had taken his overall total to 78 before being brought down by Soviet anti-aircraft fire on 14 December 1942.

16

Bf 109F 'Black Double Chevron' of Hauptmann Josef Fözö, *Gruppenkommandeur* of II./JG 51, Stara-Bychov, July 1941

Austrian-born Fözö had already claimed three I-16s, during his time with the *Condor Legion*, and 18 western victories before JG 51 was transferred to the east. There, however, two serious injuries – one as *Kommandeur* of II./JG 51, and the second when commanding I. *Gruppe* – severely curtailed his operational career. This *Friedrich* displays two points of interest. The white silhouette on the first kill bar represents a French observation balloon shot down on 13 March 1940. This profile also shows that II./JG 51 had by now discontinued its earlier practice of positioning the *Gruppe* badge on the aft fuselage in lieu of the regulation horizontal bar (see examples in *Aircraft of the Aces 11*, pages 33 and 58). Although the bar is now in evidence, the *Gruppe* – still non-conformist – have wedged it between Fözö's *Kommandeur* chevrons and the fuselage cross.

17

Bf 109G-2 'Yellow 5' of Feldwebel Anton Hafner, 6./JG 51 'Mölders', Orel-North, August 1942

One of II./JG 51's early *Gustavs* also illustrates the unit's unique custom of wearing its horizontal *Gruppe* bar ahead of both the fuselage cross and the individual aircraft number. Having already gained his first 62 Soviet victories, the pilot of this machine, Feldwebel – later Oberleutnant – Anton Hafner, would emerge as JG 51's highest scorer with a final total of 204 kills before his own death in action against a Yak-9 over East Prussia on 17 October 1944 when *Staffelkapitän* of 8./JG 51. It should be borne in mind, however, that part of Hafner's double century had been scored in the Mediterranean, and while flying the Fw 190 upon his return to Russia.

18

Bf 109F-4 'Red 12' of Oberfeldwebel Heinz Klöpper, 11./JG 51 'Mölders', Dugino, September 1942

Another of JG 51's highly successful NCO pilots whose aircraft displayed both an unusual *Gruppe* marking and an impressive scoreboard was 11. *Staffel's* Heinz Klöpper. The 65 kill bars on the rudder earned him the Knight's Cross on 4 September 1942. The smaller, simplified cross behind the fuselage *Balkenkreuz* was an uncommon, but not unique, method of identifying a IV. *Gruppe* machine. Klöpper would claim a total of 86 Soviet kills before his promotion to oberleutnant and transfer to the west as *Staffelkapitän* of 7./JG 1.

19

Bf 109G-6 'Black Double Chevron' of Hauptmann Gerhard Barkhorn, *Gruppenkommandeur* I./JG 52, Kharkov-South, August 1943

There is little to distinguish this standard, and rather plain, *Gustav* other than the name below the cockpit. 'Christl' was the wife of Gerhard Barkhorn, the second most successful fighter pilot in the history of aerial warfare. At this stage the *Kommandeur* of I. *Gruppe* was already well on the way to his double century. He would survive the war with a staggering final total of 301 kills, all scored on the eastern front.

20

Bf 109G-6 'Red 4' of Oberfeldwebel Rudolf Trenkel, 2./JG 52, Poltava, July 1943

One of Barkhorn's high-scoring, but relatively little known, NCO pilots was Rudolf Trenkel of 2. *Staffel*. This *Gustav*, which Trenkel was flying at the time of *Zitadelle*, was even more anonymous than the *Kommandeur's* machine above, and is completely lacking any unit or personal markings. Such caution was not merely a matter of denying intelligence to the enemy. Many pilots were by now wary of disclosing their identities and successes in case they were forced down behind enemy lines. In fact Trenkel would survive unscathed (despite having to bail out five times in one ten-day period), and would end the war as *Kapitän* of 2./JG 52 with a total of 138 victories.

21

Bf 109G-2 'Black Double Chevron' of Hauptmann Johannes Steinhoff, *Gruppenkommandeur* II./JG 52, Rostov, August 1942

Although giving nothing away intelligence-wise, *'Mäcki'* Steinhoff's G-2 presents a more interesting appearance with its three-colour spinner, densely dappled engine cowling and obvious signs of overpainting on its rear fuselage. Another of JG 52's solid core of 100+ *Experten*, Johannes Steinhoff amassed 148 victories in the east before transferring to the Mediterranean and thence to the Reich. He was seriously burned on 18 April 1945 when his Me 262 crashed on take-off, but survived his injuries to head the post-war German air force.

22

Bf 109G-6 'White 1' of Hauptmann Erich Hartmann, *Staffelkapitän* 4./JG 52, Budaörs/Hungary, November 1944

One pilot who positively advertised his presence in the air was the one known to the Russians as the 'Black Devil of the South'. This is the late model G-6 flown by Erich Hartmann after he relinquished his year-long command of 9. *Staffel* to set up a new 4./JG 52 in October 1944. Although the machine retains the distinctive black 'tulip-leaf' which was Hartmann's individual marking, the 'Karaya' *Staffel's* famous 'pierced heart' emblem below the cockpit is now a plain red heart bearing the name *'Usch'* (for Ursula, whom Hartmann had married two months previously). Note, however, there is no record of Hartmann's current score, which by this time was well above the 300 mark.

23

Bf 109G-4 'Black 12' of Leutnant Peter Düttmann, 5./JG 52, Anapa, May 1943

Back to 1943 and anonymity for this earlier *Gustav*, which was flown over the Kuban bridgehead by the newly-arrived Leutnant Peter Düttmann. In his two years at the front *'Bonifaz'* Düttmann was shot down, or was forced to land, no fewer than 19 times. But he gave as good as he got, however, claiming nine kills in one day alone on 7 May 1944. He ended the war as *Staffelkapitän* of 5./JG 52 with a total of 150 aerial victories (and two tanks destroyed, which were counted as kills in 1945!), plus a further 42 unconfirmed.

24

Bf 109G-2 'Yellow 5' of Leutnant Walter Krupinski, 6./JG 52, Armavir, August 1942

Still sporting the now seldom seen 'Winged sword' badge of JG 52 beneath the windscreen, 'Yellow 5' was the mount of Walter 'Graf Punski' Krupinski, who was to be a major influence on the early career of one Erich Hartmann. After a year serving as *Staffelkapitän* of 7./JG 52, Krupinski himself was transferred to the west where he commanded, in turn, 1./JG 5, II./JG 11 and III./JG 26, before ending the war flying Me 262s with JV 44. His eastern front victories totalled 177.

25

Bf 109G-4 'Yellow 3' of Unteroffizier Hans Waldmann, 6./JG 52, Anapa, June 1943

Another of JG 52's successful young NCOs, 'Dackel' Waldmann had already scored 53 kills in the nine months up to June 1943. By the end of May 1944 his final eastern front total had reached 125. He, too, transferred to the west and later converted on to the Me 262, but was killed in a mid-air collision in the closing weeks of the war when serving as *Staffelkapitän* of 3./JG 7. This particular G-4 is apparently a new delivery, hence the areas of fresh paint covering the four-letter code applied at the factory. Note also the small dimensions of the individual aircraft number common to the

Gruppe's aircraft at this period. The personal emblem is a play on the pilot's nickname, 'Waldmann' ('Woodsman') also being a favourite name for a pet Dackel, or dachshund.

26

Bf 109G-6 'Yellow 3' of Leutnant Heinz Ewald, 6./JG 52, Zilistea/Rumania, June 1944

Reflecting II./JG 52's brief period of service in the specialised anti-bomber role defending the Rumanian oilfields against high-flying US 'heavies', this G-6 *'Kanonenboot'* (Gunboat) is equipped with 20 mm underwing cannon gondolas and sports a spiral spinner (widely believed to throw off the aim of the enemy bombers' gunners). It also bears another word-play personal emblem, Heinz Ewald's nickname being 'Esau' ('E-sow'). Like Waldmann, Ewald also flew many missions as Barkhorn's wingman before he assumed command of 7./JG 52 in February 1945. His score at the war's end stood at 84.

27

Bf 109G-2 'Black 13' of Oberleutnant Günther Rall, *Staffelkapitän* 8./JG 52, Gostanovka, August 1942

The third of JG 52's triumvirate of top scorers, Oberleutnant Günther Rall flew this 'Black 13' upon his return to the command of 8. *Staffel* on 28 August 1942, exactly nine months to the day after being severely wounded the previous November. At that time he had claimed just 36 kills. He would add 235 more Soviet victories to his score (latterly as *Kommandeur* of III./JG 52) before his transfer to the west in the spring of 1944. Note III. *Gruppe's* 'Barbed cross' badge forward of the windshield, and wavy bar symbol on the aft fuselage.

28

Bf 109G-2 'Yellow 11' of Oberleutnant Hermann Graf, *Staffelkapitän* 9./JG 52, Pitomnik, September 1942

The same *Gruppe* badge adorns the *Gustav* of fellow-*Staffelkapitän* Hermann Graf. But this machine also carries 9./JG 52's famous 'Pierced heart' emblem, albeit without the word 'Karaya' – the *Staffel's* equally celebrated radio call-sign – beneath it. As with most of the 'Karaya' *Staffel's* machines, the red heart has a girl's name (*Elli?*) superimposed on it in tiny white letters. Graf reportedly scored his 150th kill in this aircraft on 4 September. After service in the west (where he claimed ten US 'heavies') Graf returned to JG 52 in October 1944, this time as *Kommodore* – a position he held until the end. His final tally of Soviet kills numbered 202.

29

Bf 109G-6 'Yellow 1' of Leutnant Erich Hartmann, *Staffelkapitän* 9./JG 52, Novo-Zaporozhe, October 1943

The mount of the 'Karaya' *Staffel's* most famous *Kapitän*, Leutnant - later Oberleutnant - Erich Hartmann. The century motif and additional 21 individual victory bars date this as 2 October 1943 (on this day Hartmann claimed four kills – a brace of La-5s, a Pe-2 and an Airacobra). But he was still 27 victories – and 27 days – away from winning the Knight's Cross! Note that the distinctive 'tulip-leaf' nose decoration has yet to put in an appearance, as has the name *'Ursel'* - for fiancée Ursula Paetsch – which would grace the pierced heart. For some reason the inscription worn on the *Staffel* emblem at this time reportedly read *'Dicker Max'* ('Fat Max')!

30

Bf 109F-2 'Black Chevron and Bars' of Major Günther Freiherr von Maltzahn, *Geschwaderkommodore* JG 53, Byelaya-Zerkov, July 1941

Although not a high scorer himself, 'Henri' von Maltzahn was one of the *Jagdwaffe's* true leaders (a quality recognised by the award of the Knight's Cross back in December 1940, when his personal score stood at just 13 – a far cry from Hartmann's 148!). Here, the tail of his *Friedrich* displays all 20 of his western victories to date, plus the additional 22 Soviet kills which won him the Oak Leaves on 24 July 1941. He would end his three years as *Kommodore* of JG 53 with a final tally of 68 victories – 35 in the west and 33 in the east.

31

Bf 109F-2 'Black Chevron and Circle/Bar' of Leutnant Jürgen Harder, *Gruppenstab* III./JG 53, Sobolevo, June 1941

Bearing a single kill bar on the rudder for his first Soviet victim (an 'I-17' claimed on the opening day of *Barbarossa*), Harder's F-2 also displays a heavily dappled cowling – the result of heavy-handed overspraying of the earlier Channel front yellow – and an unusual *Gruppenstab* symbol. It has been suggested that the latter denotes the combined duties of an adjutant and TO. One of three fighter-pilot brothers, none of whom would survive the war, the name below the cockpit commemorates the first brother to be killed in action – Hauptmann Harro Harder, *Gruppenkommandeur* of III./JG 53, who was shot down off the Isle of Wight on 12 August 1940. As *Kommodore* of JG 11, Jürgen Harder would lose his life in a crash near Berlin early in 1945. His final score of 64 included 17 eastern front victories.

32

Bf 109G-2 'White Chevron and Bars' of Major Hannes Trautloft, *Geschwaderkommodore* JG 54, Siverskaya, Summer 1942

Another celebrated fighter leader who put the welfare and success of his *Geschwader* before personal ambition, Hannes Trautloft's eastern front score of 45 was modest by some standards, but his contribution to JG 54 was incalculable. He flew at least three machines similarly (but not identically) marked to the example depicted here. All wore a non-standard segmented camouflage (of two-tone green, or tan and green) which accentuated the white *Kommodore's* insignia. Note, also, that the famous 'Green Heart' *Geschwader* badge features the crests of JG 54's three component *Gruppen* in miniature.

33

Bf 109F-2 'Black Chevron and Bars' of Hauptmann Hans Philipp, *Gruppenkommandeur* I./JG 54, Siverskaya, March 1942

Despite its *Major beim Stab* insignia, this rather worn winter-camouflaged *Friedrich* is the machine flown by Hans Philipp, *Kommandeur* of I. *Gruppe*, as he neared his century in the early months of 1942. He would be the fourth member of the *Jagdwaffe* to reach the 100 mark (on 31 March 1942), and the second to achieve the double century (behind Hermann Graf) a little less than a year later on 17 March 1943. He transferred to the west as *Kommodore* of JG 1 shortly thereafter, only to be killed in action against P-47s in October 1943. All but 29 of his 206 victories had been claimed in Russia.

34

Bf 109F 'White 8' of Leutnant Walter Nowotny, 1./JG 54, Ryelbitzi, Summer 1942

Also sporting the *Geschwader's* 'Green Heart' and the badge of I. *Gruppe*, 'White 8' was flown by 1. *Staffel's* Walter Nowotny. Although more properly associated with the Focke-Wulf Fw 190 (see *Osprey Aircraft of the Aces 6 - Fw 190 Aces of the Russian Front*), Nowotny's first half-century and more were scored on Bf 109s. The rudder of this *Friedrich* shows that he is already well on the way to his Knight's Cross, awarded on 4 September for 56 kills. Altogether, his final eastern front tally would be 255. Note, incidentally, that the green heart emblem has been embellished with Nowotny's personal 'lucky 13'.

35

Bf 109F 'Black 8' of Feldwebel Otto Kittel, 2./JG 54, Krasnogvardeisk, May 1942

Very similar to the aircraft in profile 34 (albeit minus the rudder scoreboard), and also by chance a number '8', this machine was an early mount of the NCO pilot who was destined to become JG 54's highest scorer. Before his death in action in February 1945, the little-known Otto Kittel would be credited with no fewer than 267 Soviet kills. In fact, he was the fourth most successful eastern front *Experte* after JG 52's 'top three'. Although the vast majority of his claims were made on the Fw 190, Kittel – like Nowotny – cut his operational teeth on Bf 109s. It was, however, a long and laborious process. In the eight months leading up to May 1942 he had achieved just 15 victories.

36

Bf 109E 'Black Double Chevron' of Hauptmann Herbert Ihlefeld, *Gruppenkommandeur* I.(J)/LG 2, Jassy/Rumania, July 1941

With I./JG 77 operating semi-autonomously in northern Scandinavia (where it later formed the nucleus of I./JG 5), the vacant I. *Gruppe* slot in the parent JG 77 was long filled by I.(J)/LG 2. Here, the *Kommandeur's Emil* displays both that *Gruppe's* badge – an elaborate 'L' (for Lehr) and a map of Great Britain (now somewhat out of place in Rumania) – plus 36 kill bars representing his western victories to date. To the latter a further ten Soviet kills have already been added. The fifth pilot to achieve the century (on 22 April 1942), Ihlefeld subsequently commanded various *Geschwader* in both east and west. His eastern front total was 67.

37

Bf 109F-4 'Black Double Chevron' of Hauptmann Anton Mader, *Gruppenkommandeur* II./JG 77, Stary Oskol, September 1942

Another *Kommandeur's* machine, this time of II. *Gruppe*, as witness the badge below the windscreen and horizontal bar aft of the fuselage cross. But no sign on that pristine (and rather unusual) white rudder of Mader's current tally of 62 Soviet kills. Like Ihlefeld, Mader would later command both eastern and western front *Jagdgeschwader*, ending the war with a combined total of 86 victories.

38

Bf 109F-4 'Black 5' of Oberleutnant Anton Hackl, *Staffelkapitän* 5./JG 77, Kastornoje, September 1942

No hesitation on the part of Anton Hackl, *Kapitän* of Mader's 5. *Staffel*, in proclaiming his score. All but the first four of the 117 kill bars carefully recorded on the rudder of this *Friedrich* are eastern front victories, the last two denoting a brace of Il-2s downed on 18 September. 'Toni' Hackl was yet another alumnus of JG 77 who would go on to command various *Jagdgeschwader*. Some 130 out of his final total of 192 had been claimed in the east.

39

Bf 109G-2 'White Chevron/Yellow 1' of Hauptmann Kurt Ubben, *Gruppenkommandeur* III./JG 77, Lyuban, September 1942

A distinctly idiosyncratic set of markings adorn this early *Gustav* 'gunboat' – unusual *Kommandeur's* insignia (presumably indicating Ubben's position as No 1 in the *Stabskette*), a yellow theatre band centred on the fuselage cross (a custom more associated with JG 54) and no *Gruppe* symbol on the aft fuselage (III./JG 77 appear to have discarded their oversized 'wavy bar' at the end of the Balkans campaign). What remains is the *Gruppe's* 'Wolf's head' badge and a careful record of Ubben's 84 kills to date. In all, 'Kuddel' Ubben would claim 90 Soviet kills with JG 77 before assuming command of JG 2 in the west. He was killed in action over France in April 1944.

40

Bf 109F 'White 1' of Oberleutnant Wolfdieter Huy, *Staffelkapitän* 7./JG 77, Lunga/Rumania, August 1941

Another slightly unusual, but not unique, positioning of the yellow theatre band, this time ahead of the fuselage cross. It was first introduced on III./JG 77's Bf 109s during the recent Balkans campaign. Huy's *Friedrich* also carries the *Gruppe* badge, but no aft fuselage symbol. The ship silhouettes on the rudder refer back to his anti-shipping activities off Greece and Crete. Since then he has been credited with a dozen Soviet kills. Huy would claim 37 victories in the east before III./JG 77 transferred back to the Mediterranean area, where he was shot down and captured on 29 October 1942.

Selected Bibliography

ADERS, GEBHARD and HELD, WERNER, *Jagdgeschwader 51 'Mölders'.* Motorbuch Verlag, Stuttgart, 1985

BARBAS, BERND, *Planes of the Luftwaffe Fighter Aces, Vols. 1 & 2.* Kookaburra, Melbourne, 1985

CONSTABLE, TREVOR J and TOLIVER, COL RAYMOND F, *Horrido! Fighter Aces of the Luftwaffe.* Macmillan, New York, 1968

CONSTABLE, TREVOR J and TOLIVER, COL RAYMOND F, *The Blond Knight of Germany: A Biography of Erich Hartmann.* Doubleday & Co., New York, 1970

DIERICH, WOLFGANG, *Die Verbände der Luftwaffe 1935-1945.* Motorbuch Verlag, Stuttgart, 1976

EWALD, HEINZ, *Esau: Als Jagdflieger im erfolgreichsten Jagdgeschwader 1943-1945.* Privately printed, Coburg, 1975

FRASCHKA, GÜNTER, *. . . mit Schwertern und Brillanten.* Erich Pabel Verlag, Rastatt, 1958

GIRBIG, WERNER, *Jagdgeschwader 5 'Eismeerjäger'.* Motorbuch Verlag, Stuttgart, 1976

GROEHLER, OLAF, *Kampf um die Luftherrschaft.* Militärverlag der DDR, Berlin, 1988

HARDESTY, VON, *Red Phoenix, The Rise of Soviet Air Power, 1941-1945.* Arms and Armour Press, London, 1982

HAYWARD, JOEL S A, *Stopped at Stalingrad.* University Press of Kansas, Lawrence, 1998

HELD, WERNER, *Die Deutschen Jagdgeschwader im Russlandfeldzug.* Podzun-Pallas-Verlag, Friedberg, 1986

HELD, WERNER/TRAULOFT, HANNES/BOB, EKKEHARD, *Die Grünherzjäger, Bildchronik des Jagdgeschwaders 54.* Podzun-Pallas-Verlag, Friedberg, 1985

KUROWSKI, FRANZ, *Balkenkreuz und Roter Stern, Der Luftkrieg über Russland 1941-1944.* Podzun-Pallas-Verlag, Friedberg, 1984

LIPFERT, HELMUT, *Das Tagebuch des Hauptmann Lipfert.* Motorbuch Verlag, Stuttgart, 1973

MEILLER-HAFNER, ALFONS, *Flieger Feinde Kameraden.* Erich Pabel Verlag, Rastatt, 1962

MÖLLER-WITTEN, HANNS, *Mit dem Eichenlaub zum Ritterkreuz.* Erich Pabel Verlag, Rastatt, 1962

MOMBEEK, ERIC, *Sturmjäger; Zur Geschichte des Jagdgeschwaders 4 (2 vols).* Verlag ASBL, Linkebeek/Belgium, 1997-99

NOWARRA, HEINZ J, *Luftwaffen-Einsatz Barbarossa 1941.* Podzun-Pallas-Verlag, Friedberg,

OBERMAIER, ERNST, *Die Ritterkreuzträger der Luftwaffe 1939-1945; Band I, Jagdflieger.* Verlag Dieter Hoffmann, Mainz, 1966

PLOCHER, GENERALLEUTNANT HERMANN, *The German Air Force versus Russia, 1942.* Arno Press, New York, 1966

PLOCHER, GENERALLEUTNANT HERMANN, *The German Air Force versus Russia, 1943.* Arno Press, New York, 1967

PRIEN, JOCHEN, *Geschichte des Jagdgeschwaders 53 (3 vols).* Flugzeug (vol 1) 1989/Struwe Druck, Eutin, 1990

PRIEN, JOCHEN, *Geschichte des Jagdgeschwaders 77 (4 vols).* Struwe Druck, Eutin, 1992

PRIEN, JOCHEN and STEMMER, GERHARD, *Jagdgeschwader 3* (4 vols of individual *Gruppe* histories). Struwe Druck, Eutin

PRIEN, JOCHEN/RODEIKE, PETER/STEMMER, GERHARD, *Jagdgeschwader 27* (3 vols of individual *Gruppe* histories). Struwe Druck, Eutin

RING, HANS and GIRBIG, WERNER, *Jagdgeschwader 27.* Motorbuch Verlag, Stuttgart, 1971

ROBA, JEAN-LOUIS et MOMBEEK, ERIC, *La Chasse de Jour Allemande en Roumanie.* Editions Modelism Int., Bucharest, 1994

ROHDEN, HANS-DETLEF HERHUDT VON, *Die Luftwaffe ringt um Stalingrad.* Limes Verlag, Wiesbaden, 1950

SCHREIER, HANS, *JG 52, Das Erfolgreichste Jagdgeschwader des II. Weltkrieges.* Kurt Vowinckel Verlag, Berg am See, 1990

SCUTTS, JERRY, *JG 54 Aces of the Eastern Front.* Airlife Publishing Ltd, Shrewsbury, 1992

SHORES, CHRISTOPHER, *Air Aces.* Bison Books, Greenwich, 1983

STIPDONK, PAUL and MEYER, MICHAEL., *Das JG 51: Eine Bilddokumentation über die Jahre 1938-1945.* Heinz Nickel, Zweibrücken, 1996

INDEX

References to illustrations are shown in **bold**. Plates are shown with page and caption locators in brackets.